CLOSE READING FOR THE
TWENTY-FIRST CENTURY

SKILLS FOR SCHOLARS

Close Reading for the Twenty-First Century, edited by Dan Sinykin and Johanna Winant

The Entrepreneurial Scholar: A New Mindset for Success in Academia and Beyond, Ilana M. Horwitz

How to Mentor Anyone in Academia, Maria LaMonaca Wisdom

On the Art and Craft of Doing Science, Kenneth Catania

Academic Writing as if Readers Matter, Leonard Cassuto

Thinking through Writing: A Guide to Becoming a Better Writer and Thinker, John Kaag and Jonathan van Belle

The Pocket Instructor: Writing: 50 Exercises for the College Classroom, edited by Amanda Irwin Wilkins and Keith Shaw

Stellar English: A Down-to-Earth Guide to Grammar and Style, Frank L. Cioffi

Try to Love the Questions: From Debate to Dialogue in Classrooms and Life, Lara Schwartz

The Elements of Visual Grammar: A Designer's Guide for Writers, Scholars, and Professionals, Angela Riechers

Writing with Pleasure, Helen Sword

The Secret Syllabus: A Guide to the Unwritten Rules of College Success, Jay Phelan and Terry Burnham

The Economist's Craft: An Introduction to Research, Publishing, and Professional Development, Michael S. Weisbach

How to Think like Shakespeare: Lessons from a Renaissance Education, Scott Newstok

The Book Proposal Book: A Guide for Scholarly Authors, Laura Portwood-Stacer

The Princeton Guide to Historical Research, Zachary M. Schrag

You Are What You Read: A Practical Guide to Reading Well, Robert DiYanni

Super Courses: The Future of Teaching and Learning, Ken Bain

Syllabus: The Remarkable, Unremarkable Document That Changes Everything, William Germano and Kit Nicholls

Leaving Academia: A Practical Guide, Christopher L. Caterine

A Field Guide to Grad School: Uncovering the Hidden Curriculum, Jessica McCrory Calarco

The Craft of College Teaching: A Practical Guide, Robert DiYanni and Anton Borst

Will This Be on the Test?, Dana T. Johnson and Jennifer E. Price

Close Reading for the Twenty-First Century

EDITED BY DAN SINYKIN
AND JOHANNA WINANT

PRINCETON UNIVERSITY PRESS
PRINCETON & OXFORD

Copyright © 2025 by Princeton University Press

Princeton University Press is committed to the protection of copyright and the intellectual property our authors entrust to us. Copyright promotes the progress and integrity of knowledge created by humans. By engaging with an authorized copy of this work, you are supporting creators and the global exchange of ideas. As this work is protected by copyright, any reproduction or distribution of it in any form for any purpose requires permission; permission requests should be sent to permissions@press.princeton.edu. Ingestion of any IP for any AI purposes is strictly prohibited.

Published by Princeton University Press
41 William Street, Princeton, New Jersey 08540
99 Banbury Road, Oxford OX2 6JX
press.princeton.edu

GPSR Authorized Representative: Easy Access System Europe - Mustamäe tee 50, 10621 Tallinn, Estonia, gpsr.requests@easproject.com

All Rights Reserved

ISBN 978-0-691-26569-8
ISBN (pbk.) 978-0-691-26570-4
ISBN (e-book) 978-0-691-26571-1

Library of Congress Control Number 2025937128

British Library Cataloging-in-Publication Data is available

Editorial: Anne Savarese and James Collier
Production Editorial: Jill Harris
Cover Design: Karl Spurzem
Production: Lauren Reese
Publicity: Alyssa Sanford
Copyeditor: Leah Caldwell

This book has been composed in Arno

10 9 8 7 6 5 4 3 2 1

CONTENTS

Preface ix

INTRODUCTION

What Close Reading Is 1
What Close Reading Does 11
What Close Reading Has Been 21

PART I. SCENE SETTING

1 Near Monstrous Fidelity: Erich Auerbach on Virginia Woolf 39
   Oren Izenberg

2 Touching, Reading: Eve Kosofsky Sedgwick on Henry James 46
   Jane Hu

3 A Pedicure: Angela Leighton on Alice Oswald 55
   Beci Carver

PART II. NOTICING

4 Close Reading Drama: Eric Griffiths on William Shakespeare ... 65
   Robert Stagg

5 The Poet's Choices: Helen Vendler on John Keats 72
   Jeff Dolven and Joshua Kotin

6 What Beauty Hides: Toni Morrison on Marie Cardinal 80
   Adrienne Brown

7	Grist for the Mill: Christopher Ricks on Cliché *Katie Kadue*	88
8	An Odd Way of Listening to Men: Barbara Johnson on Jane Campion *Summer Kim Lee*	97

PART III. LOCAL CLAIMING

9	The Apple of Experience: Erich Auerbach on Adam and Eve *Julie Orlemanski*	107
10	Local Claiming, Capacious Life: Kevin Quashie on Lucille Clifton *Lindsay Reckson*	116
11	Exquisite, Golden, Fragrant, Flaunting: Judith Butler on Nella Larsen *Natalia Cecire*	124
12	A Matter of Perspective: Eleni Coundouriotis on Yambo Ouologuem *Farah Bakaari*	132
13	What, What to Do with All This Black Feminine Life?: Hortense Spillers on Gwendolyn Brooks *Omari Weekes*	140

PART IV. REGIONAL ARGUMENTATION

14	The Drama of Comparison: Alex Woloch on Jane Austen *Elaine Auyoung*	151
15	Befriending Poems: Robert Penn Warren on John Crowe Ransom *Emily Ogden*	160

16 Close Reading and the General: Qolamhossein Yousefi
on Ahmad Shamlu   167
Pardis Dabashi

17 Vibe Theory: Lauren Berlant on John Ashbery   176
Brian Glavey

PART V. GLOBAL THEORIZING

18 Going Global: William Empson on William Shakespeare   187
Noreen Masud

19 Little Bit of Ivory: D. A. Miller on Jane Austen   195
Stephanie Insley Hershinow

20 Dirty Projectors: Sianne Ngai on Alfred Hitchcock   201
Kimberly Quiogue Andrews

21 The Art of Both-And: Jahan Ramazani on Daljit Nagra   209
Christopher Spaide

PRACTICAL MATERIALS

Reading Close Readings   218
Writing Close Readings   238
Using Close Readings   255

Acknowledgments 263
List of Contributors 265
Index 269

PREFACE

HOW YOU use this book will depend on who you are and what you want to learn about close reading. Whether you are an undergraduate, a graduate student, a professor, or an everyday reader, whether you are confident or anxious about your own close reading skills, whether you are thinking about how to teach close reading to yourself or to your students, we wrote this book to be helpful for you. We hope it offers useful tips and techniques along with the moments of transformative illumination and sustaining community that close reading can produce.

The introduction explains what close reading is, what close reading does, and what close reading has been. We have created new vocabulary to describe the common steps of close reading; we explain those steps here. We then describe, in the sections that follow, how close reading offers greater understanding, a demonstration of skill, and the invitation to conversation. Finally, we trace the history of close reading through the modern discipline of literary studies.

Parts I through V present twenty-one short chapters. These are craft essays, demonstrations and explications of close reading, opportunities to slow down with great close readings to see how they work and how you can do what they do. In each, the contributor takes up a close reading of their choice to demonstrate how its author accomplishes one of what we have identified as close reading's five steps. This book features established giants of close reading (though we could not have them all) across historical periods and theoretical schools. Our contributors, with their personal pantheons, represent the breadth of close reading and make the case for its future.

The final section contains practical materials—activities, worksheets, and more—for you to teach, or teach yourself, how to close read. And why.

CLOSE READING FOR THE
TWENTY-FIRST CENTURY

Introduction

What Close Reading Is

This is a book about how *reading* becomes *a* reading—a close reading. We show how you can move from an encounter with a piece of literature, following its language and figuring out what's happening, to an interpretation and an argument. How does this work?

You read a poem, play, essay, story, or novel; you start with someone else's words; you see something in those words that means something to you, though you probably don't know what yet. Maybe what you see confuses you or riles you up, maybe it surprises you, maybe it charms or delights you. You pause; you reread; suddenly the thing you noticed starts to feel central, or even crucial, like a hidden center of gravity that draws in and changes everything around it. The work of literature becomes clearer, or more complicated, or both, and is slightly or maybe tremendously reshaped. No longer just something to read, the work becomes something to study. It becomes what literary scholars call "a text"—that large category including poems, plays, essays, stories, novels, and much besides—objects of special interest and attention, things to discuss, analyze, and interpret. And now you might look up from the text because you want to show what's happened to someone else. You want to explain something to another person: your own reader. You want to persuade, to teach. You want to say, you should understand this poem, play, essay, novel, or story in light of *this* detail, you should understand it *this way*. You want to say, it matters not to miss or misunderstand this.

Understanding close reading will make you a better reader, thinker, and writer about literature. And further: understanding close reading will make you a better reader, thinker, and writer about anything that you examine in detail and explain to someone else. Literature is the most common object of attention for close reading; conversations in literary studies are where we practice close reading most frequently, though these range from high school classrooms to professional scholarship. This book is addressed to students of all levels, from those being asked to read closely for the first time to those who have already written theses or published articles but want to understand this foundational practice more thoroughly and improve further. We also address professors who teach close reading, and other practicing literary scholars and critics who close read expertly already. We welcome readers from literary studies, broadly conceived, and from the even broader university, and from the universe of readers and writers beyond it, with the enabling conviction that close reading is a skill that pays off in our discipline and also nearly everywhere.

What is close reading? *Close reading is the practice of paying attention to a passage of text to account for at least one aspect of its meaning and to make an argument about how it works.*

In literary studies, we read, then we write. And as we write, we often begin to read in new ways—ways that ultimately modify our writing. There are lots of ways to write about a novel, story, play, essay, or poem. You might describe, summarize, or paraphrase it. You might reflect upon it, evaluate it, or present the process of reading by recounting what it was like to be surprised by or be submerged in it. You might linger over particular details. You might offer larger interpretations and persuasive arguments about how to understand that piece of literature. If you do all of these—if you focus on an aspect or piece of the text and also use that to see the text as a whole, if by describing the text you tell someone else how to read it, if you say what it's like to read the text as a way of saying what to know about it—it is *a close reading*.

Close reading is the foundation of literary studies as a discipline in the modern research university. It is the basic activity that distinguishes what literary scholars do from other kinds of discussions about books. Interpreting a text is not the same thing as offering praise (or disparagement) of a book, play, or poem in response to someone asking you if you liked it—it's not a review. Nor is interpretation what you would provide if someone asked you what the novel or movie is about, nor even what it's like to read or watch. Close reading grounds general arguments in the analysis of specific details. If we compare a text to an engine, then close reading holds up one small part—say, a spark plug—and says how it works and why it's crucial—how it makes the car run.

Anyone can learn how to close read. It helps—for those who intuitively grasp how to do it and also for those who are learning—to have the process broken down into steps. This book offers you an anatomy of close reading. It's an instruction manual. If you want to bring more attention to reading literary texts, or if you already read literary texts with care and now you want to know how to take the next step in your thinking and your writing (which are closely related), or if you want to better understand the scholarly and critical articles and books you're encountering, we wrote this book to help. Close reading is a skill—a craft—and much like the work of a mechanic, or a pianist, or a dancer, you learn how to do it by doing it, assisted by the guidance we provide here.

In this first section of the introduction, we name and describe the five steps of many close readings: *scene setting, noticing, local claiming, regional argumentation,* and *global theorizing.* These steps will help you understand what a close reading is and what it is doing, whether for the essay you're writing or the article you're reading. You will be able to orient yourself better in your own writing and the writing of other scholars. You will be able to talk more clearly about what makes a close reading succeed, either your own or another scholar's. (If you write a close reading, you are a literary scholar. Welcome.)

Let's look at an example. We frequently teach close reading in our classrooms using the poem known as "The Red Wheelbarrow" by William Carlos Williams.[1] Here is the poem in its entirety:

so much depends
upon

a red wheel
barrow

glazed with rain
water

beside the white
chickens

Here is a one-paragraph close reading of this poem that we wrote:

In William Carlos Williams's "The Red Wheelbarrow," the vocabulary—chickens near a wet wheelbarrow—is simple. Kindergarteners would be familiar with nearly all of the words in this poem. They are drawn from the everyday world of agriculture. But there is one exception. Right in the

---

1. The poem didn't have a title in Williams's 1923 book *Spring and All.*

middle of the poem, one of these words is not like the others—"glazed." "Glazed" is not from the same set of vocabulary as "chickens" or even other adjectives like "red." "Glazed" comes from a different world than the rest of this scene; it comes from the world of the aesthetic, of art and beauty. By describing the wheelbarrow as glazed, by describing the rainwater on it as akin to a glass-like shine as on ceramics, the poem grants a surprising status—the status of an art object—to an ordinary gardening tool. How, then, to understand the poem's assertion that "so much / depends" upon this red wheelbarrow? The poem suggests that aesthetic beauty can be found anywhere, even in this unlikely scene. Still further: the poem insists on the importance of recognizing that anything can be art. This is not a claim that beauty is in the eye of the beholder, but rather that art is not the exclusive property of the elite. The poem's simple vocabulary, then, reinforces this idea that art belongs to the everyday world of ordinary people. Its form—each stanza has the shape of a wheelbarrow—also echoes the homely audacity of its claim that in the modern era we must rethink what art is, where it comes from, to whom it belongs, and what it should do.

What is happening in this brief paragraph? It begins by saying something so obvious that maybe you didn't even think it needed to be said because no one could disagree: the basic account of where we are and also what kind of words these are. But then the discussion homes in on a single detail, one word, and what seemed obvious is turned around, made surprising, sharpened. Then the paragraph builds an argument about how to understand the whole poem in light of just one word. The close reading ties together the poem's form and content. It reaches beyond the poem to talk about art and social class.

How does this close reading work? How does it move from its beginning to the end? Here are the five steps again: *scene setting, noticing, local claiming, regional argumentation,* and *global theorizing*. Remember: we are talking about how to organize a close reading in an essay, article, or chapter; we are talking about literary scholarship or criticism and not what the activity of reading itself is like. First we'll run through the steps, and then we'll provide concrete examples for each.

Step 1: Scene Setting. Scene setting identifies what you think matters in the text. What is relevant for the close reading that is about to arrive? Limit the information at hand, and only provide the background that makes what you will notice and argue meaningful. You are establishing common ground with your reader.

Here is the scene setting in the close reading on "The Red Wheelbarrow"—

In William Carlos Williams's "The Red Wheelbarrow," the vocabulary—chickens nearby a wet wheelbarrow—is simple. Kindergarteners would be familiar with nearly all of the words in this poem. They are drawn from the everyday world of agriculture.

These sentences mark the range of what we will pay attention to in this poem, and set the stage for the rest of the close reading.

Step 2: Noticing. Then the close reader focuses more tightly by *noticing* a detail. Noticing is often expressed as bafflement or surprise—something's missing, something's in excess, something's odd. Why this word rather than another? Why this punctuation mark? Why repeat that word? Why this ambiguity? Why this leap or lacuna? What has caught your attention, what has snagged you, where are you stuck?

In this step, you, the close reader, point to the detail that you've noticed—you identify it as specifically as possible. You usually explain why you noticed it, often with a statement of confusion, curiosity, or even annoyance. Sometimes students worry that what they notice is obvious. In our experience, the more precise the detail, the less obvious it is, and also the less likely anyone else will have also noticed it.

Sometimes experienced scholars notice details more effectively than novices, because they are more aware of literary conventions and where a text might be departing from them: they might be more skilled at scansion and so may notice where an iamb is substituted with a trochee; they might understand the generic expectations of gothic fiction and so notice when a narrator's perspective is particularly untrustworthy. But sometimes brand-new first-years notice details that experts have never stopped to consider. Don't be intimidated or feel like everything has already been seen and explained long ago—it hasn't! Trust that what surprised you will surprise your reader.

To notice well, you have to read slowly and be ready to be surprised; pay attention to your own expectations. You may even imagine writing the text as you read it. You should be able to point to what you notice: it must really be there on the page, and ideally it should be small enough to fit under your fingertip. If it's diffuse—if you notice a vibe or style or tone or even a theme—find the best example and point to that. If you're noticing ambiguity, you must be able to point to a specific detail as an example.

Here is the noticing in the close reading of "The Red Wheelbarrow"—

But there is one exception—right in the middle of the poem, one of these words sticks out, one of these words is not like the others—"glazed." "Glazed" is not from the same set of vocabulary as "chickens" or even other adjectives like "red." "Glazed" comes from a different world than the rest of this scene; it comes from the world of the aesthetic, of art and beauty.

We point out a detail—the single word "glazed." It's really on the page and small enough to fit under a fingertip. Then we explain not just what we noticed but why we noticed it.

Step 3: Local Claiming. After noticing a detail, the close reader makes a claim about how to understand what they have noticed. The close reader does this by saying how that detail is working in its immediate context of a sentence, line or stanza, moment, or paragraph. We call this step *local claiming*.

A claim is not description nor summary: it is interpretation. A claim says "understand this detail this way." Just as the detail you have noticed must be as specific as possible, your language here must be as precise as possible. Spend the time to make your account of how to understand the detail that you've noticed tight, to say exactly what you mean, and know that you may continue to tinker with the claim so that you have the right terms.

Your claim should say something along the lines of "X detail in Y text should be understood in Z way." Further, if you are saying "understand this detail this way," then you are implicitly saying "and not just that way." A claim, then, must have potential counter-arguments, and if someone could not disagree with a claim, it is not a claim at all. If you've noticed an example of the color red and you are arguing that it symbolizes blood, that is usually grounds for a weak argument, because such a claim rarely sustains reasonable counter-arguments. What would probably work better is to notice the text's use of symbolism and make an argument about why it is using figurative rather than literal language. Someone else could agree with you that red symbolizes blood, but disagree with you—usefully!—about how to understand the text's turn to figuration.

Coming up with compelling counter-arguments is a great way to test and sharpen a claim; ask yourself or someone else how the same detail might be understood differently. Don't create counter-arguments that are fake or purposefully weak—straw men that no one who has read the text carefully would be convinced by—in the hope that it will make your argument look stronger by contrast when you knock them down. The stronger the counter-argument, the stronger your claim. The reason for this is that claims offer to help the readers of your essay with their own confusion. When you say, "understand this detail this way (and not in that way)," what you're also saying is "it is *useful* to you if you understand this detail this way (and less useful if you understand it some other way)." A claim makes sense of whatever you notice; a claim offers help. You, the close reader, need to be confident and precise. You are now the teacher. You should own your own authority explicitly here; you need to recognize that you are telling your own reader that it will make a difference to them if they to listen to you.

Here is the local claiming in the close reading of "The Red Wheelbarrow"—

By describing the wheelbarrow as glazed, by describing the rainwater on it as akin to a glass-like shine as on ceramics, the poem grants a surprising status— the status of an art object—to an ordinary gardening tool.

This step is a claim that links the detail—"*By describing the wheelbarrow as glazed*"—to an interpretation—"*the poem grants . . . the status of an art object . . . to an ordinary gardening tool.*" This claim shows how the detail is working in its immediate surroundings in the text; it makes sense of what was confusing just one step before.

And the claim launches an argument. Someone could disagree with this interpretation of what the poem is doing with the word "glazed." Maybe "glazed" should be understood as a lack of focus, like when eyes are glazed. Maybe "glazed" is about use-value rather than aesthetic value, as ceramic pots that are glazed are more waterproof, or there could be a claim that aesthetic value and use-value can coincide. This one-paragraph reading does not engage with those counter-arguments, but if it were longer, it could, and discussing why those other arguments do not show what this claim does (not necessarily that they're wrong but that they're not as useful or not useful in the same way) would strengthen it.

Step 4: Regional Argumentation. The close reader now reaches beyond the immediate context to say how that detail sheds light throughout the text— *regional argumentation*—by connecting it to other details. The link between each of these steps is not "and"; it is "so" or even "because." *Because* of the background established in *scene setting*, you can see the detail that *noticing* points to; *because* you see that detail, and because you can hear this *local claim* about it, you can begin to understand how it helps us understand other aspects of the text.

Regional argumentation uses the local claim as a lens through which one can see something else about the text. You might connect the text's content to its form or style or show how two apparently unlike aspects of the text are flipsides of one another as you move toward an account of the text as a whole. This is also a step that benefits from considering possible counter-arguments. Indeed, someone might agree with the local claim but see another path than the one you're pursuing to a larger regional argument.

Your local claim says, "understand this detail this way," your regional argument says, "by agreeing with my claim, you will better understand what this concept means in this text" or even "by agreeing with my claim, you will better understand how this text conceptualizes this idea and explains how it works." That concept might be one that lots of people have written about, like love, nature, or power, or one that's been overlooked or seems too obvious to investigate. (In the third section of this book, we offer some sample close readings that invoke concepts including lyric, description, and colonialism in their arguments about texts.) Regional argumentation is where your claim gets stakes, where its implications become clear, where you say why it matters.

Here is the regional argumentation in the close reading of "The Red Wheelbarrow"—

> *The poem suggests that aesthetic beauty can be found anywhere, even in this unlikely scene. Still further: the poem insists on the importance of recognizing that anything can be art. This is not a claim that beauty is in the eye of the beholder, but rather that art is not the exclusive property of the elite. The poem's simple vocabulary, then, reinforces this idea that art belongs to the everyday world of ordinary people. Its form—each stanza has the shape of a wheelbarrow . . .*

The detail the writer has noticed and made a local claim about is connected to other details in other parts of the text, or to other aspects of the text. The argument that "glazed" gives the wheelbarrow the status of an art object is linked to the poem's simple vocabulary and its wheelbarrow-like stanzaic form. There's an account of the text as a whole, one that itself depends on textual details like the poem's vocabulary and form but links up to ideas about art and class: beauty must be common, in both the senses of being simple and widespread.

Step 5: Global Theorizing. Finally, the close reader reaches further to connect the reading to the author's body of work, the text's genre, form, or period, or historical context: *global theorizing*. Global theorizing can be extremely powerful; this step is where we locate the experience of literature telling us about the world and teaching us new ways of understanding our place in the vast reaches of space and time, and also in the confines of our own bodies. You can't skip right to this though: you have to build your way here. Most undergraduate essays do not reach global theorizing, or only gesture toward this step, even in a senior thesis. Global theorizing is the step that requires the most advanced knowledge of the field and discipline, which is, after all, one of the distinctions between undergraduate work and professional scholarship. It is worthwhile, though, for undergraduates to be familiar with global theorizing because, even if you do not plan on pursuing graduate work in literary studies, this is the horizon at which all your work is aimed. Your work, if you were to develop it further, could change how we understand other texts. It is also worthwhile to understand this last step to better recognize the stakes in the scholarship you read.

Here is the global theorizing in the close reading of "The Red Wheelbarrow"—

the homely audacity of its claim that in the modern era, we must rethink what art is, where it comes from, who it belongs to, and what it should do.

This brief paragraph-long close reading has only the most gestural global theorizing. Here, it's an idea about how art has changed in the modern era. This step is where this close reading would link up with theory and scholarship not just about William Carlos Williams or even poetry, but about modernist aesthetics more generally, as well as theories about the intersection of art and class.

We developed these names for the steps of close reading for this book by reading and rereading some of the most famous close readings from the past hundred years and discovering that they make the same moves. We named them to help us see across apparent dissimilarities that although close readings seem to work in many different ways, there is a shared methodology. The distinctions between local claiming, regional argumentation, and global theorizing are partly descriptions of scale and reach; local, regional, and global describe the deliberate extension from the particular to the abstract. But also, in showing how an interpretation grows and gathers force, we paired the geographical vocabulary with the stages of argumentation, which begins with a claim—often a single sentence—then strengthens to an argument involving the analysis of evidence and the invocation of conceptual terms, and then, working theoretically, intensifies and widens further to reach beyond the text.

Just as we can separate and identify the basic parts of a poem—lines, sounds, images—or of a lab report—methods, results, discussion—so too can we separate and identify these steps of a close reading. As with poems and lab reports, the whole exceeds the sum of the parts. But there are parts. A close reading is nearer to a proof than to a poem; a close reading turns a quotation from a literary text into evidence that can support a claim and that has stakes. The best close readings make their steps look natural, even inevitable. But like a dance, we can still discern and name the moves, however gracefully they're embodied, while affirming that, like a dance, success depends in part on the gracefulness of the performance.

Our example of a close reading of "The Red Wheelbarrow" makes the right moves, and makes them fairly gracefully as it interprets the poem's ideas about what's valued, what's art. What it doesn't show, though, is the core of why we close read: because we value art. We think so much depends upon it. Moving from reading to a close reading, then, involves *being moved*.

What Close Reading Does

A close reading offers something useful to someone else. A close reading says not just "look at this!" but also "look at it this way" and then "because that makes a difference." You have something to offer your reader, something that will help them read the text you're discussing. In this section of our introduction, we'll talk about three different ways to think about what a close reading offers: *understanding*, a performance of *skill*, and *conversation*.

Understanding

A close reading is an argument. An argument requires a claim. It extends our understanding by reasoning from what is known to be the case—what we can all see in the text—to what is claimed to be the case—how we should understand what we see.[2] A claim is debatable; you want your reader to believe it, but you are going to have to prove it. A claim shouldn't overstate the case; you should only claim what you are prepared to prove. A claim also shouldn't understate; you can and should be bold. When you're close reading, a claim points to a detail or moment in the text and then takes a leap into interpretation—in our words, it moves from *noticing* to *local claiming*. This section will discuss how to make that move, which lies at the heart of any close reading. In the previous section of the introduction, we outlined the five steps that close readings take. Argument is the route and the rationale that connects those steps; its logic underpins them.

To build toward an argument that extends our understanding, you must distinguish a claim about a text from a summary or description of it. A good summary or description is accurate and not contestable. It wouldn't make sense to call a claim "accurate," and a claim must be contestable. Understanding how to use close readings to argue is one of the fundamental skills of college-level literary studies.

Writing your own arguments is a big leap for many students. In high school, your writing assignments likely asked you to summarize and describe, to identify themes and distill main ideas. You may be familiar, maybe even have expertise, with writing five-paragraph essays. (If you don't know this term:

---

2. For an extended argument about how argument functions differently in the humanities than in the sciences, see Eric Hayot, *Humanist Reason: A History. An Argument. A Plan.* (Columbia University Press, 2021).

a five-paragraph essay comprises an introduction, three body paragraphs, and a conclusion, with the thesis, often the last sentence of the introduction, stating a topic for the essay, usually identifying a theme that the essay traces through the text with one example in each body paragraph.) This sort of writing can be a useful way to learn what an essay should roughly look like. But it is not an argument; what it shows is comprehension. A standard five-paragraph essay is nearly all summary and description. In other words: it looks like an essay but doesn't do everything an essay can do.

A five-paragraph essay might have a thesis like this: "In Shakespeare's *Romeo and Juliet*, the repeated mention of 'hours' shows that time is an important theme." The first paragraph might discuss the conversation between Romeo and Benvolio about Romeo's "sad hours" before he meets Juliet; the second, Romeo and Juliet's plan to meet "by the hour of nine" in the balcony scene; and the third, the description of Juliet as Romeo's "three-hours wife" at the time he is banished; and therefore, the essay might conclude, time is an important theme in this play. This essay might result from reading a text with attention—it might say "look at this"—but it is not a close reading: it does not explain how to understand even one detail in the text, much less the text as a whole. It is not an argument.

But you can build on the skills you already have. There's no *local claiming* or *regional argumentation* in a five-paragraph essay, but there could be. This example of a five-paragraph essay about *Romeo and Juliet* could become a strong close reading. Take the general statement that "time is an important theme" and use that as *scene setting*. Scene setting is summary or description; it's not the end of argumentation but the beginning. You could even add the detail that the whole play takes place over only a few days to focus the summary further. Then "time" is no longer the conclusion of a high school five-paragraph essay but the initial premise, the background: identifying the prominence of time in *Romeo and Juliet* prepares us to notice a detail and make a real claim about the play.

Take the more specific pointing to "Romeo's 'sad hours' before he meets Juliet" and recognize that it's *noticing*. You have paid attention not only to the text but to your response to it: maybe you were struck by the strangeness of referring to "hours," objective units of clock time, as "sad"; or maybe you were annoyed that the play jostled you out of your absorption by reminding you about the passing of time. For some reason, emerging out of your puzzlement or personal investment of one sort or another, you became attached to "sad hours."

We could generalize and say that in five-paragraph essays, *scene setting* is placed as a thesis, and then each paragraph has some *noticing*. But in a college essay—and beyond—you make a claim. You could make a claim along any number of lines, including something like: "In *Romeo and Juliet*, the hour, a shared measurement of time, is also used as a measurement of personal emotion. As a result, throughout the play, time represents an intersection between the objective and the subjective, and an examination of how characters struggle to determine a common basis for understanding each other." Or you could make a completely different argument about hours, like this: "The characters' constant discussion of time in *Romeo and Juliet*, especially in the small unit of the hour, serves to remind the audience not only of the compressed timeline of the play, but of the even more compressed—and more artificial—timeline of watching a play. They should be read as moments of self-consciousness of the play's artistry." These sketched-out close readings share the same *scene setting* and even the same *noticing* as each other—and as the imagined five-paragraph essay—but have very different *local claiming* and so then they also have different *regional argumentation*. But because they have *local claiming*, they both argue rather than just summarize and describe.

How do you know if you're making a claim? When you make a claim, you're saying not just what you see in the text, but how to understand what you see: not just "look at this" but "look at it this way." The most important parts of *local claiming* are offering that understanding to your reader and being precise and clear in your language. Getting the claim into just the right words takes time and effort; we often revise our claims until the end of the writing process. While you shouldn't write a claim with the goal of being contentious, if you're specific in what you notice and precise in what you say about it, that alone will ensure that no one else is likely to see or say it in quite the same way—your argument will be your own. If you've noticed a detail in the text because it snagged your attention but you don't know what your claim about it should be, don't worry; if you noticed something, especially something you found surprising or odd, you probably have some kind of hunch about its importance in the text that led to it jumping out at you in the first place. You may not have a claim yet, but you also probably aren't as far as you might think.

What makes a claim a good claim? A good claim is a clear claim. A claim should be specific and precise in what it says about how to understand what it notices. This is a matter of your word choice, but choosing the right words requires a lot of thinking about what you mean. For example, the claim about *Romeo and Juliet*: "In *Romeo and Juliet*, the hour, a shared measurement of time, is also used as a measurement of personal emotion." Instead of "*personal* emotion," we could have said "*private* emotion" or "*individual* emotion," and these would have been similar to our claim but each would have led in a slightly different direction. The first alternative suggests skepticism's problem of other minds; the second alternative potentially points toward people as political subjects; and the claim we made is about the relationship of feelings to being a person. You have to get your words right, which helps you get your ideas right, which in turn helps you get your words right: writing and thinking happen together. These near relations to your argument are also counter-arguments. When you engage with a counter-argument, you don't have to say that it is wrong: it might just not be all the way right. Engaging with near-miss counter-arguments, done thoughtfully, helps you bring more nuance and lucidity to your own claim.

A good claim offers fuller understanding. Good claims do not necessarily notice more or larger things in the text—often the reverse, *noticing* usually remains narrow and specific—but some arguments are stronger because their explanations are powerful. In philosophy, you can talk about how an explanation succeeds in two different ways: because an explanation is probably true since it's the most warranted by the evidence; or because an explanation might be the most broadly explanatory, which means it's not as likely to be true but if it were, it would be very powerful. The philosopher Peter Lipton, who outlines this distinction, calls the first kind of explanation *likely* and the second kind *lovely*.[3] He uses the example of a conspiracy theory for lovely explanation—not likely to be true, but proposing an explanation that has extensive reach and force. Some close readers lean likely, others lovely.

A good claim is supported not just by evidence alone, but also by the analysis of that evidence. Your claim must be warranted. We sometimes tell students to think about a lawyer in a dramatic courtroom scene holding up a piece of evidence—say, a shoe or a receipt—but then remember how that lawyer has to show exactly how that shoe or receipt matches a footprint or has a timestamp, how it clinches the case or leads to an exoneration.

Here is an example of a claim that's clear, but fails to show how the argument is supported by the evidence. We had a student who argued that Robert Frost's poem "Stopping by Woods on a Snowy Evening" was about Christmas. The poem takes place at dusk in midwinter in a rural, pre-modern landscape as a traveler pauses with his "little horse" to watch the snow fall. The student chose a striking detail—"miles to go before I sleep"—as worthy of attention and hazarded an interpretation: it is Santa Claus who has to travel the whole

---

3. Peter Lipton, *Inference to the Best Explanation* (Routledge, 2004), 59.

world in one night; the speaker of the poem is Santa Claus; the poem is about Christmas. One could certainly disagree: the speaker is usually read as contemplating suicide. But the argument, though in some ways shaped like a close reading, is weak in an instructive way. It is neither likely nor lovely. It does a poor job of analyzing its evidence. The speaker travels with a horse, not a reindeer, as the student asserted. The tone of resignation—"But I have promises to keep"—doesn't belong to the idea of Santa as we understand him.

In short, the connection between the evidence and the argument was weak: there was no possible justification for how the evidence (winter, an animal, a task) counts as evidence. The philosopher Stephen Toulmin calls this link in an argument between evidence and claim a "warrant."[4] Close reading depends on making its warrants, its connective tissue, apparent to the reader, by accounting for why the quotation from the text works to support your argument. What might be obvious to you is not obvious to your reader, and quotations aren't self-evident as evidence. Notice and make your local claim—but also connect those for your reader. *Make your evidence into evidence* to support local claiming and regional argumentation. A large part of any close reading is showing how you're moving from one step to the next. You don't disappear from one step and reappear on the following one; you construct the route between them.

When students are confused about how argument works, they sometimes treat the text as a puzzle to be decoded, asserting, for example, that blue symbolizes peace. Such claims are typically unwarranted. Why should blue symbolize peace and not sadness, or sadness and not the ocean? But also, although decoding the speaker of "Stopping by Woods on a Snowy Evening" as Santa Claus is weak, it offers some new understanding. The poem does have a mythic quality: its attention to the solstice is interesting, its vague placelessness is strange, its vocabulary is childish or for children. A more successful essay that began with noticing that the poem takes place during the winter solstice and beyond "the village" might have argued, for example, that the poem is a critique of organized religion and its control over society. This argument could have connected the location of the poem to the poem's form to think more about how the poem investigates control as it keeps a tight, but slipping, grip on its meter and rhymes, and even argued that the blank white page stretching around the poem could be read as the solstice's white landscape and a place where there are no rules.

Finally, a good claim has stakes. It's not just noticing—"look at this"—nor just local claiming—"look at it this way"—but also the follow-through of

---

4. Stephen Toulmin, *The Uses of Argument* (Cambridge University Press, 2003), 135–36.

"because that makes a difference." The argument about *Romeo and Juliet* has stakes; if you argue this claim—"In *Romeo and Juliet*, the hour, a shared measurement of time, is also used as a measurement of personal emotion. As a result, throughout the play, time represents an intersection between the objective and the subjective, and an examination of how characters struggle to determine a common basis for understanding each other"—then the stakes will be about how language fails to communicate. You might end up arguing that Romeo and Juliet are the exception to this, that they are able to use words to establish their common world . . . or you may argue that the play's tragedy is that they ultimately cannot, and their misunderstandings doom them. But the stakes are about how the argument shifts our understanding of the play; they are a claim for the importance of the argument.

What counts as stakes? Stakes are calibrated skillfully, neither so immense to be implausible nor too inconsequential to matter. You don't need to solve world hunger or revolutionize our sense of Shakespeare. But you do need to give yourself credit for the power of what you are arguing. Stakes are often expressed via a conceptual term; for example, the stakes of the *Romeo and Juliet* argument are about *communication*—how it works and how it fails in this play. The "Stopping by Woods on a Snowy Evening"/Christmas essay doesn't have stakes because it doesn't have a strong argument. But an argument like "the poem's taking place during the solstice and beyond 'the village' is a critique of organized religion and its control over society," the stakes would be about *control*—its powers and its limits.

Figuring out what counts as stakes is part of learning the expectations, assumptions, and methods of the discipline of literary studies. It means recognizing how what matters to you in literature connects with the discipline's rules and sense of itself; it means entering our community of literary scholars. The philosopher of science Thomas Kuhn coined the term "paradigm" to describe when science has an "accepted practice" and "coherent traditions of scientific research."[5] For example, Ptolemaic astronomy, with the earth at the center of the solar system, was one scientific paradigm, and, in the Renaissance, it was replaced by Copernican astronomy, with the sun at the center. Kuhn calls working in an established paradigm "normal science," our typical practice. In literary studies, close reading is part of our normal science. So when we say that an argument based on close reading is useful, we mean that we believe it to be making new knowledge because it is playing by our rules. In the discipline of literary studies, you show the truth of an argument by demonstrating

---

5. Thomas Kuhn, *The Structure of Scientific Revolutions* (University of Chicago Press, 1996), 7.

how your evidence supports your claim and how your claim makes a difference in how we understand a text or term. If your argument is useful to other people—to your own readers—in offering greater understanding of a text in precise and clear language—it counts as good.

Skill

When we sit down to write, we often find ourselves uttering the phrase, "writing is hard." Your professors—we assure you—often struggle with it, writing some sentences, some paragraphs, even many pages again and again, trying to get it right. We did so with these pages. And close reading is a complex genre of writing. Sometimes students feel like they ought to excel at close reading from the start. That's almost never the case, even if you read attentively, even if you have lots of ideas about the text, even if you have always been a superb student and always loved literature and writing. This is a complex genre that requires knowing *how* to make the kinds of arguments we describe above; to do so requires a set of skills specific to the genre that you have (almost certainly) not yet mastered. In short: it's okay if it's hard; it's hard for a reason; one of those reasons is that writing close readings takes practice. We wrote this book to help you improve.

What does it mean that close reading is a craft and a skill?[6] As a craft, close reading shares qualities with knitting, pottery, and woodworking; you show you know how to do it and in knowing how you reveal deeper knowledge of yarn, clay, wood—or words.[7] As a skill, close reading is akin to practicing a sport or a musical instrument; your practice makes you stronger, more confident, more careful. No one can pole vault without instruction and practice. Close reading is more than a set of steps with an argument. Even if you have the elements of a good argument, you can communicate them poorly, and the argument can be less effective than it should be.

Apt execution matters. For your *scene setting*, you might need to provide plot summary in just a sentence or two, or to capture the implicit occasion for a lyric poem; you might embed a quote among your own language; you might delimit your intellectual terrain by pointed exclusion; and this is just *scene setting*. You reveal the nuance of your understanding in the nuance of your prose. And not only your understanding: a pianist is bound to a score but a good pianist imprints her own style. A close reading is also a creative act. In the precise choice

---

6. For an account of close reading as a "cultural technique," see John Guillory, *On Close Reading* (University of Chicago Press, 2025).

7. See also Jonathan Kramnick, *Criticism and Truth* (University of Chicago Press, 2023).

and order of words and punctuation you put your own mind on display. The best close readings dazzle with both their careful attention to the text and to their own thinking and writing. The best close readings have command, style, even fun.

But how are you supposed to know what a dazzling close reading looks like? It's impossible to write poetry well if you never read it, never find poets who show you, say, what a single line can do. Because you need examples, this book is not just a presentation of the steps, not just us telling you how to accomplish them; it also includes many examples, examples where you see a dazzling close reading nested in an account of how it was done. Reading these is, we hope, like a football player watching classic game tape with a coach to isolate opportunities for instruction.

The contributors to this volume isolate many different skills. For example, to move from *local claiming* to *regional argumentation*, you might rely on the side-by-side comparison of details—such as, say, the description of two characters—to "identify abstract underlying patterns" and to "detect subtle differences in gradation," as Elaine Auyoung demonstrates. Under Auyoung's guidance, the familiar task of compare-and-contrast—which can thwart a strong argument if it substitutes for a claim—becomes an analytical tool of great power, fueling the argument. But it takes practice to develop the specific acuity required to know when differences are salient, and how. Auyoung's comparison is a learned skill that enables the inferential, inductive logic of argumentation. The selection of fruitful details, or what we call *noticing*, is the fundamental skill of close reading, the ground upon which the rest is built. Among many techniques, you might, as Jeff Dolven and Joshua Kotin suggest, imagine yourself as the author of a text, making decisions word by word. Why, if you were the author, would you follow that word with this one?

Undergirding *noticing* or any other skill is the most fundamental skill of all in the study of literature: you must train yourself to be aware of your experience when reading. Normally, we read to enjoy a text, which often involves a sense of immersion where we pleasurably lose ourselves. It is difficult to learn to watch yourself reading, which, to be valuable, ought to be at once analytical, in the sense that you are observing yourself, and naive, in the sense that you are also the object of your observation—and the you who is observed ideally preserves her immediate responses of pleasure and surprise. Some sometimes worry that this most fundamental skill can alienate students from the joy of reading, kill pleasure, ruin books; but, when done right, close reading preserves the old pleasure while doubling it with a new satisfaction: the pursuit of knowledge, the accomplishment of skill, the thrill of discovery, and a deeper intimacy with literature.

Conversation

You might read alone. But we close read with other people. Close readings emerge out of conversations and they flow back into conversations. They are products of and offerings to a community.

When you read literary criticism in academic journals or books, you might feel like you are eavesdropping on a long-running conversation between scholars where close reading is part of what they offer to each other. You are—and as you respond to their arguments, you are joining their conversation. You might find yourself agreeing, or not. You might want to respond "yes, and. . . ." You can build on or alongside or back down from someone else's scene setting, noticing, local claiming, regional argumentation, or global theorizing. (Look in the last section of this book to see how scholars situate close readings as part of longer genres of writing.)

You can also build your own close reading from the ground up. But that still does not have to mean doing it alone. Once you can identify the steps of close reading, you will see how good class discussion can take the shape of a collaborative close reading: one student notices a detail, another makes a local claim about it, another offers a counter-argument, another student connects that first detail to a second, another links them by arguing regionally. When we teach, we often prompt students to begin our conversations in exactly this way. "What did you notice?" we ask. "What's the local claim?" "Are there counter-arguments?" "What else does that detail connect to?" "How can we argue regionally?" "What terms are at stake?" "How can we theorize this argument globally?" Even if your teacher doesn't ask discussion questions using our vocabulary, you can still map how a conversation moves forward—and how you can help it move forward—with the steps from this book.

You might go from classroom conversation—or any conversation, really—to writing your own close reading, which you might then send to someone: an instructor, probably, but maybe also an editor or a family member or a friend. To send someone a close reading—or anything you've written, really—is an act of hope. Hope entails risk, and risk makes it nerve-wracking to send someone your writing. You can mitigate risk by making strong and skillful arguments with the help of this volume. But risk always remains in asking for a conversation. For such a request to succeed, you need to demonstrate that you really want a conversation, that you care about the matter at hand. Your interlocutor needs to hear you saying something like: I want you to see what I see because it matters to me; I care about it, and I care about whether you care about it. For an invitation to conversation to work, you need to write about something that matters to you: you think something about a text should be understood a certain way, and you put in the time and effort and care to say so. After all, as Jeff Dolven and Joshua Kotin write in chapter 5, "one of the things that close reading is" is "a way of figuring out how to talk about how a poem makes you feel." You figure out how you feel and think and you ask your reader if they feel how you do, think how you do, and if not, why not?

When we get stuck in our own writing, we remember that Dante has his beloved Beatrice say something of a motto: "Amor mi mosse, che mi fa parlare"—*love moved me, that makes me speak*. This might sound very far away from a homework assignment, but can you think about how love makes you speak? What do you see in the text that you care about? What are you compelled to say about it to someone else who might not see it, or see it the way you do? When we get stuck, we like to begin a new paragraph as if it were a letter addressed to someone we love: *Dear* _____ . . .

Close reading *should* entail risk. Everything valuable does. We encourage you to take seriously the task of standing between, and thinking with, two other people. Someone has invited you to think with them: whoever wrote the text under consideration. Allow something about the text to matter to you. Write about what matters to you. You enter the conversation in good faith and invite a third: your reader. Each makes themself vulnerable to misunderstanding. But the reward, if it works, is intellectual community.

What Close Reading Has Been

In the first two sections of this introduction we aimed to teach you what close reading is and what it does—and also to invite you to care about it. We hope you feel that it is a practice worth cultivating. This section depends on your interest. Our tone changes—it becomes a little more technical—because we are addressing you now as a close reader or aspiring close reader who wants to situate yourself in the history of literary studies, who wants to know how its practitioners have practiced so that you can be an informed practitioner yourself. Whether you know it or not, your ideas about how to read have been shaped by the theories we discuss in this section, so it helps to be self-aware about how you're already thinking about what art is and how it works.

You will encounter references in this book to schools of thought that have been influential for close reading: New Criticism, deconstruction, New Historicism, Marxism, postcolonialism, psychoanalysis, and others.[8] When we were literature students, these were often taught as options on the menu of methodologies—choose one and do a reading with it—which frustrated us because it obscured what made these movements matter: what motivated their founders, who they were arguing against, why they cared. In the next few pages, we provide some of this context. It's often the case that literature professors tightly associate close reading with New Criticism. But many other movements, including those most critical of New Criticism, developed the practice in subsequent decades and depend on it, even if our account of close reading hasn't kept pace.

New Criticism

Imagine your professor hands you a set of poems and asks you to analyze them. But their authors and titles have been redacted. This is the storied origin of close reading, an experiment conducted by I. A. Richards at Cambridge University in the 1920s. Even strong students with experience reading poetry struggled. They failed to make out the plain meaning of the poems, the foundation for any

---

8. For classic overviews that remain salient, see Terry Eagleton, *Literary Theory: An Introduction* (University of Minnesota Press, 2008), and, specifically on deconstruction, Jonathan Culler, *On Deconstruction* (Cornell University Press, 2008). For postcolonialism, see Leela Gandhi, *Postcolonial Theory: A Critical Introduction* (Columbia University Press, 2019). For reassessments of practical criticism and New Criticism, see Andy Hines, *Outside Literary Studies: Black Criticism and the University* (University of Chicago Press, 2022), and Joseph North, *Literary Criticism: A Concise Political History* (Harvard University Press, 2017).

further study. They went wrong variously, which Richards recorded: among other errors, they gave stock responses; pursued irrelevant personal associations; indulged in sentimentality; and did not feel the poems' sensual qualities, such as rhythm. These problems persist one hundred years later.

Richards was astonished at the extent of misapprehension, and he made it his project to document it. Curiously, though credited as the founder of close reading, he did not practice it much, neither as a writer nor as a teacher. Instead, he wrote and taught as part of a collective experiment in studying our habits of reading. We should remember that close reading, although central to literary studies, is not without alternatives.[9] We might study genres, or authors' biographies, or texts' relations to context, or, like Richards, we might conduct experiments belonging to a larger research project—all of which are compatible, too, with close reading.

Though not much of a close reader himself, Richards inspired an influential generation of scholars to address common errors of misapprehension by developing the practice of how to do it persuasively, skillfully—correctly. Noreen Masud, in chapter 18, wrestles with a student of Richards, William Empson, who accomplished dazzling, intimidating interpretations of texts, shucking tight clams to present us glistening pearls of insight. Already in Empson, close readings become artworks worthy of close reading, an argument Katie Kadue picks up in chapter 7 on Christopher Ricks, an inheritor of Empson, showing that their style of close reading—in which the analyst mimics the style of the text at hand—thrives in the twenty-first century. A protégé of Ricks, Eric Griffiths, demonstrates the power of stripping back to the basics—who says what when and where to whom—as Robert Stagg presents in chapter 4. A later student of Richards, Helen Vendler, proposed close reading by identifying with poets, by *becoming* them, imagining how they wrote their poems, word by word, a technique Jeff Dolven and Joshua Kotin explore in chapter 5.

Richards's legacy persists in the United Kingdom under the name practical criticism and in critics such as Angela Leighton, who, as Beci Carver shows in chapter 3, argues that the sounds of literature are indispensable to understanding its meaning. When Richards's scholarship traveled to the United States, it evolved into New Criticism, which conservative intellectuals established in the 1930s and

---

9. For an account of some of those alternatives, see Rachel Sagner Buurma and Laura Heffernan, *The Teaching Archive: A New History for Literary Study* (University of Chicago Press, 2021).

1940s, and which held sway as a dominant movement into the 1960s.[10] Whereas Richards taught students to infer a poet's intention from a poem (a practice taken to its limit by Helen Vendler), New Critics argued that intention was irrelevant to the critic—a debate that continues today. New Critics emphasized the uniqueness of literature. They argued that the orderly form created by an exact sequence of words, placed precisely, enables unique effects, such as irony and paradox, which make literature a rich source of knowledge about humanity.

According to New Critics, to paraphrase literature deprives it of its power. Consider Robert Frost's poem "The Road Not Taken":

Two roads diverged in a yellow wood,
And sorry I could not travel both
And be one traveler, long I stood
And looked down one as far as I could

To where it bent in the undergrowth;
Then took the other, as just as fair,
And having perhaps the better claim,
Because it was grassy and wanted wear;

Though as for that the passing there
Had worn them really about the same,
And both that morning equally lay
In leaves no step had trodden black.

Oh, I kept the first for another day!
Yet knowing how way leads on to way,
I doubted if I should ever come back.
I shall be telling this with a sigh

Somewhere ages and ages hence:
Two roads diverged in a wood, and I—
I took the one less traveled by,
And that has made all the difference.

We might say the poem is about *how we'll never know what might have been had we made a different choice at a crucial juncture when we were younger*, but that

---

10. New Criticism continued to travel internationally. For an account that traces its worldwide influence, see Yael Segalovitz, *How Close Reading Made Us: The Transnational Legacies of New Criticism* (SUNY Press, 2024).

we'll nevertheless think back on that juncture longingly. And we might get at something of the gist of the poem. But no matter how well we summarize it, the summary will be fundamentally weaker than the poem, because the poem's strength is in how Frost crafts it with rhymes on simple words and lines that sometimes end with grammatical stops and sometimes are enjambed, calling on us to feel the poem with our ears and the hair on our neck as we think about it with our mind. The art of noticing as a close reader involves learning to recognize how the elements of a text's form make it function as a work of literature.

Belief in the uniqueness of literature lends itself to aesthetic judgment.[11] If you think literature is distinct from other kinds of writing, it's a short step to arguing that what makes a work of literature good is its commitment to those qualities that make literature distinct. Thus John Crowe Ransom, a leading New Critic, argued for the superiority of the metaphysical poets, such as John Donne, because of their deft deployment of paradox, over the Romantics, such as William Wordsworth. Similarly, Cleanth Brooks, resuscitating one Romantic in Ransom's wake, argued that John Keats's "Ode on a Grecian Urn" is the apex of poetry because it brings paradox to its apotheosis. By enacting paradox, an irreducible truth of human experience, and by making paradox beautiful through a text's harmonious unity, literature makes life bearable: an argument that Emily Ogden makes in chapter 15, following Robert Penn Warren in his reading of a poem by Ransom.

New Critics worried that the rise of scientific authority and expertise, in public and in universities, would limit our understanding of truth to what science can prove, leading us to forget about the truths to which literature testifies. They argued that literature offers unique access to truth through irony, paradox, and its powers of directing our attention. As reactionary white men, especially in the earlier years, Brooks, Ransom, Warren, and their fellow New Critics, went further, using the harmonious unity of poems to argue against what they saw as the fragmentation of industrial modernity, preferring the agrarian past of the racist US South. Whether they embrace or reject New Criticism, subsequent scholars have grappled with its legacy of racism.[12]

11. For a study of practical critics, New Critics, and the problem of judgment, see John Guillory, *On Close Reading* (University of Chicago Press, 2025).

12. See Niall Munro, "Neo-Confederates Take Their Stand: Southern Agrarians and the Civil War," *European Journal of American Culture* 39, no. 2 (2020): 141–62; Andy Hines, "New Criticism and the Object of American Democracy," in *Outside Literary Studies* (University of

Arguing with and against New Critics, the question of context became a core concern for future close readers.

Deconstruction

If you were to close read like a deconstructionist, you might notice when a text is self-referential, such as when the speaker of Frost's "The Road Not Taken" says, near the end, "I shall be telling this with a sigh / Somewhere ages and ages hence." Now, as you read the poem, *is* that telling, that ages and ages hence. Or you might notice when a text contradicts itself, such as when Frost's speaker says he took the road "less traveled" even though earlier he'd noted that "the passing there / Had worn" both paths "really about the same." Or you might notice how a text sets up binaries that it can't maintain, such as Frost's less and more (or equally?) traveled roads. Noticing these details might lead you to theorize that poetry, like life, is never one thing, never unified in some pure present, but is always divided from itself.

Deconstruction arrived in the United States in October 1966 when a charismatic French philosopher named Jacques Derrida spoke at a conference at Johns Hopkins University. Its influence grew across the 1970s. Deconstruction rejects tenets of New Criticism, above all the idea that a work of literature is a unified whole that provides access to enduring human truths. Instead, deconstructionists argue that every literary text is in conflict with itself, inescapably fragmented, porous with its context. If, for New Critics, the unit of literature is the *work*, for deconstructionists, signaling their difference, it is the *text*.

Early New Critics looked back longingly to a preindustrial past. Early deconstructionists looked ahead in anticipation of a future when we will have transcended myths of individuality, knowing that language governs us more than we govern it. For deconstructionists, language is the context for a text. Theirs is a Nietzschean world where God is dead, truths are socially constructed, and we must overcome two millennia of Platonic metaphysics with its privileging of spiritual, timeless essences in favor of the pre-Socratic chaos and flux of a will to power. One American scholar remembered the excitement many felt at the time: "Just when New Criticism was looking old,

---

Chicago Press, 2022); Matt Seybold, host, *The American Vandal*, podcast, season 9, episode 5, "The Racist Interpretation Complex," Center for Mark Twain Studies, August 28, 2023, 1 hr., 21 min., 21 sec.; Miranda B. Hickman and John D. McIntyre, eds., *Rereading the New Criticism* (Ohio State University Press, 2012).

deconstructionism came along to make close reading chic and smart and potent again."[13]

Deconstruction gained institutional strength in the 1970s and 1980s, girded by its uptake in new academic fields: Black studies, postcolonialism, feminism, queer theory. These fields recognized the force of deconstruction's identification and disruption of binaries that give one side power over the other: white/Black, empire/colony, man/woman, straight/gay. The potential for using deconstruction to intellectually dismantle social boundaries was always latent given the continuity between text and context. Summer Kim Lee brings us an example in chapter 8 from Barbara Johnson. Johnson noticed something different in a favorite New Critical poem, John Keats's "Ode on a Grecian Urn." She noticed that the poem's speaker idealizes the urn's silence—but refuses to be silent about it. From there, Johnson builds a staggering reading that reveals the force of patriarchy as a hidden structure informing the history of art, enabling men to adopt the position of the victim in relation to women, and entrapping women in a double bind.

Henry Louis Gates Jr. adopted deconstruction for Black studies. Earlier critics, including deconstructionists, had identified what they called the master tropes of figurative language: metaphor, metonymy, synecdoche, and irony. Gates argued that "we might think of these as the 'master's tropes,'" referencing slavery to argue that figurative language is imbued with race in service of white supremacy.[14] Meanwhile, he argued that race—a social construction we treat as real, founded on a white/Black binary that cannot withstand pressure without falling apart—"is the ultimate trope of difference."[15] In a classic deconstructive inversion, he asserted that African American writers are the true masters of refusing closure and celebrating difference. In chapter 13, Omari Weekes demonstrates how Hortense Spillers—a former colleague of Gates and a foundational figure in Black studies who drew inspiration from deconstruction—explored the consequences for literary theory of centering Black women. Whereas Gates and Spillers focused on texts by Black authors, Toni Morrison accomplished an inversion in how we understand canonical white American

---

13. Jane Gallop, "The Historicization of Literary Studies and the Fate of Close Reading," *Profession* (2007): 181–86.

14. Henry Louis Gates Jr., "The 'Blackness of Blackness': A Critique of the Sign and the Signifying Monkey," *Critical Inquiry* 9, no. 4 (June 1983): 686.

15. Henry Louis Gates Jr., "Editor's Introduction: Writing 'Race' and the Difference It Makes," in *"Race," Writing, and Difference*, ed. Henry Louis Gates Jr. (University of Chicago Press, 1986), 5.

literature by placing race at its center. She turned our attention from the victims of racism to its perpetrators. "The subject of the dream is the dreamer," she wrote.[16] We should notice, then, what few bothered to notice before: how white writers imagine race. In chapter 6, Adrienne Brown pays attention to how Morrison close reads for "when and how race shows up in texts."

It has become increasingly common in some contexts to identify as nonbinary and to provide one's pronouns, part of a large cultural shift in our collective understanding of gender since the 1990s. Inspired by deconstruction and the work of French philosophers, especially that of Michel Foucault, scholars in gay and lesbian studies, literary studies, women's studies, and philosophy created queer theory. Since the 1970s, feminist scholars had used close reading to show how men degraded women with misogynistic stereotypes in their fiction. Literature by women, often newly rediscovered, offered an alternative with, some argued, powerful stylistic implications. Judith Butler intervened in feminist theory to argue that gender is not an essence at the core of our identity but a performance we must enact every day when we put on a skirt or slacks or inflect our voice this way or that—even if our performance is coerced and policed by social rules. We learned from Eve Kosofsky Sedgwick to take seriously her first axiom: "People are different from each other."[17] Sedgwick invited us to proliferate the possibilities for gender identifications and sexual orientations. The founding figures of queer theory were superb close readers. They show the transformative social potential of careful attention to a short passage of a text.

By 1990, when Butler and Sedgwick published landmark books, deconstruction was in retreat. It had been twenty-four years since Derrida delivered his groundbreaking paper at Johns Hopkins. Deconstruction had displaced New Criticism. But critics argued that deconstruction had too much in common with New Criticism. Barbara Christian, a Black feminist critic, argued in 1987 that deconstruction focused on dead white men from the Western tradition to the exclusion—possibly tactically, she suggested—of flourishing new writing from women of color. Those Black scholars who adopted deconstruction, she wrote, had been co-opted "into speaking a language and defining their discussion in terms alien to and opposed to our needs and orientation."[18] She called for attention to the sensuousness of African American literature. Natalia Cecire writes, in chapter 11, about how Butler, who previously close-read philosophy more than literature, heeded Christian's call, offering a

---

16. Toni Morrison, *Playing in the Dark* (Harvard University Press, 1992), 17.
17. Eve Kosofsky Sedgwick, *Epistemology of the Closet* (University of California Press, 1990), 22.
18. Barbara Christian, "The Race for Theory," *Cultural Critique* 6 (Spring 1987): 52.

close reading of Nella Larsen's *Passing* whereby Butler could theorize sex, gender, and race together.

Others, in the 1980s, argued that both New Criticism and deconstruction sanctified the aesthetic object, the literary work or text, by treating it as distinct from other historical documents. Both New Criticism and deconstruction declared the author irrelevant, dead. Both paid such close attention to literature that, even as they attended to race, sex, and gender, they elided history, the fundamental source of context. By eliding history, they missed—their critics said—everything.

Historicism

The turn to history was not a turn away from close reading. But the new movements needed to find a new tradition that reconciled history and literature. They found it in the work of Erich Auerbach.

Auerbach was a German Jewish philologist steeped in the work of Italian philosopher Giambattista Vico, whose *New Science* (1725), which Auerbach translated, countered his era's leading theory, which asserted that truth is timeless and universal, by arguing that truth is particular to historical time. This was a revolutionary claim. Auerbach was further trained in a tradition of close reading that held that texts emerge from human experience and thus contain the world of that experience; it is the task of the critic to join extensive interdisciplinary knowledge, personal intuition, and precise attention to language to conjure that world from the text. In *Mimesis*, which Auerbach wrote from Istanbul, exiled by Hitler's Third Reich, he did so brilliantly, beginning with Homer and the Old Testament, describing their synthesis with Dante, and narrating the eventual disintegration of experience in modernity with James Joyce and Virginia Woolf. In each case, and with the figures he explicates in between, Auerbach close reads patiently to show how reality appeared in a series of historical moments, caught in the amber of literature.

Reading Auerbach can be intimidating. Not because he is difficult—he is easier to read than, say, Jacques Derrida—but because he makes extraordinary close reading look simple. He walks us from scene setting through global theorizing, allowing us to follow his inductive logic to awe-inspiring ends. Oren Izenberg and Julie Orlemanski, in chapters 1 and 9, explain how he does it: through rhetorical sleights of hand.

Izenberg notices something odd in Auerbach's scene setting when it comes to Virginia Woolf. Auerbach changes one small detail, which makes a big difference for his reading. Rather than see this as cheating, Izenberg argues that misdescription is often revelatory of the perspective that close reading demands of a reader. Orlemanski argues that though Auerbach presents us with a clear, direct path, his investigative process of clearing it was meandering, requiring he travel hermeneutic circles. Auerbach interprets a passage from a medieval French play about Adam and Eve. His local claim relies on previous knowledge he holds about medieval French peasants. If, as Emily Ogden shows us, New Critics supplement interpretation with social knowledge—how we read people in life—Auerbach supplements interpretation with historical knowledge: moving cyclically between history and text. Auerbach inadvertently shows us that every close reading is partial, but no less true for its partiality.

Auerbach inspired at least three traditions of close reading: New Historicism; Marxism; and postcolonialism. He showed that with enough erudition and stylistic verve, a scholar could reveal the world embedded in a short passage from a historical literary text. Scholars who shaped these traditions were undergraduates when New Criticism was dominant, and they found in Auerbach a refreshing opening from the cloistered text onto the world. (If you are an undergraduate reading this, you, too, belong to the continuing history of literary criticism and should carry yourself with the poise of your participation.) These traditions resisted deconstruction in different but important ways—and not without adopting something from French philosophy.

In the 1980s, a group of scholars in California, impatient with the persistence of New Criticism and opposed to how deconstruction "seems to re-erect the hierarchical privileges of the literary," came to be associated with New Historicism. *Came to be associated* because New Historicists are eclectic, pluralistic, and non-programmatic. Two commitments unite them: the refusal to separate literary from non-literary texts; and a resistance to the abstract, the general, and the theoretical in favor of the "singular, the specific, and the individual." They took from Auerbach the practice of finding in a brief passage "a vast social process."[19] They tend to resurrect the author muted by New Criticism and killed by deconstruction. Without agreed-upon principles, New Historicism, more than most methods, depends on the virtuosity of scholarly performance.

New Criticism advises us to notice irony and paradox, deconstruction binaries and self-referential moments. New Historicism, in contrast, suggests that the decision about what to notice is not very important.[20] Whatever we

---

19. Catherine Gallagher and Stephen Greenblatt, *Practicing New Historicism* (University of Chicago Press, 2000), 14, 6, 45.

20. Those of us experienced with New Historicism might notice that its claim that it matters little what we notice is an assertion of a methodological tenet following from a philosophy of

choose, we will discover language that belongs to some larger discourse from the time the text was written: maybe theological debates about the eucharist from language about the defilement and rot of bodies in *Hamlet*, from one celebrated essay.[21] Or to return to "The Road Not Taken," we might notice that it was published in 1916 and only recently had Americans begun to see woodland paths that were "grassy and wanted wear" as attractive and worth pursuing rather than frightening and in need of domination. Moving from noticing to theorizing—their resistance is to the deductive application of theory, not to inductive reasoning—New Historicists, like queer theorists, often bring to their close reading a philosophy drawn from Michel Foucault: the most insidious forms of power in contemporary society are not obvious but operate subtly through language, serving to control and govern people. New Historicists reject the concept of *reflection* as too simple. That is, texts do more than show us some social discourse; they themselves operate on discourse, becoming social agents whose actions reverberate in the world. The nineteenth-century novel disciplines bourgeois women into the domestic, gendered worldview necessary for the expansion of capitalism: take care of the house so your husband can be productive in society. Or "The Road Not Taken" instills in readers an ironic detachment in response to the increasing life decisions one—here, white men—could make in an industrializing, secularizing society. To make these arguments persuasive requires historical knowledge, conveyed to one's reader through elaborate scene setting.

"Always historicize!" exclaimed Fredric Jameson in 1981. He meant it differently from the New Historicists then formulating their ideas. They hew closely to Auerbach and Vico, understanding history as endowing texts with the spirit of the age. Jameson supplements Auerbach, whom he studied with at Yale, with Karl Marx.[22] G.W.F. Hegel subsumed Vico's theory into a teleological progression where the spirit of the age guides us toward ever greater knowledge; Marx inherited Hegel's historicism, keeping the teleology but installing a new guide, capitalism, leading us not toward knowledge but toward the limits

---

language rather than a faithful observation of actual practice; in practice, New Historicists tend to notice details that emerge as salient in the process of following Auerbachian hermeneutic circles from text to history and back again.

21. Catherine Gallagher and Stephen Greenblatt, "The Mousetrap," in *Practicing New Historicism* (University of Chicago Press, 2000), 136–62.

22. Jameson wrote an extensive critique of New Historicism. See Fredric Jameson, *Postmodernism, or, The Cultural Logic of Late Capitalism* (Duke University Press, 1991), 181–219. Jameson was also influenced by the genre criticism of Northrop Frye, in addition to Auerbach and Marx.

of its own constitutive contradictions that the proletariat will one day tip over into revolution. For Jameson, History with a capital *h*—which for him means class struggle and the mode of production, in the form, for the last several centuries, of capitalism—is what literature is ultimately about.[23]

The truest interpretation explains how a text's genre, plot, style—its form—crystallize an imagined resolution to the intractable obstacles of capitalism in a historical moment. Jameson's critic functions kind of like a psychoanalyst for texts, evoking their political unconscious, the historical truth obscured by their desire but that, when unlocked, gives uniquely potent if fragmentary access to capitalism's totality. Whereas the New Historicists find greatest meaning in the particular, Marxists find it in the structure, the system, the universal. Jameson criticizes New Criticism and deconstruction, both of which, he argues, believe they can make arguments while fixated solely on the text, a belief Jameson says is a mirage, because history is already in the text, and a refusal to acknowledge it results in failures of interpretation. What exactly was happening in 1916, a Jamesonian critic might ask—amid the rapid industrialization of the United States, including the expansion of roads to provide infrastructure for the flourishing young automobile industry—such that a poet in New England could write a nostalgic fable in rhyming verse about the fantasy of the importance of choosing the correct grassy woodland path; and what can close attention to the structure of that fable tell us about the history of industrialization?

Fifteen years after his book *Orientalism* launched postcolonial criticism, Edward Said, in *Culture and Imperialism*, published in 1993, wrote:

> To read most cultural deconstructionists, or Marxists, or new historicists is to read writers whose political horizon, whose historical location is within a society and culture deeply enmeshed in imperial domination. Yet little notice is taken of this horizon, few acknowledgments of the setting are advanced, little realization of the imperial closure itself is allowed for.[24]

---

23. Fredric Jameson, *The Political Unconscious: Narrative as a Socially Symbolic Act* (Cornell University Press, 1981), 20. "Here also Auerbach comes to mind; yet surely Vico's model, as suggestive as it may be, is an anachronistic one which fails to come to terms with the specificity of the modern situation," in Fredric Jameson, "Demystifying Literary History," *New Literary History* 5, no. 3 (Spring 1974): 609.

24. Edward Said, *Culture and Imperialism* (Knopf, 1993), 56.

He assessed literature and literary criticism written from current and former empires—the United States and the United Kingdom—and found them unaware of how profoundly their worldviews were limited by imperialism. Said shares much with New Historicists: a debt to Auerbach; a sense that, politics and culture "are not only connected but ultimately the same"; and a debt to Foucault that results in claims for literature's role not just in registering history but in producing it.[25] But Said brings colonialism to the center. Novels, he argues, assisted "the formation of imperial attitudes, references, and experiences" and accomplished "society's consent in overseas expansion."[26]

The postcolonial critic is attentive to setting: geography, history. Said notices a few passing references to Antigua, a British colony in the Caribbean, in Jane Austen's *Mansfield Park*, which punctures Austen's famous insularity. Wealthy estates such as Mansfield Park instill the habits of mind, manners, and worldview specific to a life of balls and courtship, insulated from the harsh realities of most. Mentions of Antigua reveal that this life, these manners, rest on a foundation of distant slave labor. *Mansfield Park* taught its contemporaneous readers to be good imperialists, ignoring empire; it teaches us today how, no matter how much Austen might have neglected it, empire shaped the practicalities of everyday life and the intimacies of courtship and marriage.[27] Or to turn once more to the New England woods, might we notice a peculiar American fantasy in the vision of a woodland road that "no step had trodden black"? How did that road get there in the first place? Might a repressed fantasy of vanished Native Americans serve as a secret key to the possibility of the poem's existence? Christopher Spaide shows how postcolonial criticism moves from noticing small poetic details to ambitious global theorizing and back again in chapter 21 on Jahan Ramazani.

What we observe, then, among historicists, is a set of expanding contexts. New Historicists open the text to contemporaneous anecdotes that reveal a shared discourse. Marxists situate discourse within capitalism. Postcolonial critics argue that Marxists nevertheless remain constrained within the West and have been unwittingly shaped by imperialism. Our next turn in this tour of literary criticism returns us from such sweeping vistas back to the place from where they are experienced: the individual psyche.

---

25. Said, *Culture and Imperialism*, 14, 57.
26. Said, *Culture and Imperialism*, xii, 12.
27. Said, *Culture and Imperialism*, 84–97.

Psychoanalysis

Sex, desire, secrets, death: we have written little about these, though they are the stuff of literature. Psychoanalysis has given us rich language with which to think about them. We must first avoid a common pitfall: we should not attempt to psychoanalyze the author or her characters. We don't have access to the author's mind. And characters don't *have* minds: they are verbal constructions. Instead, psychoanalysis teaches us how literature organizes the chaotic, at times unspeakable, material of human life for us as animals with instinctual drives on an inexorable path toward personal extinction. Literature veils what we must repress, but it also leaves clues—arguably more clues than most kinds of writing—to lead us toward its unconscious. The critic notices these clues, "evasions, ambivalences, and points of intensity in the narrative—words which do not get spoken, words which are spoken with unusual frequency, doublings and slidings," and investigates these symptoms that, upon analysis, reveal how literature works.[28]

Consider: "Two roads diverged in a yellow wood." These roads stand in for life trajectories. Which to take? How to decide? Ah, perhaps we should take the road less traveled. That way, someday, we can tell ourselves it made all the difference. The poem is less about our decisions than what we tell ourselves about our decisions. It is about the fantasy that our choices matter. It ends "Two roads diverged in a wood, and I   / I took the one less traveled by, / And that has made all the difference." We might notice Frost's em dash, his enjambed repetition of "I." Why that pause, that hitch, that repetition? Why is it there? Might it be a symptom of anxiety about the poem's fantasy, the em dash as a gash where the darkness enters? Where we might get caught on the fantasy of an "I" itself, a coherent sense of self, an ego that we must constantly reiterate to keep coherent? But quickly the speaker catches himself, gets back on track, finishes the fantasy, even as Frost gives us enough clues—the two roads aren't so different at all, really—to see it *as* fantasy. Even the rhyming serves to suggest a calming sense of order instead of a forest's feral chaos. The poem is *about* poetry's therapeutic service in the face of our animalistic, ineffable, horrifying drives.

Often we want things that make our lives worse. Lauren Berlant called this "cruel optimism."[29] Berlant coupled psychoanalysis with feminism and

---

28. Terry Eagleton, *Literary Theory: An Introduction* (University of Minnesota Press, 1996), 158.
29. Lauren Berlant, *Cruel Optimism* (Duke University Press, 2011).

Marxism in affect theory, which, when used to read literature, can provide, as Brian Glavey calls it in chapter 17, a literary vibe check. Glavey shows us how Berlant susses out the desires, the fantasies, and their implications for flourishing in a poem by John Ashbery. In chapter 20, Kimberly Quiogue Andrews investigates how Sianne Ngai discovers a theory of anxiety in Alfred Hitchcock's *Vertigo* and Herman Melville's *Pierre*. Andrews elucidates Ngai's challenging argument that anxiety, as classically theorized by Sigmund Freud, put in conversation, here, with Jamesonian Marxism, is about space. But shame, according to Eve Kosofsky Sedgwick, is about time, about looking back, and, in the case of Henry James, about looking back at his earlier writing—a potentially shame-inducing act many of us might relate to. Jane Hu, in chapter 2, investigates how Sedgwick sets the scene for thinking through shame.

The Twenty-First Century

The legacies of Marx, Nietzsche, and Freud dominate twenty-first-century literary studies. Fewer scholars today identify as deconstructionists or New Historicists than as Marxist or psychoanalytic critics; regardless, these methodological assumptions and procedures have become the status quo, ready to be deployed in permutations with one another. As a close reader, you are entering into conversation with these thinkers, so it is valuable to understand how and why they write like they do, whether or not you adopt these models yourself.

You don't have to adopt them. Scholars continue to pursue alternatives. In recent years, to gesture briefly toward several new directions, scholars have turned to Pierre Bourdieu's sociology, Ludwig Wittgenstein's philosophy, and the technologies of computational modeling and machine learning. Pardis Dabashi, in this volume, looks beyond Anglophone and European criticism to Persian traditions of literary criticism, here as practiced by Qolamhossein Yousefi. Dabashi teaches us, through Yousefi, the power of thinking with genres and what we might gain by resisting the impulse to move from regional argumentation to global theorizing—and the slipperiness such resistance entails.

Narratology, with its long history, offers another model for close reading. Narratologists look for patterns in narratives that explain how techniques of pacing and perspective make meaning. How do writers manipulate language to give the impression of time passing?[30] What do we really mean when

---

30. Gérard Genette, *Narrative Discourse: An Essay in Method* (Cornell University Press, 1983).

we describe a narrator as omniscient?[31] Elaine Auyoung, in this volume, investigates—through reading Alex Woloch reading Jane Austen—how authors give space to their various characters to lend them illusions of shallowness and depth. Also reading Jane Austen, D. A. Miller—read in this volume by Stephanie Hershinow—moves from noticing the most minor details about characters and narrators and pieces of jewelry to theorizing about something as diffuse as style. Farah Bakaari shows how Eleni Coundouriotis unites narratology with postcolonialism in analyzing point of view in Yambo Ouologuem's *Le Devoir de violence*, demonstrating how attention to perspective can reveal much about power.

Some of the most original, influential interventions in literary studies in the twenty-first century have come from Black studies: Afropessimism and critical fabulation. Afropessimism argues that the "event" of slavery "has yet to end"; it is an "ongoing disaster."[32] Slavery continues "unfolding" because the United States subjects Black people to the "normative terror" of mass incarceration, premature death, and "the diffuse violence and the everyday routines of domination," but also because, ontologically, slavery ensured and ensures "blackness's ongoing and irresolvable abjection," a fundamental exclusion from the category of the human.[33] This is a very different basis for Black studies than Henry Louis Gates's deconstructive focus on the fictionality and fluxion of race, which has given way to the demanding exigencies of the reality of the terror of Black being. Gently countering Afropessimism while sharing its concern for Black being, Kevin Quashie argues that African American poetry reveals what he calls Black aliveness, attentive especially to the sonic registers of poems, as Lindsay Reckson demonstrates in this volume.

Afropessimism inverts normal critical procedures with its call to become "undisciplinary."[34] As often as Afropessimists close read literary texts they close read their own lives and fragmented, lost lives discovered in or absent from archives. Critical, literary autobiography—or autotheory—is one Afropessimist mode used by Saidiya Hartman, Christina Sharpe, and Frank Wilderson, where their lives become the text in which they notice details that become an occasion for theorization.

---

31. Jonathan Culler, "Omniscience," *Narrative* 12, no. 1 (January 2004): 22–34.
32. Saidiya V. Hartman, "The Time of Slavery," *South Atlantic Quarterly* 101, no. 4 (Fall 2002): 758; Christina Sharpe, *In the Wake: On Blackness and Being* (Duke University Press, 2016), 5.
33. Sharpe, *In the Wake: On Blackness and Being*, 14.
34. Sharpe, *In the Wake: On Blackness and Being*, 13.

Another mode is critical fabulation, a term coined by Hartman for the practice of narrating lives only captured in fragments in archives. Hartman observes how little archives hold about enslaved people and former enslaved people on their own terms. "There is not one extant autobiographical narrative of a female captive who survived the Middle Passage," she writes. Studies of slavery tend, then, to repeat the quantification of Black lives originally perpetrated by slaveholders: a record of silence and violence. "The archive is, in this case, a death sentence, a tomb, a display of the violated body, an inventory of property," she argues. In response, Hartman tells the stories of lost lives, "listening for the unsaid, translating misconstrued words, and refashioning disfigured lives."[35] The ambition is to make new, make visible. Critical fabulation inverts standard disciplinary protocols: usually the scholar writes nonfiction about a fictional text in an attempt to persuade readers of the likeliness of their interpretation; here, the Afropessimist fabulates a text on the basis of a fragment of the historical record.

We began this section by expressing the hope that you feel that close reading is worth learning and learning about. We hope you feel that way in part because you think literature is worth it. At the heart of close reading is our commitment to literature's value, our conviction that literary texts matter. All the different scholarly traditions of close reading share that foundation. What varies is how literary texts matter: through language, history, psyche.

Close reading emerged from the scholarship and classrooms of literary studies, but it's been enriched by thinking that began elsewhere. An imported conceptual context can show us new aspects of literary texts we thought we knew well, and it can use the interpretation of literature to get purchase on larger worlds beyond the text as well as the luminous ones within ourselves. Close reading involves looking at literature and looking with literature—through literature, via literature—and you won't succeed unless you think that literature has things to show us.

Investigate the traditions of close reading that compel you and learn how they operate through practice. Or draw from intellectual passions left unmentioned here as occasions to imagine your own method of reading. Let yourself be inspired by the work you find most invigorating, then write with both rigor and vim.

---

35. Saidiya Hartman, "Venus in Two Acts," *Small Axe* 12, no. 2 (June 2008): 2.

PART I
Scene Setting

1

Near Monstrous Fidelity

ERICH AUERBACH ON VIRGINIA WOOLF

Oren Izenberg

When it was unpopular to perform close readings with attention to history, Erich Auerbach (1892–1957) wrote Mimesis, *a paragon of historicist close reading. Maybe he couldn't escape history. He was a German Jew living in Istanbul, exiled from Hitler's Germany, writing from 1942 to 1945.* Mimesis *travels from Homer and the Old Testament through Dante to Virginia Woolf to argue that literature reveals the reality of its time. He influenced major figures who popularized historicist close reading in the United States. Here, Oren Izenberg shows us how Auerbach sets the scene for his reading of Woolf—and argues that scene setting, too often overlooked as mere exposition, becomes in Auerbach's hands an opportunity to sow the seeds of the argument to come. Izenberg also shows us how even Auerbach, one of the greatest close readers, made mistakes—and that mistakes, well read, can teach us truths about the text at hand and ourselves.—DS + JW*

THE NOVELIST Henry James famously described the novel as a "loose baggy monster." Literary scholars have tried to tighten things up somewhat; most will stipulate that the novel is a *fictional narrative* in *prose* (thus not every text you will encounter in a literature class is a "novel"!), and many will also note that novels are are *long*. Given everything that there is to read in a novel, what does it mean to read one *closely*? For a master class in the close reading of novels, I tend to consult Erich Auerbach's "The Brown Stocking," a study of Virginia Woolf's *To the Lighthouse* that forms the nineteenth chapter of his book *Mimesis*; we can learn a great deal from his way of addressing the critical challenges presented by novelistic length.

What do we learn? First, reading closely means reading *selectively*. This is true, Auerbach tells us, of both art and life. Or, it is true of art *because* it is true of life, a (hopefully) long story that can only be rendered whole by being partially rendered: "He who represents the course of a human life ... from beginning to end, must prune and isolate arbitrarily."[1] Accordingly, Auerbach begins by selecting—and quoting in full—a substantial passage from *To the Lighthouse*. At four pages of the novel, it is longer, by a fair bit, than the excerpts of the previous nineteen texts Auerbach has treated up to that point in *Mimesis*, but still only a small fragment of Virginia Woolf's three hundred and twenty pages.

What else? Auerbach acknowledges the "arbitrariness" of selection. And it is true; nothing of obvious interest happens in the scene Auerbach has chosen: a mother knits a stocking for the child of a distant stranger and tries it out for size against her fidgety son. But if a reading is to have some stakes beyond mere ingenuity, you must make the case that your selection is not *wholly* arbitrary, but in some way representative: of this novel's particular achievement ("a tendency which is particularly striking in our text from Virginia Woolf"); of the novel as a form ("The distinctive characteristics of the realistic novel between the two great wars"); of transformations happening in the world beyond fiction that you take the novel to somehow encompass ("The spread of publicity and the crowding of mankind on a shrinking globe sharpened awareness of the differences in ways of life and attitudes, and mobilized the interests and forms of existence which the new changes either furthered or threatened" [546, 550]).

Auerbach argues all of these things; but he is particularly concerned with the last. This is, as Julie Orlemanski also explains in chapter 9, Auerbach's largest point in *Mimesis*: *whatever* arbitrary things great works of literature represent, they also represent something fundamental about "reality": the "ways of life," or "forms of existence" specific to the the eras and cultures within which they are written. Our volume calls these moves—from instance to genre, from text to world—"global theorizing," and notes that they are "risky" moves with high stakes. As the culminating chapter in an ambitious book; as an essay that takes up a novel very nearly contemporary to the critic (*To the Lighthouse* was published a mere fifteen years before *Mimesis*); as an attempt to encapsulate what Auerbach calls "our epoch," and its aspirations toward finding an alternative

---

1. Erich Auerbach, *Mimesis: The Representation of Reality in Western Literature* (Princeton University Press, 2003), 548. All subsequent citations given in text.

to the seemingly endless conflicts caused by "a shrinking globe"—the stakes of this move are unusually "global," and thus the risks are unusually high.

The last move to "global theorizing" depends (more than you might think) upon the first—"scene setting." Scene setting, as our volume defines it, "establishes where, who, what information we have; ... how much and which context is necessary for the reading to follow." If your reading is going to argue that a novel is a "representation of reality"—that somehow, despite being a *fictional narrative*, the novel as a whole makes a claim about how the world you live in really is—it must do more than give us one part among its many. It must, somehow, make the whole present to justify the significance of your selection. Put another way, you are going to have to begin by dealing with the novel's length.

Auerbach is aware of this obligation, and states it explicitly, and in much the same terms as we do: "I shall ... briefly summarize what the *situation* is at the beginning of our passage" (528, emphasis mine). And he does offer a brief paragraph establishing the whos of the characters (Mrs. Ramsay is "the wife of an eminent London professor of philosophy; she is very beautiful but definitely no longer young"; James is "her youngest son—he is six years old"); the wheres of the action ("by the window in a good sized summer house on one of the Hebrides islands"), and the whats that have precipitated the scene ("people at the lighthouse are to receive various presents"; "James has been looking forward to this trip for a long time") (528–29).

Auerbach asserts that everything we need to know in terms of scene setting about this moment in *To the Lighthouse* is *self-evident* in the passage. "The situation in which the characters find themselves can be almost completely deduced from the text itself." But then, having dismissed the need to set the plot or characters in the context of the larger narrative, having told us that the text is, in some sense, obvious, he proceeds to *re-narrate* it at great length. In my edition, this eerily close paraphrase runs from page 529 to 534, with only occasional pauses for questions ("Who is speaking in this paragraph"?) up to the point where he writes: "Our analysis of the passage yields a number of distinguishing stylistic characteristics, which we shall now attempt to formulate."

At this point, the reader may be brought up short. Whatever has happened in the essay until then has only a loose relation to anything I would call "analysis"; I'd barely call it "paraphrase"—since it has just given us the text again, and with a near monstrous thoroughness and fidelity. Where Woolf has Mrs. Ramsay wondering of her fidgeting son: "what demon possessed him, her youngest, her cherished?" Auerbach writes: "What is the matter with

James, her youngest, her darling?" Woolf has Mrs. Ramsay lament "It's too short . . . ever so much too short." Auerbach repeats and ever so slightly lengthens the observation of shortness: "it is found that the stocking is still considerably too short."

We might even be tempted to write off such minor alterations to the intervention of translation; Woolf writes in English and Auerbach writes in German. And yet translation cannot explain *all* the changes that Auerbach introduces. Here is Auerbach, rendering Mrs. Ramsay's thoughts about the library of her home, back in London, that she is glad to be away from: "Books—it is ages since she has had time to read books, even the books which have been dedicated to her (here the lighthouse flashes in for a second, as a place where one can't send such erudite volumes as some of those lying about the room)." But what we know from Woolf is something different: that Mrs. Ramsay has *never* read those books. "She never had time to read them. Alas! even the books that had been given her, and inscribed by the hand of the poet himself . . . disgraceful to say, she had never read them."

Auerbach has altered several details: first, and most obviously, he seems to have invented out of whole cloth the idea that Mrs. Ramsay was *once* a reader but is no longer. Second, he has moved some of Woolf's prose—the part about the characters' anticipated journey to the lighthouse—into parentheses. This might seem like an insignificant intervention—even less important than the change of "cherished" to "darling." After all, a parenthesis is, virtually by definition, an intervention that doesn't change anything. Syntactically, parentheses are set off from the ordinary business of a sentence (enclosed, as here, within the rounded brackets that share their name). And even when they contain their own grammatical structures (Here! Do you see what I am getting at?) they do not interrupt the grammatical flow of the prose. Semantically, they work similarly. The information sequestered inside parentheses (the English use of the word dates back to the sixteenth century) may be relevant and interesting (or not!), but it is, in some sense, "extra"—a less-than-fully consequential afterthought or aside to the main event.

Parentheses, as it happens, *are* a significant stylistic feature of Woolf's novel. Though they do not appear at *precisely* this moment, they aren't far off; you can find them at the end of the very passage that Auerbach is rewriting: "('My dear stand still,' she said)." Unlike the bit about Mrs. Ramsay reading, Auerbach's addition of parentheses isn't really an invention; it calls our attention to the real existence of parentheses in Woolf's prose and highlights their function in the novel, which is to distinguish things that objectively take place in the novel's "outside" world (the lighthouse flashing, Mrs. Ramsay speaking) from the things that take place "inside": the perceptions, thoughts, and feelings in the minds of characters who inhabit that world. As Auerbach puts it in one of the few analytic moments in the early part of the essay, "The continuity of the section is established through an exterior occurrence involving Mrs. Ramsay and James: the measuring of the stocking.... This entirely insignificant occurrence is constantly interspersed with other elements which, although they do not interrupt its progress, take up far more time in the narration than the whole scene can possibly have lasted" (529).

Auerbach's word, "interspersed," is interesting. It is self-evidently true about ourselves: we contain at every moment a great heaving ocean of thought interspersed with *and simultaneous to* the relatively straight course of our lives. The interior world of thinking, we might say, is parenthetical to the outside world of living. But he also prompts us to see something that now seems self-evident *in the text of the novel*, even if we had not quite registered it: there is a massive disparity between the number of words given over to the narration of thoughts and the number given over to the narration of things. *To the Lighthouse* is long, in other words, not because a lot happens in it, but because a lot happens inside the characters who inhabit it. From the perspective of someone interested in the unfolding of plot or action, such a lengthy narration of thoughts is not going to look like "interspersal"; it is going to look like *interruption*. And in fact, "interruption" is Auerbach's preferred word for describing Woolf's toggling back and forth between inner and outer life. Sometimes the narration of inner life is the interruption: "Here the second interruption comes to an end and we are taken back to the room where Mrs. Ramsay and James are" (533–34). More often, as with the lighthouse "flashing in," it is the outside world that interrupts the characters' thinking. Though "thinking" and "living" may happen at the same time (and take the same *amount* of time) in your life, Auerbach shows us that there is a kind of competition between them in Woolf's art.

To summarize what I've said so far: under the auspices of "giving us" the text as "self evident," Auerbach has, in subtle ways, set the scene for us to see in it two kinds of events—"external" ones and "internal" ones. Auerbach has prompted us to see a novel itself as a kind of scene, or space: a theater of representation. The important "where" of the action in *To the Lighthouse* is not a house in the Hebrides, where characters come into contact or conflict; it is the *page*, where two different kinds of representation are jockeying for priority.

This way of setting the scene of the novel ultimately will be the groundwork for Auerbach's "global" accounts of its significance. Some of these will be claims about the history of the novel. Virginia Woolf is not alone, or first, in her interest in narrating the inner life. But where past novels have given us "stream of consciousness," Auerbach notes that they have tended to do so from the authoritative perspective of a single, often unusual, character. What is new in Woolf is not so much the interiority itself, but the degree to which multiple, conflictual, ordinary interior lives expand to fill the whole of novelistic space in what Auerbach calls "a method which dissolves reality into multiple and multivalent reflections of consciousness" (551).

Some of Auerbach's claims are claims about transformations in "the representation of reality." As Auerbach understands it, novels that dissolve reality into multiple reflections of consciousness emerged in Europe after World War I ("a violent clash of the most heterogeneous ways of life and kinds of endeavor") to represent a world that could share no single objective account of what reality is. In such a world, even Virginia Woolf, who has *created* a fictional world and all the people in it, might not be the final authority over the interior lives of its inhabitants.

I began by pointing out that Auerbach has changed a fact about Mrs. Ramsay's past: that she used to read books. This is actually a *mistake*. Woolf's Mrs. Ramsay is kind, but as her embarrassed ("Alas!") admission that she has never read the books poets have dedicated to her suggests, she can be a little shallow. She has a gentle ability to provide what people most need in the moment; but she is most fully "active" in the novel as the object of people's imagination, desire, and fantasy. That is why her death midway through the novel (spoiler!) renders her no less alive on the page. She remains an ongoing presence in the inner lives of the characters who survive her. Auerbach's Mrs. Ramsay is all of this—but she is something more besides. Auerbach has read Woolf, closely: he has read the long, poetic passages of Mrs. Ramsay's thoughts. And while he may have *imagined* her "very beautiful" exterior self, he has seen, directly on the page, an inner life of staggering, surpassing beauty. Perhaps for Auerbach, one of our most serious and searching of readers, it is unthinkable that anyone could have such a rich and reflective inner world of her own without a relation to literature. Such a person *must* have been a reader. Even if she no longer has the time or leisure to do it, *having been a reader* is the mark, for Auerbach, of having been somebody. Time and circumstance may have conspired to interrupt Mrs. Ramsay's inner life. But look at the page; it is self-evident. There is someone in there. Auerbach's "misdescription," like the rest of his descriptions of the text, is scene setting. To make an argument, he has rebuilt the passage so that the quality he finds is everywhere self-evident within it. The Mrs. Ramsay that Auerbach invents—who once had poetry in her head and now has no time for it—is, one might say, truer to the world Virginia Woolf has made than the Mrs. Ramsay Woolf describes; for she has lived in her life the same conflict between exterior action and inner landscape that we have read in her thoughts.

I'll conclude by pointing to one more instance of Auerbach's reading practice; both to indicate his great ambition and power as a reader, and as a kind of cautionary tale about the relation between global ambition and close reading. Auerbach's *most* global claim in "The Brown Stocking" is not really about the novel, or about the history of representation. It is about reality itself. As Auerbach understands it, whatever uncertainties exist in our present epoch, from which authoritative accounts of and agreements about reality have fled; whatever conflicts have arisen from the multiplicity of worldviews competing for space on our shrinking globe; this is not how things *really* are. Beneath the competition of life and mind, within the cacophony of competing consciousness, there is unity: what Auerbach calls the "elementary things which our lives have in common," and which might serve as a ground of hope in the present, and a direction for the future. In his view, *this* is what Virginia Woolf makes present in *To the Lighthouse*; *this* is the novel's central "insight and mastery." In it, as nowhere else, "something new and elemental appeared: nothing less than the wealth of reality and depth of life in every moment to which we surrender ourselves without prejudice."

It is a mysterious claim. Whatever this new elemental thing might be, it seems to be embodied in the kiss that Mrs. Ramsay gives to her son at the end of the scene Auerbach has quoted. "And the kiss she gives her little boy, the words she speaks to him, although they are a genuine gift of life, which James accepts as the most natural and simple truth, are yet heavy with unsolved mystery" (534). No effort is made to connect this account to the words on Woolf's page, which simply read "Mrs. Ramsay . . . kissed her little boy on the forehead." Auerbach does no close reading to explain why we ought to regard Mrs. Ramsay's kiss as the bearer of a "natural truth," or as a "gift of life" (528); he offers no explicit reason to see it as an emblem of the common world whose existence he insists upon at the essay's end. Properly situated, Auerbach seems to suggest, this way of seeing things will be self-evident—which is to say, so pervasive in all this long novel's particulars that it needn't be connected to any particular in the novel at all. It is perhaps a testament to Auerbach's greatness as a critic that I'm inclined to think he succeeds in making this claim stick. (But don't try this one at home.)

2

Touching, Reading

EVE KOSOFSKY SEDGWICK ON HENRY JAMES

Jane Hu

As Hu quotes Henry James in this chapter, relations stop nowhere. Neither do texts. The work of scene setting is to make it seem as if they happily appear *to do so, by priming your reader for what you deem salient. A good scene setting, as Hu observes here, is already building an argument—even if your reader doesn't know it yet. Scene setting often requires description, summary, contextualization, splicing your language with quotes from the text. In addition to mastering these, Eve Kosofsky Sedgwick (1950–2009) pulled off another tricky maneuver: scene setting by personal anecdote. Instructors warn against personal anecdotes because they can easily grow irrelevant or self-indulgent. Hu shows how Sedgwick—one of the founding queer theorists; a brilliant, capacious, eclectic close reader—turns personal experiences into the occasion for her reading. Sedgwick narrates her shame to prepare us to see James's shame—and to theorize shame itself. In doing so, Sedgwick licenses you to make the personal the literary critical.—DS + JW*

WHEN WE talk about close reading a literary text, we rarely associate it with literal, physical closeness. If anything, my students seem to encounter their readings from a mediated distance—increasingly engaging them over tablets and screens. But as someone who only really begins to grasp a text after I've held it in my hands—scribbled in its margins, fondled its pages—the act of close reading has always been, for me, more than a metaphor. If I can read a piece of writing and leave it untouched—unmarked and unremarked upon—then I was probably not reading all that closely.

The first time I read Eve Kosofsky Sedgwick, one of my favorite close readers, was over a computer screen. My college professor had recommended her influential essay "Paranoid Reading and Reparative Reading," which one can, these days, easily pull up online. I began reading the essay—itself a theory about the politics and stakes of close reading—until, about a third of the way through, I realized the PDF format could not sustain the kind of annotational damage I felt the piece demanded from me. I printed it out and proceeded to scrawl all over it: underlining critical phrases, circling keywords. By the end, my marginalia consisted almost solely of hearts, stars, and the periodic triple exclamation mark: "*!!!*"

Sedgwick's literary criticism precipitated not only my strong personal feelings, but the feeling that to read criticism closely was to bring it somehow personally, materially close. I learned this from reading Sedgwick, whose close readings dare to sidle up to their textual objects with intense, sometimes even inappropriate, intimacy. This makes a kind of intuitive sense, given that Sedgwick was, besides a "masterful close reader" (as David Kurnick calls her), also a theorist of embodiment and affect, performance and queerness, touching and feeling.[1]

This chapter gets cozy with Sedgwick's close reading of Henry James's prefaces to his novels in her essay titled "Shame, Theatricality, and Queer Performativity: Henry James's *The Art of the Novel*."[2] As an exemplar of close reading, Sedgwick's essay deviates from some other prominent cases in this collection: not only is it a close reading of a fiction writer's *nonfiction*, it's also, in a way, a close reading *of a close reading*. James's prefaces, written for the New York editions of what he considered to be his most important novels and stories, show the older writer rereading and reflecting on his earlier work. Subsequently

---

1. David Kurnick, "A Few Lies: Queer Theory and Our Method Melodramas," *ELH* 87, no. 2 (2020): 361.

2. A version of the essay first appeared in 1993 under the title "Queer Performativity: Henry James's *The Art of the Novel*," in the inaugural issue of the influential journal *GLQ: A Journal of Lesbian and Gay Studies*, though the version I'll discuss in this chapter is the much longer revision that appears in Sedgwick's essay collection *Touching Feeling: Affect, Pedagogy, Performativity* (2003), which also contains the "Paranoia" essay.

collected and published in 1934 as *The Art of the Novel*, the prefaces are now considered canonical texts of novel theory. Yet if James's prefaces are often cited as about the novel writ large, its global theories are inseparable from the localized scenes and settings of James's fiction—and even, the scenes from which James wrote them.

Henry James is known to have authored some of the most difficult works of literature in the English language. His novels are imposingly dense: narratively, grammatically, philosophically. There's a reason, after all, he's referred to as "The Master." But in Sedgwick's hands, he is brought down, and somewhat dirtily, to earth. In her close reading of James's abstruse and aestheticizing language, Sedgwick gets up close and personal with the Master himself—fixating, in particular, on how James's bowel movements influenced his prose style. Connecting James's linguistic abstractions to his literal ass remains one of the essay's most memorable moves, partly because the gesture seems so counterintuitive, if not perverse or simply unfounded. But if Sedgwick's redirection of critical attention makes you blush, that's also partly the point. An organizing theme of "Shame, Theatricality, and Queer Performativity: Henry James's *The Art of the Novel*" is, well, shame—an affect that Sedgwick understands as crucial for getting deep into Henry James.

Shame informs not only the content of Sedgwick's argument, but also the experience—we might say feeling—of reading it. I've personally felt shame reading Sedgwick's essay, because, despite considering myself a scholar of both Sedgwick and James, I'm regularly flustered by it. Sedgwick's metabolization of James's personal shame through his chronic constipation, closeted gayness, and creative output is virtuosic—a master class in critical proficiency and dexterity. But when I try to reiterate her argument, I become flushed with frustration, quickly lapsing into convoluted circles trying to capture the complexity of her moves, the full terrain of her expertise. There are just too many scenes to set, too many throughlines, too many exclamation marks. I'm left feeling, you could say, *!!!* "You'll just have to read it yourself," I often concede.

Because even before arriving at Sedgwick's central argument (that James's shame as a queer, constipated, creatively blocked young man is precisely what animates his prolific output of fictional prose and nonfictional prefaces), I find myself struggling to stage the coordinates through which her reading will make sense. To be fair, Sedgwick's scene setting is extensive, requiring us to grasp psychoanalytical theories of shame, the biographical context around James's queerness and failures, and the basic premise of many of his novels (which his prefaces later opine on). It also asks that we understand Sedgwick's investments in the formation of queer theory in the late 1980s, and the history of the AIDS crisis during which she wrote much of her scholarship. Part of what makes reading Sedgwick so thrilling is how she takes a writer as difficult as James and seeks to match his difficulty. The climax of her close reading is so dazzling that I often forget how much intellectual labor goes into setting it up. The remainder of this chapter seeks to shift that balance in attention—forgoing the brilliance of Sedgwick's arguments and theories to linger instead on the quieter, but no less ingenious, seductions of their scene setting.

"Shame, Theatricality, and Queer Performativity: Henry James's *The Art of the Novel*" opens with what is conventionally the first step of close reading—scene setting—though it does so in a somewhat unconventional style. The essay begins with what we're often advised to avoid in literary criticism: a personal anecdote. Its first paragraph goes like this:

> In the couple of weeks after the World Trade Center was destroyed in September 2001, I had a daily repetition of an odd experience, one that was probably shared by many walkers in the same midsouthern latitudes of Manhattan. Turning from a street onto Fifth Avenue, even if I was heading north, I would feel compelled first to look south in the direction of the World Trade Center, now gone. This inexplicably furtive glance was associated with a conscious wish: that my southward vista would again be blocked by the familiar sight of the pre-September 11 twin towers, somehow come back to loom over us in all their complacent ugliness. But, of course, the towers were always still gone. Turning away, shame was what I would feel.[3]

I often tell my students to begin their essays by staging the key terms of their argument: *who, where, what, when*. But in an essay with "Henry James" in the title, Sedgwick opens not by telling us about Henry James, but about Eve Kosofksy Sedgwick. Here's the first hint of Sedgwick's unorthodox approach—which comes at things sideways, from a queer angle. Yet when I read her, never do I doubt that I am in a master's hands. While Sedgwick's first paragraph doesn't explicitly set the scene for James's *The Art of the Novel*, it nonetheless performs the work of scene setting. It tells us *who* (Sedgwick as well as "many walkers" like her), *where* (the "midsouthern latitudes of Manhattan"), *when* ("weeks after the World Trade Center was destroyed in September 2001"), and

---

3. Eve Kosofksy Sedgwick, *Touching Feeling: Affect, Pedagogy, Performativity* (Duke University Press, 2003), 35.

for *how long* ("couple of weeks"). Sedgwick's anecdotal scene is not only contextual, but also literal. Her scene is itself about a change of scenery: a "southward vista" that she knows is "now gone" yet can't look away from.

Sedgwick's reader might not know it yet, but changes in scenery are exactly what will come to haunt the essay's subsequent theorization of shame and James. Like those memes staging the difference between "expectation" and "reality," Sedgwick keeps finding herself embarrassingly hoping for the former (the "twin towers . . . in all their complacent ugliness"), despite being always met with the latter ("But, of course, the towers were always still gone"). And the more Sedgwick keeps looking back for "the familiar sight of the pre–September 11 twin towers," the more shame she feels when she finds it "of course . . . still gone." Shame, as an affect, hinges not on a single scene, but in the contrast *between* scenes. Like my renewed disorientation each time I reread Sedgwick's essay, my shame emerges from the gap between feeling like I know this essay well and realizing that perhaps I don't know it at all.

There's a kind of disarming vulnerability, even stupidity, in how Sedgwick begins her essay. Her opening anecdote about shame makes me feel, in many ways, ashamed on her behalf. Sedgwick, however, soon interrupts my first impressions. Regarding the "despoiled view" of the post-September 11 Manhattan skyline, she goes on to write:

> [T]hough it was I who felt the shame, it wasn't especially myself I was ashamed of. It would be closer to say I was ashamed *for* the estranged and denuded skyline; such feelings interlined, of course, the pride, solidarity, and grief that also bound me to the city. The shame had to do, too, with visibility and spectacle—the hapless visibility of the towers' absence now, the shockingly compelling theatricality of their destruction.[4]

Sedgwick's shame is something personally felt, though it's not of herself that she's personally ashamed. Instead, shame unfolds as an affect Sedgwick feels "*for* the estranged and denuded skyline" that sits alongside other feelings of "pride, solidarity, and grief." In clarifying her felt sense of shame *for* this scene, Sedgwick describes herself as moving "closer" to a more precise description of her experience. In other words, in finding "closer [ways] to say" what she feels, Sedgwick's description of the scene also approaches, in a way, a close reading of it.

What I love about Sedgwick's opening paragraphs is how seamlessly she moves from anecdote to analysis, from setting the scene to close reading it, from

---

4. Sedgwick, *Touching Feeling*, 36.

description to global theorization. Scene setting is often seen as that which must be completed to move on to the more significant and substantial forms of analysis: noticing, local claiming, regional argumentation, global theorizing. Yet if we consider scene setting as often the first—and seemingly simplest—step of close reading, Sedgwick's essay shows how to set the scene is always already to begin to close read. Even to know which initial scenes to present involves critical judgment; it primes the reader for *how* to read by showing us what to look at. By beginning with a scene of personal shame, Sedgwick sets the stage not only for *what* she'll notice in James (feelings of shame), but also *how* she'll do so (filtered through scenes of James's own personal shame).

Scene Changes

Sedgwick's scene setting through the unfolding of personal scenes is strategic, even necessary, given how shame is a deeply social and interpersonal affect—one through which "the *question* of identity arises most originally and most relationally."[5] In doing so, her autobiographical and affective scene setting becomes a form of argumentative scene setting; the personal becomes the literary critical.

When Sedgwick finally turns to James, six dense pages into the essay, her delayed introduction hardly makes me blink. For while she must set the scene anew, the mode through which she does so—the personal anecdote—chimes with her own opening:

> Henry James undertook the New York edition of his work [...] at the end of a relatively blissful period of literary production ("the major phase")—a blissful period poised, however, between two devastating bouts of melancholia. The first of these scouring depressions was precipitated in 1895 by what James experienced as the obliterative failure of his ambitions as a playwright, being howled off the stage at the premiere of *Guy Domville*. [...] The next of James's terrible depressions was triggered, not by humiliation on the stage, but by the failure of the New York edition itself: its total failure to sell and its apparently terminal failure to evoke any recognition from any readership. When we read the New York edition prefaces, then, we read a series of texts that are in the most active imaginable relation to shame.[6]

---

5. Sedgwick, *Touching Feeling*, 37.
6. Sedgwick, *Touching Feeling*, 38–39.

As with her own anecdote, Sedgwick introduces her reading of James's prefaces by describing not just when and where he wrote them, but emphasizing how he *felt* while writing them. (The New York editions required James reread and reflect on what was considered his best work—emotionally treacherous terrain for any writer who's looked back.) Sedgwick resets the scene to focus on James's personal shame—a scene where James is already trying, and somewhat failing, to reset the scene of his own uneven reception. James's prefaces work, from the beginning, to contextualize his earlier writing process (often described as his famous "scenic method," which seeks to *show* rather than *tell*).[7] But Sedgwick's essay introduces this context by drawing the curtain back even further to provide the unhappy and demoralizing circumstances driving James's own self-contextualization. It's important to read the New York prefaces as "in the most active imaginable relation to shame," because this context changes how we might read—through what we might notice or register in—the prefaces.

When Sedgwick begins to close read the actual language from the prefaces, she focuses on scenes where James gets intimate, even indulgent, with his past self. In particular, she spotlights instances in which James describes his earlier work as though addressing his "inner child." James's recurring figure of the inner child, Sedgwick explains, "opens out a rich landscape of relationship positionalities—perhaps especially around issues of shame."[8] What's more, Sedgwick close reads these figurations to further note how James often describes his juvenilia as though they were *literal* children, variously referring to them as, for instance, "uncanny brood," "awkward infants," and "the unlucky or unlikely child."[9] By speaking of his past writing in anthropomorphized terms, James is also, Sedgwick argues, speaking about his younger self as a writer.

The "sanctioned intergenerational flirtation" between James and his earlier work, as Sedgwick puts it, "represents a sustained chord in the New York edition."[10] And to give readers a sense of its ongoingness, her essay cites extensively from the prefaces, presenting scene after scene in which this relation gets staged and restaged. In doing so, Sedgwick's scene setting does not simply provide textual evidence, but channels the sustained rhythms and undulations

---

7. For more of the extensive scholarship on James's "scenic method," I recommend the introduction to David Kurnick's *Empty Houses: Theatrical Failure and the Novel* (Princeton University Press, 2011), which sets the scene for close readings of James's investment in theatrical scenes.

8. Sedgwick, *Touching Feeling*, 40.

9. Sedgwick, *Touching Feeling*, 42, 40.

10. Sedgwick, *Touching Feeling*, 43.

of James's prose—of its linguistic *texture*. Her reading not only tells us what James says, but shows us how. To give readers a sense of this texture, Sedgwick must also consider to what degree—and lengths—she must redescribe James's own scenes. And as Sedgwick continues to describe scenes from James's prefaces, she also begins to describe scenes from it that further redescribe scenes from James's novels.

As Sedgwick proliferates examples, it becomes hard to unsee (to *not* notice) how the figure of the inner child permeates James's prefaces. This too is one of the magic tricks of a good and sustained close reading. What begins as perverse, even counterintuitive, ends up feeling, if not always inevitable, then at least obvious. For Sedgwick, it's important that James's doting, paternalistic relation to his earlier work is obvious, because part of her argument is that James is no longer ashamed—is in fact "unshamed"—in the prefaces. Instead, the constant display of an imagined relationship with his inner child becomes a writerly strategy: James uses "reparenting or 'reissue' as a strategy for dramatizing and integrating shame, in the sense of rendering this potentially paralyzing affect narratively, emotionally, and performatively productive."[11]

Throughout her essay on James, Sedgwick repeatedly models how personal scene setting—even as it retreads one's own intimate past—can be productive for close reading. Like shame, personal anecdotes can be volatile and unwieldly in scholarship—seeping illicitly across the usual norms and boundaries of what counts as critical analysis. But as Sedgwick and James both show us, such risks of self-exposure can also be richly rewarding. Another way of saying this might simply be to follow your hunches: know that whatever you're inclined to notice will already be a product of where you've been and what you feel, even as what you end up saying need not be determined by your first impressions.

Henry James wrote in *The Art of the Novel* that "relations stop nowhere, and the exquisite problem of the artist is eternally but to draw, by a geometry of his own, the circle within which they shall happily *appear* to do so." The same might be said of scene setting. As I often tell my students, close reading is rarely just the burrowing in of a localized scene. Instead, the recollection and gathering of key words or images from across a text is also crucial to the work of reading closely. Close reading always involves moving from small to large, from concrete to abstract, but it's a movement that happens not linearly—in a single direction—but recursively. As Sedgwick's essay shows us, the movement from

---

11. Sedgwick, *Touching Feeling*, 44.

small to large, concrete to abstract, might all be happening already at the level of setting the scene. As others have written in this collection, it's an ongoing and circular project—reading that almost always invites rereading or more readings. Like shame, and like scene setting, close reading is never fixed nor final. Critics set scenes and make arguments in hopes that someone else might look back and respond in kind, re-setting the scene again.

3

A Pedicure

ANGELA LEIGHTON ON ALICE OSWALD

Beci Carver

When Dan was in graduate school, he heard the great critic M. H. Abrams, then ninety-nine years old, deliver a lecture called "The Fourth Dimension of a Poem." The first dimension is the look of the poem on the page; the second is its sound; the third is its meaning; the fourth is the oral act of enunciation. Abrams enunciated and interpreted poems by W. H. Auden, Emily Dickinson, and William Wordsworth, observing the feel of the poems as his tongue hit his teeth and his lungs grabbed for air. Poetry, that is, should be spoken; and, spoken, it should be listened to. So, too, argued Angela Leighton (1954–) in her 2018 study Hearing Things. Carver, here, picks up Leighton's work and shows us how she sets scenes. The duty of scene setting is to delimit information for the close reading to come, narrowing from the near-infinite options to just the salient data, which for Leighton includes both Abrams's second (sound) and fourth (oral enunciation) dimensions. Carver invites us to feel the drama of scene setting, which can also mean inviting one's reader to see (and hear!) the actual setting, the location where the close reader reads (and listens!) from, and the setting where the poem takes place.—DS + JW

I'M RUNNING up a stone spiral staircase in stilettos. I'm about twenty minutes late. I get to two tall doors, think, "This is it," crook my ear to the wood, and listen, and hear Angela Leighton's familiar chocolate alto reading a poem from her newest collection. Nervously, I lean forward and the door wheezes open. To my horror, I am exhibited to the whole audience of a large, well-lit room.

I spot an empty seat at the back and make my way there. But as my feet meet the polished floor, they click-clack, click-clack, click-click: a monstrous solo in the high-ceilinged hall. Someone giggles. Then something mad happens. Angela catches my footfall in the air, imitating each step, exaggerating the clumsiness but getting something about the rhythm fiendishly right. The room breaks out in laughter. I dive to my seat, bright red.

Footfall is a prominent recurring theme in Leighton's book, *Hearing Things: The Work of Sound in Literature*. You could say it is a book that likes feet, and not just for the obvious pun they permit on metrical feet—our traditional measuring tool for micro units of poetic sound. Leighton is also interested in the book in real footfall: how arresting it can be, holding the attention of a room, how haunting, and mostly how strange: how at the same time that a heel tap or hoofbeat may sound rhythmical, their rhythms remain nonetheless stubbornly unlike those of the mouth and voice. We put our feet in our mouths all the time (or at least I do) but it is almost impossible to make our mouths sound like feet, repeating what one end of the body does automatically at its other extremity. What poets do when evoking footfall, what Leighton did on that blush-worthy evening, is attempt the feat (pun intended) of reproducing with one kind of sound-making instrument (the voice) the ways and wanderings of another sound-maker (the foot). What foot-interested critics do in their turn, what she does in *Hearing Things*, is analyze the end product, alert to "tiny incompatibilities," "syncopation," "counterpoints."[1] Between them, poets and critics recuperate the sounds of the foot as sounds for the voice. You could call it "pedicure."

Often in *Hearing Things*, footfall offers Leighton a way into interpreting a poem. But she also understands that to hear feet or "feet" as she hears them and appreciate the technical significance of her claims we may need handholding. In her close reading of Alice Oswald's "A Greyhound in the Evening After a Long Day of Rain," she cuts into the poem halfway through, at the tetrametric line: "Listen Listen Listen Listen," inviting us to hear it with her.[2] This interjection is then framed with terms and justifications that let us into her thinking. In other words, she sets the scene. Wanting to ensure that we are there with her, equipped to make the same intellectual moves as she does, she supplies the word "tetrameter" and explains how it works: "This is a hexameter

---

1. Angela Leighton, *Hearing Things: The Work of Sound in Literature* (Belknap Press of Harvard University Press, 2018), 229, 231, 228. All subsequent citations given in text.

2. Alice Oswald, *The Thing in the Gap-Stone Stile* (Faber & Faber, 2007; first published, 1996), 4.

tick-tock already softening to [...] tip-tap" (243). Scene setting can be like a stiletto solo in a crowded room in making you look up and take notice, and inviting you to recreate the rhythm for yourself in your own mental voice or even out loud, taking your lead from the critic. Angela had vocally imitated me that night years ago, and if you attend to the language of her reading of Oswald's poem you will be able to join in (as I do) in her imitation of Oswald's feet. Leighton writes: "Rhythm is not an abstract rule [...] applied after the event; rather, it is the articulation and stress brought to language at each specific reading" (230). In setting the scene of her "specific reading" of Oswald, Leighton involves us as readers in her mental-vocal performance, so that we may tip-tap too.

By this point in Oswald's poem—when the "Listen" sequence unfurls—we have hit a sudden downpour, and the gardener-narrator is waiting it out in shelter, musing on the misfortune of her leaky wellies. Skipping this preamble though, Leighton's ear flies to "Listen Listen Listen Listen" because of its strange walk. How do you measure a disyllabic foot with no end, or a series of feet with no full stops or exclamation marks or even question marks between them to hold in their sound? Every "Listen" is capitalized and as such syntactically self-contained, but there is no mark to break its fall. It freefalls; but for how long? It is as though the command were meant as a provocative contradiction in terms, saying on the one hand: listen indefinitely, fall into listening; and on the other: know when to stop listening and start again with each new "Listen." It is as if different intensities of listening were expected of the reader at the beginning and end of each iteration of the word, as if each one said "Listen," leaving us ready for a refresh. Yet we receive no direct instructions to this effect. The reading voice, too, has intuitively to clip off the sound like clipping toenails. In the nineteenth century, Alfred Lord Tennyson played a similar trick with the opening line, "Break, break, break," which needs somehow to fold into the anapestic, triple-beat norm of the rest of the poem but is just three monosyllabic words, all of them breathy and weighty and urgent-sounding.[3] It is too little *and* too big. The answer must lie in the punctuation. How to measure the commas? Tennyson's critics are still scratching their heads.

Yet Oswald's freefalling tetrameter is significant not just for the time-keeping challenges it poses to the reader, but for the way it illuminates the next

---

3. Alfred Tennyson, *Selected Poems*, ed. Christopher Ricks (Penguin, 2007), 89.

three-line stanza. Leighton quotes the line and stanza together, retaining Oswald's asterisk between them (interpreted as a rain splash):

Listen Listen Listen Listen
*
They are returning to the rain's den,
The grey folk, rolling up their veils,
Taking their steel taps out of their tips and heels.[4]

Foot-focused, Leighton skips downward from the rain's veils to its figurative feet, which are stilettoed at first (like me earlier) with steel-tapped tips and heels but gradually muted. She comments: "The once cleated rain now goes on tiptoe" (243). "Cleated" here is an important rethink of Oswald's metaphor, bringing a whiff of the sea air and an atmosphere of practicality. For centuries the place where you would most likely find cleats was a ship deck, where the metal wedges were (and still are) used to gather and secure rope. Another likely scene for the cleat is the stable, where the cleats on horses' hooves act as buffers between their raw soles and the ground. Cleats characteristically contain, hold steady, protect. Moreover, it is steel cleats too, combined with the wholly singular muscular mechanism of a horse-walk, that lets us hear hooffall. Leighton begins one of the chapters of *Hearing Things* by attempting to catch this singular pattern in rhythmical formulations she knows, scanning the trot of a horse in the street. It "sounds like a beat of four," she writes, thinking aloud, "but at a gallop, like three, in a dotted rhythm, each footfall a double note as the iron shoe strikes the surface of the road" (97). Slipping between four and three, like intermittent tripods, the trot may just about be musically analyzed. And, in the sense that they are legible in this way, amenable to capture, the horses have an advantage over the fading rain. Oswald's pun in the line: "Taking their steel *taps out* . . ." speaks to this difference between cleated and uncleated sound. Rain with its "tap" taken out "goes on tiptoe," whereas to "tap out" is to ring out, sound out, bang out. It suggests a blast with a definite stop. Listen.

Oswald's ambition to, in Leighton's words, hear "what rainfall stopping may still sound like" could seem nonsensical. For how can a finished sound sound like anything at all, or even constitute sound? But Leighton's present participle, "stopp*ing*," is crucial here. It is not quite the case that the rain has stopped but

4. Oswald, *The Thing in the Gap-Stone Stile*, 4.

rather that the cleats by which you might hear it stopping have been taken out. It is a naked hoof, a sentence with no ending, a welly with a hole in it, a fall into what sounds like silence but is not. There is no such thing as real silence, Leighton writes, since everything that exists physically must make sound: "The tiniest moving particle must emit some noise" (4). Silence is an invention of our laziness, meaning that our ears and aural imaginations have it in them to hear *into* seeming silences flickerings of undiscovered sound. This could strike us as thrilling, a new beginning for peeled ears. Leighton writes that poems "create a promise of listening beyond listening's scope," encouraging that part of us that wants to hear more than we can, to hear imaginatively (245). And Oswald echoes this optimism in her account of the sunrise after the rain: "tiny begins-again danc[e] on the night's edge." But the promise of a deepened listening may be as alarming as it is enlivening. Paraphrasing an essay of Oswald's on garden noises, Leighton makes a distinction between the safety of vision versus the risks of the ear: "While the eye meets surfaces and can therefore be assured of encountering empirical things as they are, the ear meets depths, which are less encountered than surmised or gauged."[5] That sensation of a depth confronted, of sounds under sounds under sounds, can make Oswald's work eerie. In another poem of hers from later in the same volume, "The Three Wise Men of Gotham Who Set Out to Catch the Moon in a Net," she tells a story of helpless searching. The men are on a fool's errand, as the title suggests, wanting to reach, wrap up, and take home the moon. But nothing whatsoever in their world may be held on to. "It was deafman's buff," Oswald writes, conjuring up a life-or-death auditory version of "blind man's buff" where the object is not to catch opponents while blindfolded but to anticipate the unthinkable without the aid of one's ears.[6] Rowing in the dark with the moon as their one bright principle of orientation, the journeyers' hearing is a guesswork with nothing to stop speculation. Anything could be anything and none of them has the intuition to know what. One exclaims: "I'm frightened. There's no end to where we are."[7]

The men's oars imprint and dissolve their trail with each sweep. They leave no footprint, nothing by which they may be tracked. Their interpretative troubles are mirrored in their predicament. Oswald, though, has higher hopes for

---

5. Oswald, *The Thing in the Gap-Stone Stile*, 5.
6. Oswald, *The Thing in the Gap-Stone Stile*, 49.
7. Oswald, *The Thing in the Gap-Stone Stile*, 51.

the rain. Leighton, again foot-curious, zooms to the walk with which her earlier poem ends:

> But what I want to know is
> Whose is the great grey wicker-limber hound,
> like a stepping on coal, going softly away . . . [8]

There should grammatically be a question mark here; it is another unfinished, un-cleated sentence. However, rushing to fill the pause, the ellipses claim the footsteps for themselves in the act of imitation; they too are "stepping [. . .] softly away," an unstopped stop-stop-stopping, a stepping *as* stopping, like a rhyme gone wrong. Leighton suggests that there is something preposterous about the effort of ellipses to put in print a sound going out of earshot, print being itself a silent medium, as silent as the blank page. In aural terms, the only difference between a block of text and the white margin surrounding it is one of aspiration: the text wants you to hear it, the margin for you to hear nothing. Ellipses put on airs (or ears), trying to hear what not even our ears can hear, trying to leap from an image into sound's depths. In any case, Oswald's implied question overflows the dots. Whose, *whose*, is the hound?

One answer might be: Stevie Smith's. In "Pad, Pad," a poem about the fade-out of a love affair, Smith's second stanza muses:

> All I know is, if you were unkind now I should not mind.
> Ah me, the power to feel exaggerated, angry and sad
> The years have taken from me. Softly I go now, pad pad.[9]

Listen *into* the "stepping away" of Oswald's hound and you will hear Smith's poem.

"All I know is" comes back inverted in "what I want to know is," while "Softly I go now" returns as "softly going away," with Smith's "now" reintroduced in the suggestion, in Oswald's "go*ing*," of a continuous just-as-we're-looking walk off. Even the flutter of "pad pad" may be read as a model for Oswald's ellipses, in that they both re-perform a stepping action described a moment before. Both the dots and the pads attempt to be feet. At the same time, however, within the echoey allusion to Smith, a vivid discrepancy jumps out. Most obviously, Smith's speaker is unmistakably feline, with her padded

---

8. Oswald, *The Thing in the Gap-Stone Stile*, 5.
9. Stevie Smith, *The Collected Poems and Drawings of Stevie Smith*, ed. Will May (Faber & Faber, 2015).

paws and weaving, slick withdrawal, while Oswald's hound is irrefutably a dog. The hound is also highly energetic. Oswald's phrase "wicker-limber" tricks you into mishearing "wicker-limbed," so that your tongue clasps a limb that melts limberly away. "Limbed"-becoming-"limber" has a ghosting effect too, turning a body into a ripple of motion, absorbing that motion into a momentary, understated rhyme: wick*er*-limb*er*. Everything about the hound moves. Smith's cat, on the other hand, moves "softly" not from litheness but from total emotional exhaustion. You almost feel that if she were "stepping on coal" as the hound figuratively does she would not speed up but wilt, defeated, into the blaze. How do you make a hyper dog hear the steps of a drained cat?

A few years ago, I was at a party with Angela and a few others, listing and reciting poems we loved. We had detached from the main scrum in the kitchen, were growing conspiratorial, and getting noisier and gigglier, entering the spirit of the game. Suddenly Angela volunteered the first lines of a poem I had never heard before, by Tudor poet Thomas Wyatt. Immediately, as if challenged to a memory test—and surely too because of the sheer pleasure of enunciating Wyatt's rhythms; so old, so unlike any rhythms with which we are familiar, embedded as they are in a time before prosody was standardized and giving as they do, in Oswald's words, "more to the eye than the ear"[10]—everyone joined in with her. Out rolled the words: "They flee from me who sometime did me seek / With naked foot stalking in my chamber."[11] The poem is about an ex-lover, formerly keen, formerly prowling a bedroom, now gone. It is a heartbroken poem, though not defeated like Smith's, more like Oswald's hound in its limber, spectral intentness. It is unreconciled to loss, still attempting to hear the woman's naked footstep. Intently listening too, myself, since I could not participate vocally and the sounds were wonderfully new to me, I remember how everyone stumbled, blindsided, by Wyatt's over-quick and abruptly long vowels and the little shocks of his k's. You cannot help but search for traditional metrical feet in poems; our ears are trained to. But the shoe doesn't fit with Wyatt; he gets away. Likewise, the ex in these lines. I remember everyone pouncing, emphatic, on the word "naked" in "with *naked* foot stalking my chamber," as though we had caught her at it, whatever it was: that mysterious act of lust lurking in the adjective, bared to a man in the past. But

---

10. Alice Oswald's "Introduction" to *Sir Thomas Wyatt: Poems Selected by Alice Oswald* (Faber & Faber, 2008), xii.

11. Thomas Wyatt, *The Complete Poems*, ed. R. A. Rebholz (Penguin, 1997; first published, 1978), 116.

a naked foot is *less* audible than a shoe, its softness making it ethereal for all its corporeality, all its show of passion. It is a limb too limber to be grabbed, a ghost of the floorboards. How do you catch the echo of a muffled foot, once a declaration of desire—naked, honest, in pursuit—now an ellipsis? Impossible. Even so, this is the foot you want: this and no other, the one you cannot get.

At the party, we felt we could catch elusive feet. I listened, enchanted, as tongues curled and sizzled and teeth percussed, and the gorgeously odd poem fell in and out of range. Wyatt writes in another poem, again musing on the uncapturability of a lover: "I leave off therefore / Sithens [meaning 'since'] in a net I seek to hold the wind."[12] There is no point trying to hold what cannot be held, yet you sense that, despite this, the speaker will keep on trying, that the net and wind experiment is an old habit of his. Oswald's moon-catching poem ends hopefully. The boatmen are close, they can feel it. If they can only get to the horizon where the wind shatters the water's surface and the giant moon, split by the commotion, is accessible at last. They will net and scoop up the big white-silver shards, a fortune's worth. They will take them home in bowls.

---

12. Wyatt, *The Complete Poems*, 77.

PART II
Noticing

4

Close Reading Drama

ERIC GRIFFITHS ON
WILLIAM SHAKESPEARE

Robert Stagg

A former student of Eric Griffiths (1953–2018) wrote upon his death that, for Griffiths, "the study of English literature mattered."[1] *It mattered "in a way that affirmed what it is to be alive and to process mute swirls of consciousness into words on the page." Himself a protégé of Christopher Ricks (read in chapter 7 by Katie Kadue), Griffiths satirized the literary theory that was ascendant as he was coming up in the 1970s and 1980s. He preferred the practical criticism of Ricks and William Empson (read in chapter 18 by Noreen Masud). He was a passionate and popular lecturer, and it is a lecture on* Hamlet *that Stagg takes up here. Most readers and viewers probably hurry past the first few lines of Shakespeare's play, deeming them trivial. Stagg, through Griffiths, shows the power of slowing down with the dictum, who says what when and where to whom. Suddenly, the opacity of the opening of* Hamlet *appears: we notice it. Students sometimes believe they must rush to identify imagery, metaphor, symbol. But linger on* who says what when and where to whom *first. As Stagg demonstrates, this simple instruction is surprisingly complex to enact—and rewarding.—DS + JW*

---

1. Hugh Thomson, "Once in a Lifetime: Eric Griffiths (1953–2018)," *The White Rock*, November 9, 2018.

IT IS often said, rightly, that close reading is "as close to a shared methodology as literary study is ever likely to have."[2] Yet no matter how many share in it, that word "methodology" is a broad one and the sorts of close reading we train on a lyric poem can be substantially different to those we train on a narrative poem or an epic poem, let alone a novel or a short story. It can sometimes seem that close reading is suited to (or designed for) the lyric poem above all other modes, chiefly because the phenomenon of "lyric time"—that "intensified awareness" of "temporal condensation" supposedly characteristic of lyric poetry—invites a slow reading that must also involve a kind of close reading.[3] But what happens when our close reading cannot be slow? For example when a drama is playing out before our eyes and ears in a theater, when critical judgment must be exercised at some speed, and when we are reading (or "reading") a stage rather than a page. And even when we have the text of a play in front of us, not yet incarnated by performance, how can we ensure that our reading is properly close to the playtext's essential nature, its status as a play rather than a lyric poem? What might we notice in a play that we wouldn't, or shouldn't, or couldn't, in a novel or a sonnet or a short story? In other words, how should we close read drama?

At least one good answer to this question is offered in Eric Griffiths's "A Rehearsal of *Hamlet*." Fittingly, the printed text of "A Rehearsal of *Hamlet*" originated in a performance of sorts: it was given as part of a lecture series about *Hamlet* in the Cambridge University English Faculty (and then gathered into a collection of Griffiths's lectures by Freya Johnston). Although the lecture tends to fizz centrifugally, it has a chief centripetal concern: that is, "the perpetual situatedness of utterance in a play."[4] Griffiths clarifies this compacted phrase by way of a complaint: "A principal weakness of much comment on Shakespeare's plays is that the commentators pay little attention to what a figure in a play is doing by uttering *these* words at *this* point; commentators are often preoccupied rather with such things as imagery, or with what they take to be the philosophical suggestiveness of what is said, as if it were a secondary

---

2. Russ McDonald, Nicholas D. Nace, and Travis D. Williams, "Introduction," in *Shakespeare Up Close: Reading Early Modern Texts*, eds. McDonald, Nace, and Williams (Arden, 2012), xxiii.

3. Howell Chickering, "Lyric Time in 'Beowulf,'" *Journal of English and Germanic Philology* 91, no. 4 (1992): 489–509, 493; David Nowell Smith, "Parsing Time in the Lyric," *Critical Quarterly* 64, no. 4 (2022): 138–54, 139.

4. Eric Griffiths, "A Rehearsal of *Hamlet*," in *If Not Critical*, ed. Freya Johnston (Oxford University Press, 2018), 91. All subsequent citations given in text.

consideration who says what when and where to whom, whereas it is not secondary, not at all, but rather the drama itself" (106). The consequence of this critical "weakness," Griffiths concludes, is that some "commentaries on Shakespeare seem to me like treatises on sculpture which never deign to mention stone" (107). On first reading, it may appear that Griffiths is rebuking those critics (or, presumably worse, "commentators") who do not read Shakespeare's plays closely, who "pay little attention." But close readers are not exactly spared Griffiths's rebuke, for he regards "such things as imagery," a typical domain of close readers, as being also inessential to "the drama itself." To understand "the drama itself," we need to read closely for the "situatedness" of speech in the playtext, to notice the sheer practical business of "who says what when and where to whom" (these questions being not unique to drama but acquiring a particular shape and significance in a playtext that is distinct from the varieties of speech, or "speech," we encounter in a poem or novel).

If this sounds like a kind of Cluedo criticism—it was Colonel Mustard talking to Professor Plum in the Library—Griffiths makes good on his readerly principles in a diffusely illuminating account of the first few lines of *Hamlet*:

1.1 Enter BARNARDO and FRANCISCO, two sentinels.

BARNARDO
 Who's there?
FRANCISCO
 Nay, answer me. Stand and unfold yourself.
BARNARDO
 Long live the King.
FRANCISCO
 Barnardo?
BARNARDO
 He.
FRANCISCO
 You come most carefully upon your hour.
BARNARDO
 'Tis now struck twelve. Get thee to bed, Francisco.
FRANCISCO
 For this relief much thanks. 'Tis bitter cold
 And I am sick at heart.
 (*Hamlet* 1.1.1-7, as printed in the Arden Third Series)

These will be familiar lines to some readers, and it takes effort to consider them afresh. One way to do this is to read the lines with Griffiths, noticing "who says what when and where to whom." Griffiths first notices "the special twist Shakespeare has given the opening exchange by transferring the formulaic challenge of a sentry on guard, 'Who's there?,' from the sentry who is actually on guard, Francisco, to the one just arriving to take up his watch, Barnardo" (105). Griffiths is far from the first critic to have spotted this unnerving reversal, and it is an open question—open to performance, that is, as well as to readerly interpretation—quite how unnerving the reversal needs to be, since some productions emphasize it more than others and some audiences (or audience members) appear to notice it more than others. A lot depends on how the actor playing Francisco stresses his opening words. Does he say "Nay, answer ME" as though asserting that it is his job to pose the questions, or does he say "Nay, ANSWER me" as though indicating that he is about to ask a question, of sorts, in his ensuing challenge to "Stand and unfold yourself"? Close reading theatrically, we might also wonder what Barnardo's word "there" is supposed to mean. Where is "there"? Are Francisco and Barnardo close together or far apart? Could it be hard to tell in a darkly lit modern-day theater? This little undoing of deixis, where an act of lexical pointing need not be indicating anywhere specific at all, is quite as unnerving as the reversed role of the sentinels. Nor does the stage direction before their speech clarify matters. We are told nearly the bare minimum: "Enter BARNARDO and FRANCISCO, two sentinels." We are not told whether the sentinels enter together, or from separate entrances, or at the same time, or in short or prolonged succession. "Who's there?" could almost be the stage manager's (or, in early modern terms, the prompter's) question to the playwright. By contrast, in an early, textually corrupt version of the play (the First Quarto or Q1) Barnardo opens the drama by saying "Stand: who is that?"—a somewhat less unsettling because more direct query (even if the latently absurdist quality of the opening exchanges is emphasized by Q1's speech prefixes refusing the sentinels their names, marking them instead as "1." and "2.").

Noticing "who says what when and where to whom" can illuminate the play's initial obscurity—not to resolve or dissolve that obscurity, but to see it the better for what it is. Francisco's "Stand and unfold yourself" might sound like a challenge to the obscurity, but is itself quite obscure. It is long-winded, periphrastic, almost as though the character feels a need to comfort himself by padding out his verse line to a regular ten syllables or to fill out his social posture with orotund utterance. Is unfolding yourself the same thing as identifying yourself? Or does it go beyond simple identification? (And is this a joke about Barnardo and Francisco's names recalling Bernardine and Franciscan monks, "folded" up in their habits? If so, it is a joke for readers who can see the characters' names printed in speech prefix but not yet for audience members who will have to wait a few lines to hear Barnardo and Francisco called by their names.)

Barnardo's response to Francisco's challenge (if it is a challenge) is to say "Long live the King." The Arden editors describe this as a "password," formulaically clarifying Barnardo to Francisco. However, the following lines do not straightforwardly bear out the password's efficacy. The play of *Hamlet* exists in three different versions, and the First Folio version has Francisco ask "Barnardo?" right after the "password," indicating that he is still not quite certain of his fellow sentinel's identity. Even if Francisco speaks without a question mark, as in the quarto texts of the play, Barnardo's ensuing utterance "He" carries with it a note of reassurance, seeming to answer a question that Francisco has not quite asked. (It is worth noting here that question marks and exclamation marks were somewhat interchangeable in early modern punctuational practice.) The Arden editors have formatted these three utterances as one verse line, distributed between the two speakers, which comes to look "stepped" or "shared" on the page. However, these words are not presented thus in any of the early modern texts of the play, and if the syllables are added together they are still two syllables short of a pentameter (perhaps allowing space for edgy, nervous pauses in performance). The Arden editors would presumably argue that Francisco's speech on either side of this exchange ("Nay, answer me . . ." at one end and "You come most carefully . . ." at the other) is in verse and that these quick-fire or agonizingly slow exchanges between the sentinels should likewise be in verse. Yet to set these exchanges as verse is to steady them, so that the play settles into an order and a structure immediately after its first line. If these opening exchanges instead shiver between prose and verse, never quite consolidating into the latter, a different feeling emerges. The question of "who says what when and where to whom," then, is also an editorial question; it gets answered by Shakespeare's editors (and early printers) as well as by Shakespeare himself.

Griffiths has an acute ear for the conversation between Francisco and Barnardo. He describes them, and other characters in the play, as "individuals in pitilessly nervy relation to each other, entangled in backchat, constantly looking out of the corners of their eyes at those around them" (96). We can hear some of this in Francisco's next line to Barnardo, "You come most carefully upon your hour." Is it a compliment or a rebuke? Does Francisco intend to say that Barnardo has been heedful and attentive, or circumspect and cautious (these being the Oxford English Dictionary's four synonyms in its entry for the word "carefully")? Much hinges on Barnardo's reply (for, in drama, the assessment of one voice cannot be enough): "'Tis now struck twelve. Get thee to bed, Francisco." How soon is "now"? Are we to hear a bell chiming at this point in the play, or immediately beforehand, to verify Barnardo's timekeeping? And if not, or if the bell chimes sometime before Barnardo and Francisco first speak, are we to discern that Barnardo is late and Francisco therefore sarcastic or reproachful in his speech? In other words, in close reading drama we will often have to read moments that are not entirely visible or audible on the page, no matter how closely we scour it. These moments will have their realization only on stage (or in an imagined performance) although such realization will also decisively narrow the range of possibilities intimated by the playtext. Indeed we might think of performance, whether in terms of an actorly rendition or a directorial design or a readerly imagination, as being a species of close reading: the actor Simon Russell Beale has aptly described his performances as being attempts at "three-dimensional literary criticism," a sort of noticing achieved by or through the actor's body.

By line 5 Barnardo appears to be taking control of the conversation and the scene, properly assuming his role as the nightwatch by commanding (however sternly or gently) Francisco to "Get thee to bed." At this point in the scene Griffiths notices another "twist" in "who says what when and where to whom." Francisco's statement "For this relief much thanks" turns on the meaning of the word "relief." In a functional sense he is thanking Barnardo for having relieved him of his duties (partly owing to the "bitter cold"), yet the line that follows suggests the relief is more than professional or meteorological. Francisco tells Barnardo, or us, or himself, or all of the above, that he is "sick at heart." Since Francisco never expands on the subject of his sickness and will soon disappear from the play, it is easy not to notice (or to notice and then disregard) this curious little half-line. Griffiths, however, registers this as one of the play's many "hints of unrecounted lives, like snatches of conversation overheard in the street, inviting speculation, with the poignancy of scenes glimpsed from a passing train, scenes we are not allowed to dwell on" (notice how his own writing flits from street to train, not allowing his reader to dwell on either) (109). Separately and together, Griffiths argues, these "hints" fashion a "depth-of-field," an impression that the play's characters have lives quite their own, happening offstage as well as onstage, before and after the action of the drama. Sometimes close reading can notice things far away or out of view—for attention to a play's surface begets a proper awareness of its dramatic depth and width, with each inevitably depending on the other.

Natalie Phillips has described close reading as a "style of focus," succinctly suggesting some ways in which close reading is as much a manner as a methodology.[5] Close reading can often be detected in the style of a critic's writing; some close-readerly prose can be "close" in the atmospheric sense of being dense or humid, stuffed with noticings that are complemented by the critic's own tumid repertoire of wordplay. In other words, we might think of close reading as incurring a close writing. Griffiths's noticings are of a somewhat different kind. There is nothing conspicuously stylish about them. They are as much about the disposition and negotiation of expressions as the expressions themselves. Griffiths implies that the question or questions of "who says what when and where to whom" are the mechanics of drama that then allow a style to take place, "Vorsprung durch Technik" as a certain car manufacturer might put it. It is easy to neglect such mechanics, or to consider them beneath critical notice; even "professional noticers," as Stephen Booth referred to literary critics, can close or squint their eyes and ears to some aspects of the text they have before them.[6] It is also hard to notice such mechanics in part because they are so patently visible, so obviously part of a play's infrastructure, so quintessentially the business of drama, and thus sufficiently subdued into the text as to be almost invisibly flush with it. But then, as one professional noticer George Orwell had it, "To see what is in front of one's nose needs a constant struggle."[7]

---

5. Natalie Phillips, "Literary Neuroscience and History of Mind: An Interdisciplinary fMRI Study of Attention and Jane Austen," in *The Oxford Handbook of Cognitive Literary Studies*, ed. Lisa Zunshine (Oxford University Press, 2015), 59.

6. McDonald et al., "Introduction" to *Shakespeare Up Close*, xviii.

7. George Orwell, "In Front of Your Nose," *Tribune*, March 22, 1946.

5

The Poet's Choices

HELEN VENDLER ON JOHN KEATS

Jeff Dolven and Joshua Kotin

The headline for a New York Times *profile of Helen Vendler (1933–2024) dubbed her "The Closest Reader."*[1] *A student of the original "practical critic," I. A. Richards, Vendler has carried his prescriptions for students—tight focus on the words on the page, in dialogue with other works of literature, bracketing history and theory—into the twenty-first century. She is a consummate noticer, which she achieves through a practice Dolven and Kotin call empathetic reading. Vendler identifies with the writer and considers why they chose each word, word by word. Dolven and Kotin present, here, a starter kit to begin to notice like Vendler: read aloud, read to a friend, write the work out longhand. Imagine a counterfactual text. Close reading becomes an act of attention tantamount to authorship.—DS + JW*

IN THE essay "How Should One Read a Book?" (1926), Virginia Woolf answers her own question in this way:

> To read a book well, one should read it as if one were writing it. Begin not by sitting on the bench among the judges but by standing in the dock with the criminal. Be his fellow worker, become his accomplice. Even, if you wish merely to read books, begin by writing them.[2]

---

1. Rachel Donadio, "The Closest Reader," *New York Times*, December 10, 2006.
2. Virginia Woolf, "How Should One Read a Book?" *The Yale Review* 16, no. 1 (Autumn 1926), https://yalereview.org/article/virginia-woolf-essay-how-should-read-book.

There is no literary critic more committed to this practice than Helen Vendler. In *The Odes of John Keats* (1983), she takes Woolf's recommendation to what must be its limit: "The poet is so unconscious of his reader that we have only the choice of becoming him [...] and losing our own identity."[3]

In this chapter, we attempt to describe what it means for Vendler to become Keats: how she does it and what it can do for readers to, as it were, identify with her as she identifies with the poet. We recognize that reading in this way may not be obvious or easy, and may even seem nonsensical. You're signing your name to the paper you're writing—why attempt to lose yourself? What can you see as Vendler or Keats that you can't see as you? Vendler's book—as well as all her writing about individual poets from George Herbert to Emily Dickinson to Wallace Stevens—makes a case for bringing a writerly attention, a sense of agency, responsibility, and choice, to the interpretation of someone else's words. The practice is worthy of study for the light it brings to specific poems, and for its general lessons about the techniques and value of reading closely.

One of the first things that Vendler does in *The Odes of John Keats* is set the boundaries of her enterprise. "I propose," she writes, "the conceptual frame of authorial choice and the contextual frame of the Keats canon (supplemented by some of Keats's sources)" (5). We'll return to the idea of "authorial choice" in our next paragraph. By the "Keats canon" and "Keats's sources," Vendler means that her interpretation of each of the six odes will draw on the others, on Keats's poetry at large, and on the work of the writers Keats most often invoked: Spenser, Shakespeare, Milton. Notice that poetry itself is her world of reference. This is the data she uses to get to know Keats, to get inside his head. Another term for this "frame"—the one proposed by the book you're reading—is scene setting: orienting your reader both to the poem at hand and to the resources you will bring to it. Vendler's scene is Keats's writing and Keats's reading.

When you write about a poem, your contextual frame will likely be narrower than Vendler's. It will possibly include other poems you have been assigned or a critic or historian you have read, or both. It might only include the particular poem you are interpreting. Let us work with Vendler's boundaries. What questions does she ask within them, and what questions can we ask? The main guidance she offers is that phrase, "the conceptual frame of authorial choice." (You didn't have to wait long for that phrase to reappear.) Just as her

---

3. Helen Vendler, *The Odes of John Keats* (Belknap Press of Harvard University Press, 1983), 246. All subsequent citations given in text.

contextual frame excludes many texts, so this emphasis on choice excludes many questions. She is not concerned with the influence of larger social and political discourses (as a historicist would be). She is not inclined to view language as at play free of its speakers (as a deconstructionist would). She does grant special authority to Keats's unconscious drives and impulses (like a psychoanalytic critic). It is a lot to set aside, but within its boundaries is a world of intentional language. "[A]n artist's choices are never haphazard," she writes (5).

You can enter this world by small acts of noticing: noticing something surprising, something strange, something you didn't expect. This advice will be familiar to any close reader: mind the details, pay attention to your own surprise and confusion. To wake ourselves up to these possibilities, we rely on a few strategies. For example, reading the poem with a friend and talking about it. (Hence our collaboration on this chapter.) Even reading the poem aloud to yourself is useful: you will likely notice many choices when you hear how the poem sounds and how it departs from everyday speech. Vendler likes to write the poem out by hand—to pretend that she is inventing it as she goes. Slowing things down, tuning your senses, reading in company, you will notice whether anything in the poem seems off, or wrong, or goes against common sense, or if the poet seems uncertain about anything. Does a line contain an extra beat? An archaic word or an anachronism? Any small, telling swerve from the familiar, the expected?

The value of Vendler's practice depends on what you do when you've noticed that surprising detail. It is her reflex to ask not just what that detail means, but why did Keats choose to include it instead of something else? Why put those words in that order and not another? Why choose that image or that rhyme or that punctuation mark among all those available—available, for example, elsewhere in his poems, or sources, or everyday language? All these questions invite us to imagine a different poem, a counterfactual poem. By comparing the poem we have to the poem that could have been, we learn to see through the poet's eyes, because it was exactly that contingency that Keats faced when he was writing and revising. (Although it should be said, Keats was not much of a reviser!) For Vendler, every choice a poet makes is important and, in Keats's case, correct. Our job is to find out why he did just what he did.

Reading Keats's final ode, "To Autumn," Vendler notices many surprising features of the poem and its connection to the other odes. We will focus on one: a simple problem with profound consequences. The activities of the harvest as represented in the poem—reaping (cutting and gathering the wheat), gleaning (collecting what is left in the field), and threshing (separating the grain from the straw)—happen out of order. In the poem, the threshing happens first, then the reaping and gleaning. The reordering is subtle and easy to miss. Keats uses a series of keywords to mark the actions: "winnowing" (a near-synonym for threshing), "hook" (an instrument for reaping) and "half-reap'd," and "gleaner" (a person who gleans). The reordering is also easy to miss because all three actions take place in an environment of inactivity—of sleep and drowsiness, of carelessness. Indeed, the actions, as we will see, might not even be actions at all.

The relevant stanza of "To Autumn" is the second. (The poem has three.) Keats is addressing a personified autumn:

> Who hath not seen thee oft amid thy store?
>   Sometimes whoever seeks abroad may find
> Thee sitting careless on a granary floor,
>   Thy hair soft-lifted by the winnowing wind;
> Or on a half-reap'd furrow sound asleep,
>   Drows'd with the fume of poppies, while thy hook
>   Spares the next swath and all its twined flowers:
> And sometimes like a gleaner thou dost keep
>   Steady thy laden head across a brook;
> Or by a cyder-press, with patient look,
>   Thou watchest the last oozings hours by hours.[4]

The stanza imagines Autumn "sitting careless on a granary floor." The wind does the winnowing—or threshing—and its object is not the wheat, but Autumn's "hair." Continuing this portrait of active inactivity, Keats describes how Autumn's "hook / Spares the next swatch and all its twined flowers." The word "spares" allows Keats to imply reaping even as Autumn abstains. Finally, Keats compares her to a gleaner alternately dozing by a brook and watching the "last oozings" of a cider press. (Like almost all critics of the poem, we use she/her pronouns for Autumn.) The harvest is at once out of order and not quite happening.

Vendler develops her account in one long paragraph. We track her close reading over four stages or movements. First, she notices the inactivity:

> We see in this poem a thresher who does not thresh, a reaper who does not reap, a gleaner who does not glean, a cider-maker who does not turn her press. (251)

---

4. John Keats, *Complete Poems*, ed. Jack Stillinger (Belknap Press of Harvard University Press, 1982), 360.

Already an act of noticing sets the stage for a claim—an act of local claiming, to adopt the terminology of this book. "Autumn," Vendler writes, "acquiesces in but does not enact her own dissolution. Her tresses are the winnowed grain, her life-blood the last oozings" (251). In other words, Autumn passively accepts the transitions that make autumn autumn. What is autumn if it doesn't lead to winter?

So far we only have an account of the harvest being stayed, paused. These acts of noticing and local claiming lead to bigger questions. In the second stage of her close reading, Vendler notices something else: "Keats's rearrangement of the normal order of the grain harvest":

> Where we would expect (in this minutely conscious poem) first reaping, then gleaning, then threshing, we find instead first threshing, then reaping, then gleaning, a sequence invented, I believe, to show the difficulties of presenting an inactive harvest, one imbued with pathos. (251)

Again, an act of noticing leads to a claim. Provoked by an unexpected fact, Vendler attempts to explain why Keats would have chosen to write the poem in this way. Her claim: he meant to imbue the "inactive harvest" with "pathos," a quality, the dictionary tells us, "that evokes pity or sadness."

The third stage of her close reading begins to explain the significance of this claim. She describes an association that was almost certainly in Keats's mind between threshing and the apocalypse, the end of time in Christian history and the day of final judgment, when the saved are winnowed from the damned. For Keats, the apocalypse—its violence and terror—interferes with the production of a more temperate, melancholy, even sustainable pathos:

> Though the archetypal image of harvest is that of reaping, the most energetic single harvest image is that of threshing: when "the stars shall be threshed, and the souls threshed from their husks," then, as Yeats and Blake knew, would come the trampling out of the vintage where the grapes of wrath are stored. Keats wishes to avoid any appearance of apocalypse, and so the season, far from herself wielding the flail, becomes in the threshing scene entirely passive, and is herself, in her metamorphosis into grain, "winnowed" by the soft wind. (251)

Vendler talks through how a harvest works—how it culminates, in energy and productivity, with the violent act of threshing. She mentions two poets, W. B. Yeats and William Blake, to show how Keats inhabits a particular tradition.

(Keats didn't read Yeats or Blake—indeed, Yeats was born forty-four years after Keats died.) Keats, she argues, wants to evade this tradition to "avoid any appearance of apocalypse."

In the fourth stage of her close reading, she completes her act of theorizing, which now becomes regional and global. To do so, she adds a final turn that tempers her account of pathos, capturing Keats's unique and precise vision:

> Gleaning must occur last in the series of scenes from the grain-harvest because it is by definition the most pathetic of harvest-phases, associated as it is in Keats's mind with the image of Ruth, in tears amid the alien corn. And yet, refusing to succumb to the pathos inherent in the image of gleaning [. . .] Keats permits himself to show the gleaner only as a careful tributary presence on her way to the granary, a presence steady and skillful, not homesick and estranged. In the arrested motion of the stanza, the thresher sits, the reaper drowses, the gleaner balances her laden head, and the cider-maker watches in vigil. (251–52)

In this passage, another biblical association comes to Vendler's aid: the Book of Ruth, to which Keats alludes in his "Ode to a Nightingale." (Vendler is making characteristic use of the contextual framework of Keats's writing and reading.) The story once again offers a contrast that clarifies the poet's choices. The biblical Ruth is in exile after a famine in Judah, and is now gleaning in an alien field, "homesick and estranged." Keats's gleaner, by contrast, is a figure of poise and balance, carrying a basket of grain safely across a brook. This stanza is no apocalypse; the poet has not followed his precedents, either about the order of the harvest or its meaning. The stanza sustains instead a kind of mellow sadness, time passing but somehow not running out, the harvest's events loosened from the order that would drive the season to a final winter. You might have something like this feeling when you first read the poem without being able to say exactly what it is or why you feel it. Or perhaps it might grow on you as you reread, as details that at first are just puzzling start to make sense. It can work both ways: but that's one of the things that close reading is, a way of figuring out how to talk about how a poem makes you feel.

Vendler's close reading of the out-of-order harvest reflects a life of studying poetry. She was fifty when *The Odes of John Keats* was published. She had been reading Keats for most of her life, and teaching him, too. It can seem like she knows more than you will ever know. (It still seems that way to us.) But she is committed to a basic set of questions that we can all ask and all begin to answer. In the case of "To Autumn": Why this word, John Keats, rather than another? Why that word after this one? What were you thinking when you made that choice? To close read in this way is to become like Keats, and to make Keats a little more like you. He is not a man struck by lightning: he is a writer making choices, solving problems, just as you are in writing an essay about him.

There are many critics who want to understand the poets they read and write about better than the poets understood themselves—critics who aspire to say something that the poet could not have known about the motives and even the structures of their art. Not Vendler. In an interview for *The Paris Review* in 1996, she told the poet Henri Cole:

> What I would hope would be that if Keats read what I had written about the ode "To Autumn," he would say, Yes, that is the way I wanted it to be thought of. And, Yes, you have unfolded what I had implied, or something like that. It would not strike the poet, I hope, that there was a discrepancy between my description of the work and the poet's own conception of the work. I wouldn't be very happy if a poet read what I had written and said, What a peculiar thing to say about this work of mine.[5]

Vendler is not a suspicious reader, reading for what is hidden behind the poet's words; she is also not a surface reader, merely describing those words. She aspires to give an account of a poem as an instance of how the poet has figured out how to think and live and feel. In the process, she can try out those ways of being for herself. "I feel close to Keats [...] by temperament," she explains in the same interview. Vendler might be best described as an empathetic reader.

Empathetic reading is often a way to care for one's subject. (For a very different—but equally thrilling and attentive—example of empathetic reading, read Hugh Kenner's book about Ezra Pound, *The Pound Era* [1971].) When Keats wrote "To Autumn" in September 1819, his brother Tom had died of tuberculosis the year before, and he himself would die, at the age of twenty-five, seventeen months later. He already suspected he might not live long. To articulate the pathos of rich suspension that Keats achieves, by pausing or holding back the momentum of autumn, is a gift to the poet—a recognition

---

5. Helen Vendler, "The Art of Criticism No. 3," interview by Henri Cole, *The Paris Review* 141 (1996): 170.

that, in the poem at least, he has solved the problem of death itself, turning it from a grim appointment to an enduring feeling. Vendler gives Keats's short life its completion and its eternity at once. To write such an essay (Vendler herself observes that she gives more than a page to each of the poem's thirty-three lines) you have to care so much about the poet. That may be daunting, for a critic starting out. But reading is one way to learn that care. Reading as a writer, Vendler shows us how poetry can pass from a bewilderment to a passion.

6

What Beauty Hides

TONI MORRISON ON MARIE CARDINAL

Adrienne Brown

What makes American literature American? A country founded on the ideal of freedom and the reality of slavery makes "a singular landscape for a writer," wrote Toni Morrison (1931–2019). The Nobel laureate is best known as a novelist, but she was also a critic. Her Playing in the Dark *(1992) argued that American literature's preoccupations—with, for example, individualism and innocence—are not self-made nor sui generis, but produced in differentiation and opposition to the repressed presence and history of African Americans. Noticing race in a time of liberal color-blindness was, for Morrison, as Brown observes here, not a game of gotcha, but a pursuit of the obliquities of literature, what makes its effects possible. Brown draws from Morrison much practical advice for noticing. What makes a text feel familiar, or not? Is there a gap between your investment in a scene and a text's? Trust your gut. Read first for plot and feeling, then revisit passages to engage. The process is messy, but you can make the final project polished, dramatic, beautiful.—DS + JW*

NOTICING TRANSFORMS readers from passive consumers of a text—largely at its mercy—into active co-producers of knowledge *with* a text in engaged conversation with it. To notice is to meditate on the choices that comprise a work of literature. Just like you might strike up a conversation with someone at a party by complimenting their shoes—or, gossip with someone else at that same party about why said shoes are tacky—noticing is a way of beginning a dialogue with a text or with others that might turn into something more. And, as at a party, where an initial observation may pave the way for a deeper, more meaningful exchange, in close reading, noticing is the necessary first step to building an impactful claim about a text.

One way to begin the work of noticing is to describe what is familiar about a passage as well as what might be defamiliarizing about it. If you know exactly where a scene is situated in time, space, or emotional register, you can start by noting what precisely the text has done to make you feel so. Perhaps a story mirrors in either content or style an established genre—a fairy tale, an epic, a noirish mystery, or gothic horror. Familiarity may come from having access to the interiority of a character in which a character's feelings and thoughts are described in a way that sparks the reader's empathy. But such access can also breed disjuncture when the reader observes a gap between thought and action or a schism between how a character feels about themselves and how the reader is scripted to feel about them.

If a text refuses to locate you in time, space, or feeling, this, too, is a starting point for taking stock by pinpointing what expectations or conventions it eschews in doing so. More commonly, a work of literature will mix the familiar with the unfamiliar within a single passage, scripting the reader to reflect on their expectations and how they are being either met or undermined. Too many details presented by a work may feel stabilizing; or they may produce a disarming sensory overload making it hard to sense the greater whole. Starkness in description and plot can feel withholding; or it may strike you as refreshingly to the point, conjuring an ease that may later twist into accumulating unease. No detail on its own is inherently familiar or defamiliarizing—it only becomes so in context, either in relation to the formal or social expectations a text deploys and reflects back to us, or in relation to the larger work as a whole. Everything on the page is a choice, and the first step of close reading is inquiring about those choices against the backdrop of all other possibilities.

It tracks that writers are often very good readers. Nothing primes you more to appreciate the choices a writer has made than facing off with your own blank page that must be filled up by making choice after choice. Writer Toni Morrison suggests as much in her 1992 book of literary criticism, *Playing in the Dark: Whiteness and the Literary Imagination*. Before publishing her 1970 novel, *The Bluest Eye*, Morrison earned a master's degree in English literature from Cornell University for her thesis on William Faulkner and Virginia Woolf and worked as an editor at Random House. Rather than siloing her training as a literary critic and editor from her work as a writer, Morrison insists in *Playing in the Dark* upon the intimate and irreducible relationship between these acts and what they together make possible. "Writing and reading are not all that distinct for a writer," she writes, since both "require being alert and ready for unaccountable beauty, for the intricateness or simple elegance of the writer's imagination, for the world that imagination evokes."[1]

And yet, as Morrison also insists, being alert to "unaccountable beauty" or "simple elegance" is only one aspect of appreciating the "world that imagination evokes." Bringing that beauty to account or revealing the effort behind the appearance of simplicity is the necessary next step when reading critically. Learning to pay attention to what beauty hides or the complexities nestled in what can seem quite simple teaches us something about not only how a text works but how the world the text aims to reveal also functions.

In *Playing in the Dark*, Morrison performs close readings of heralded works of American literature to show just how much "the world that imagination evokes" has relied upon renderings of what she calls the "Africanist presence"—naming the "denotative and connotative blackness that African peoples have come to signify as well as the entire range of views, assumptions, readings and misreadings that accompany Eurocentric learning about these people" (6). Starting with her own "early assumptions as a reader" that "black people signified little or nothing in the imagination of white Americans," Morrison demonstrates just how much American literature has needed such presences for its own coherence. She mines American literature's figuration of blackness—from how black people are depicted to more symbolic intrusions of dark forces—to chart "the impact of notions of racial hierarchy, racial exclusion, and racial vulnerability and availability on nonblacks who held, resisted, explored, or altered those notions" (11). Written in the 1990s, when a certain kind of polite color-blindness made "the habit of ignoring race" seem like "a graceful, even generous, liberal gesture," Morrison urges readers instead to vociferously notice when and how race shows up in texts. "Through significant and underscored omissions, startling contradictions, heavily nuanced conflicts, through the ways writers peopled their work with the signs and bodies of this presence," Morrison insists, "one can see that a real or fabricated Africanist presence was crucial to their sense of Americanness" (6). "Even, and especially, when American texts are not 'about' Africanist presences or

---

1. Toni Morrison, *Playing in the Dark: Whiteness and the Literary Imagination* (Harvard University Press, 1992), xi. All subsequent citations given in text.

characters or narrative or idiom," Morrison writes, "the shadow hovers in implication, in sign, in line of demarcation" (47).

Playing in the Dark, then, is largely a book dedicated to teaching us to read the shadow from the sign. Through a series of close readings, Morrison models how we, too, might notice the presence of race in texts where it is not often meant to be noticed. But she is also quick to insist that the end goal of such a reading practice is not to more skillfully "cancel" writers for being racist (she wouldn't have used that term in 1992, but we can). For instance, in attending to a short story by Willa Cather that had been "virtually jettisoned from the body of American literature by critical consensus" because of its problematic rendering of black characters, Morrison insists that "simply to assert the failures of Cather's gifts [...] evades the obligation to look carefully at what might have caused the book to fail" (18). Morrison's aim is neither to distinguish "good" depictions of race from "bad," nor racist writers from righteous ones. Rather, she is more interested in what figurative renderings of race make possible within a given work.

"My project rises from delight, not disappointment," Morrison is thus careful to note. "It rises from what I know about the ways writers transform aspects of their social grounding into aspects of language, and the ways they tell other stories, fight secret wars, limn out all sorts of debates blanketed in their text" (4). We are all inheritors of racial structures and Morrison is particularly interested in the work it takes all writers to both inhabit and transform language in light of this social and cultural legacy. "For both black and white American writers, in a wholly racialized society, there is no escape from racially inflected language," Morrison writes, "and the work writers do to unhobble the imagination from the demands of that language is complicated, interesting, and definitive" (13). It is from trying to do this unhobbling in her own writing, Morrison explains, that she has learned to attend to just how much of our language is tethered to racial forms and norms. Learning to read for race is the first step in being able to understand how race works or fails to work. To return to the opening of this chapter, Morrison asks us to notice how race has been made familiar to us within literature in order to then defamiliarize its appearance. Whether you are a writer trying to transform the language you've inherited, or a reader working to understand what this language has enabled—or, like Morrison, you are both—noticing is a revelatory tool that can make the familiar suddenly unfamiliar and vice versa, creating the conditions for producing new understandings of old texts or creating new texts that transform old understandings.

Now that we've glossed what Morrison is up to, let's look at how she introduces us to the revelatory work of noticing. In her hands, noticing is itself a storytelling tool filled with drama and intrigue. I'm particularly partial to the close reading with which Morrison begins the book, drawing her reader in by asking them to read alongside her. While *Playing in the Dark* goes on to wrestle with some of the most canonical writers of American literature—Edgar Allan Poe, Willa Cather, William Faulkner, Ernest Hemingway, and Herman Melville—she opens by close reading something far less familiar to the average American reader: a contemporary French memoir by Marie Cardinal. It is in some ways the arbitrariness of this text, even its banality, that makes it a useful example. By choosing a text the reader is likely to be unfamiliar with, Morrison can begin to build her argument about the centrality of the Africanist presence to Western literature on relatively neutral ground.

Morrison moves through scene setting in relation to Cardinal's book in less than a page, swiftly glossing its title, *The Words to Say It* (five words she says speak to "the full agenda and unequivocal goal of a novelist"), genre (she describes the book as an "autobiographical novel" shaped by "scenes and dialogue selectively ordered and situated to satisfy conventional narrative expectations"), and purpose (to document the author's "madness, her therapy, and the complicated process of healing"). Morrison's scene setting emphasizes the utter ordinariness of Cardinal's memoir, noting of the text that "clearly her preoccupations, her strategies and her efforts to make chaos coherent are familiar to novelists" (vi). Cardinal's efforts to "make chaos coherent" draw upon the established protocols and familiar repertoires that writers have long used to accomplish such a feat. Nothing to see here, folks, Morrison seems to say here.

But, just as quickly, Morrison upsets this familiar terrain by asking a question that begins to defamiliarize Cardinal's memoir for us. "From the beginning," Morrison queries, "I found one question insisting itself: when precisely did the author know she was in trouble?" (vi). From having read similar stories centered on a protagonist's journey from madness to healing before, Morrison has come to expect that at some point, Cardinal will describe her initial realization that something within her psyche was off-kilter and in need of adjustment. Morrison's question anticipates this scene on our behalf and, by extension, primes us to be curious about how Cardinal will tackle this expectation. Morrison then takes us to this moment, reproducing a lengthy passage from Cardinal's book recounting her first anxiety attack at a concert by Louis Armstrong, a black jazz musician heralded as one of the genre's greatest performers. Narrated in the first person, the passage Morrison quotes at length finds Cardinal describing the intensity of this experience in which she comes to feel almost tortured by Armstrong's willingness to break the limits of musical equilibrium. His playing causes her heart to speed up, her ribs to shake, and her lungs to gasp for air. "Gripped by panic at the idea of dying there," Cardinal writes, "I ran into the street like someone possessed" (vii).

Immediately following this passage, Morrison recounts her own experience encountering it for the first time. "I remember smiling when I read that, partly in admiration of the clarity in her recollection of the music—its immediacy—partly because of what leaped into my mind: what on earth was Louis playing that night?" (vii). While Morrison takes for granted that we can all agree that Cardinal's panic-filled response at the concert is out of proportion, Morrison dramatizes the gap between what interests Cardinal about this scene—her own response and the trouble it causes her—and what interests Morrison—how Armstrong could have incited such a response from Cardinal. Morrison asks us to not only notice what's happening within the text but to notice with her noticing, enacting what we call second-order noticing. It is the gap between Morrison's investments in this scene and Cardinal's—but also her therapist, and even the famous doctor who wrote the preface for the book—that Morrison is most committed to interrogating. "Enunciating that incident was crucial in the launching of her therapy," Morrison notes, "but the imagery that worked as a catalyst for her anxiety attack goes unremarked—by her, by her analyst, and by the eminent doctor" (vii). Morrison's questioning of the role Armstrong played in inciting Cardinal's panic begins to defamiliarize the text and its choices, as we, too, now wonder not only about what Armstrong is doing here but why this detail is brought up only to be abruptly dropped and ignored by everyone else who has engaged Cardinal's tale.

Morrison builds upon this observation by showing us the work it takes for Cardinal and others *not* to notice this imagery. She starts by cataloging all that these other readers have failed to notice: "None of them is interested in what ignited her strong apprehension of death ('I'm going to die!' is what she was thinking and screaming), of physical power out of control ('nothing could appease me. And so I continued to run'), as well as this curious flight from the genius of improvisation, sublime order, poise, and the illusion of permanence" (vii). Here, Morrison describes the severity of Cardinal's response, supporting her readings with short but effective quotes from the text attesting to these descriptions. She then underscores how much of Cardinal's visceral experience of the Armstrong concert is described in terms of violence, noting Cardinal's apperception of his music's skillful precision as being so "painful" to her, it "tore at the nerves" (viii). Tracing the enormity of Cardinal's response to Armstrong's live performance leads Morrison to ask what exactly about this scene could have so triggered Cardinal: "Would an Edith Piaf concert or a Dvorak composition have had the same effect?" (viii). Cardinal's memoir doesn't answer this question and Morrison acknowledges her own uncertainty by answering that "certainly either could have." But in asking the question, she leaves open the possibility that Armstrong's specific presence does, indeed, matter for understanding Cardinal's breakdown. With this possibility on the table, Morrison begins to theorize locally about what this detail might open up: "What solicited my attention was whether the cultural associations of jazz were as important to Cardinal's 'possession' as were its intellectual foundations" (vii). Morrison follows this localized query with a more global gambit: "I was interested, as I had been for a long time, in the way black people ignite critical moments of discovery or change or emphasis in literature not written by them" (viii.) From noticing Cardinal's outsized response to Armstrong, Morrison walks us step by step through an interpretation of this passage that tees us up for this larger claim about the importance of black presence to writing at large that will organize the rest of the book.

Morrison goes on in this section to further close read Cardinal's memoir in ways that verify and deepen her original hunch about the racial logic accompanying Cardinal's anxiety. At the conclusion of this series of readings, Morrison stops to reflect on the utility of such an exercise: "These musings on Marie Cardinal's text are not in themselves wholly necessary for the book's appreciation, being simply illustrations of how each of us reads, becomes engaged in and *watches* what is being read all at the same time" (x). While Morrison uses her close readings to pursue broader claims about race's central place within Western literature, she also frequently brings us back to the intricacies of reading itself as a tool for knowing. Morrison parses reading into two acts, distinguishing between the act of "watching what is being read"—which I take to denote the baser practice of consuming a text passively to simply know what happens—and the work of "becoming engaged" with a text—interacting with it to question its assumptions and choices. Morrison approaches watchful reading and engaged reading as simultaneous, if distinct, activities. And while this may be true for experienced close readers, for the newbie, it can be much easier to separate out these forms of reading as sequential acts. I tell my students to read first as watchers—to orient oneself within the text by reading hungrily, even greedily, for plot and feeling—before revisiting key moments in the work as an engager, someone who now has the patience to slow down, ask questions, and dwell in details the author may themselves breeze past but may prove stickier for them.

I suspect that Morrison—a master storyteller herself—finessed her own revelatory account of close reading to most effectively help us to arrive where she does. She admits as much when she reveals she read Cardinal's memoir around the same time that she had "started, casually like a game, keeping a file of such instances" of epiphanic encounters with black presence in the work of nonblack writers. Sometimes we come to the text with a specific case to support or an underlying set of commitments shaping how we attend to any set of texts. Other times, we don't. We read something because we've been told to, or we're just curious, or someone suggested we might like it. But whatever the conditions that cause us to start reading, to notice is to go from watching a text to engaging it—allowing yourself to get tripped up in the details, to sense when something fits or doesn't and to follow that hunch. Not everything you notice will pan out by leading to a larger claim, but noticing remains a necessary starting point. Even if your own narration of noticing isn't always as gripping or lyrical as Toni Morrison's, her attention to the artfulness that can accompany engaged reading teaches us to treat the work of observation as an ongoing practice that can be both functional and beautiful.

7

Grist for the Mill

CHRISTOPHER RICKS ON CLICHÉ

Katie Kadue

Christopher Ricks (1933–) is a wildly stylish yet pointedly unfashionable close reader, even old-fashioned. A practitioner of practical criticism—the British predecessor to America's New Criticism—Ricks rejected the theory revolution of the 1970s, preferring to work in the lineage of Samuel Johnson, F. R. Leavis, and William Empson. He resists abstraction and writes with "lexicographical dedication," a love for the precision of language that makes him an exemplary noticer; he himself, as Katie Kadue notes, has called criticism "the art of noticing." Ricks teaches us that we can notice through stylistic imitation and through engaging the language we study cooperatively, awakening meanings for our reader who will then notice what we've noticed. Imitation breeds intimacy: when you imitate another's style, you come to know it inside out. Watch how Kadue deftly, playfully imitates Ricks, demonstrating the serious fun of noticing, and licensing us to do the same.—DS + JW

> The only way to speak of a cliché is with a cliché.
>
> —CHRISTOPHER RICKS, "CLICHÉS"

SINCE THE dawn of time, English teachers have instructed students to "avoid cliché." Clichés kill the imagination; they arrest thought; Hannah Arendt blamed them, in part, for the Holocaust.¹ Once a phrase has been stamped with the stigma of "cliché," the thinking goes, it is no longer available to either the creative writer or the close reader. Writers on the verge of cliché should quickly swerve before getting caught in its thought-quashing quagmire, and readers who come across it should write it off as hackneyed, outworn, and tattered.

And yet, as the critic Christopher Ricks points out in his essay "Clichés," which is the primary focus of my chapter, "what, as a metaphor, could be more hackneyed than *hackneyed*, more outworn than *outworn*, more tattered than *tattered*?" What could be more well-trodden than the well-trodden ground of complaining about phrases like "well-trodden ground"? Why does the contempt for cliché seem to inspire such uninspired critique? Is it possible to speak of cliché without cliché?

Ricks reminds us that George Orwell, in his famous essay "Politics and the English Language," joins the long line of thinkers who have had the unoriginal idea of trashing cliché. The essay's closing salvo drills readers in giving such "verbal refuse" the boot:

> From time to time one can even, if one jeers loudly enough, send some worn-out and useless phrase—some *jackboot, Achilles' heel, hotbed, melting pot, acid test, veritable inferno* or other lump of verbal refuse—into the dustbin where it belongs.²

---

1. Arendt traced the Nazi bureaucrat Adolf Eichmann's unquestioning obedience of genocidal orders to his fundamental unoriginality: "he was genuinely incapable of uttering a single sentence that was not a cliché." Arendt notes "the striking consistency with which Eichmann, despite his rather bad memory, repeated word for word the same stock phrases and self-invented clichés (when he did succeed in constructing a sentence of his own, he repeated it until it became a cliché).... The longer one listened to him, the more obvious it became that his inability to speak was closely connected with an inability to *think*, namely, to think from the standpoint of somebody else." Hannah Arendt, *Eichmann in Jerusalem: A Report on the Banality of Evil*, revised and enlarged edition (Viking, 1965), 48, 49. The famous phrase from the book's subtitle, "banality of evil," has itself become a cliché. (Pointing out that the phrase has itself become a cliché has arguably *itself* become a cliché.)

2. George Orwell, "Politics and the English Language," in *The Orwell Reader: Fiction, Essays, and Reportage* (Harcourt, 1984), 366.

After quoting this sentence near the beginning of "Clichés," Ricks decides to do a bit of dumpster diving. In the depths of the dustbin, he finds that "Orwell's darkest urgings" are borne by "a weirdly bright undertow":

> For what is most alive in that sentence is not the sequence where Orwell consciously put his polemical energy—his argumentative train of serviceable clichés from "worn-out" and "useless" through "lump of verbal refuse" to "the dustbin where it belongs"—but rather the sombre glints lurking in the sequence of the scorned clichés themselves: the way in which, even while he was saying they were useless phrases, Orwell used them so as to create a bizarre vitality of poetry. The *jackboot* has, hard on its heels, *Achilles' heel*; then the *hotbed* at once melts in the heat, into *melting pot*, and then again (a different melting) into *acid test*—with perhaps some memory of Achilles, held by the heel while he was dipped into the river Styx; and then finally the *veritable inferno*, which not only consumes *hotbed* and *melting pot* but also, because of *veritable*, confronts the truth-testing *acid test*. Orwell may have set his face against those clichés, but his mind, including his co-operative subconscious, was another matter.[3]

Here Ricks takes seriously—his tenacious playfulness is a kind of seriousness—what Orwell would have us simply laugh off. This is an exaggerated version of what all good close readers do, and what Ricks has elsewhere defined as "criticism": "the art of noticing things"—a slightly unusual word choice, an unacknowledged contradiction, a subtle intertextual allusion, a surprising relation between form and content—"that the rest of us may well not have noticed for ourselves and might never have noticed," or, in this case, things that we have been explicitly instructed are not worthy of our notice.[4]

Ricks's reading of Orwell argues by way of inflected imitation: he helps us notice what he has noticed by playing it back to us at a slightly different frequency. His near-mimicry is a kind of intimacy, making close reading about "closeness" in the sense of emotional bonds as much as of microscopic precision, even if those bonds are ambivalent.[5] He integrates numerous short

---

3. Christopher Ricks, "Clichés," in *The Force of Poetry* (Oxford University Press, 1984), 357. All subsequent citations given in text.

4. Christopher Ricks, *Along Heroic Lines* (Oxford University Press, 2021), 139.

5. Less ambivalently, D. A. Miller describes close reading as "an almost infantile desire to be *close*, period, as close as one can get, without literal plagiarism, to merging with the mother-text." *Jane Austen, or The Secret of Style* (Princeton University Press, 2003), 58.

quotations from Orwell's sentence into his own prose and—with the phrase "his argumentative train of serviceable clichés from 'worn-out' and 'useless' through 'lump of verbal refuse' to 'the dustbin where it belongs'" suspended between em dashes, just like Orwell's avowed list of clichés—mirrors Orwell's syntax with his own.

Even as Ricks seeks to expose Orwell's "co-operative subconscious," "co-operative"—referring to how Orwell is working together with his linguistic material, but also how he makes language work with itself—is the more operative term than "subconscious." Ricks sets his sights primarily on the text's surface, less on plumbing the author's psychic depths than on recording the conversations and confrontations in the social scene of co-operating components that Orwell has assembled: *jackboot* has *Achilles' heel* "hard on its heels" (a cliché introduced by Ricks, but a welcome latecomer to the affair), *hotbed* is melting into *melting pot*, *acid test* joins in and calls back to the "memory" of Achilles, who was also soaked in a special solution, and finally *veritable inferno* arrives to blow up the hot and heavy affair of *hotbed* and *melting pot* and also "confront" *acid test* with its veritable claim to truth. Ricks, in turn, co-operates with Orwell's language, and it's in this uneasy co-operation between critic and text that the truth-testing chemical reaction of close reading occurs. Sometimes, as here, the co-operation is so uneasy that it slides into something more like co-optation, the critic using the text for ends beyond the author's conscious intent. What Orwell tries to cordon off as isolated and inert prison cells of language Ricks reveals to be communicating with each other, sending signals that bounce off one another at lightning speed, through a kind of echolocation that we have only to attune our ears slightly to hear.

Ricks's metaphors for his own close reading are perhaps too much like lightning, more about sight than sound. They suggest that close reading is a matter of illumination: of highlighting the "glints lurking" in the verbal shadows, the "weirdly bright undertow" beneath "darkest urgings," the "vitality" of Orwell's stock phrases simmering on the stove, burning with all the light and heat of a *hotbed*, a *melting pot*, an *acid test*, a *veritable inferno*. As I try to write about Ricks, his metaphors start to flicker in my brain, and my own metaphors to fluoresce, as if his lurking glints have sparked a chain reaction in my own co-operative subconscious. I start to imagine that, somewhere between Orwell's melting pot and his dustbin, Ricks has come across a discarded metal cup, dusted it off, held it up to the light, and revealed (perhaps with the help of an acid wash) what had been etched into its surface. Like such old dusty engraved cups, or like the cupboarded-up household objects that emerge and break into song in *Beauty and the Beast*, words are not endowed with life by close reading so much as their existing but dormant life is activated by the co-operative process of noticing what's already there.

Ricks is a critic best known for his writing on canonical poets such as John Milton, Andrew Marvell, and John Keats, all of whom would seem to contribute a lot more poetic vitality to the co-operative enterprise of close reading than Orwell. But reading Orwell's cliché collection against the grain lays the groundwork for Ricks to go on to show, later in the essay, how more self-consciously poetic writers—his main examples are the poet Geoffrey Hill and the songwriter Bob Dylan—put clichés to more deliberate use. This opening gambit also works to expand our expectations of what is worth noticing. If even someone who demonized doublespeak as doggedly as Orwell can be close-read to reveal ambivalence ("even while he was saying they were useless phrases, Orwell used them so as to create a bizarre vitality of poetry") and multiple significations (examples of cliché, or elements of an accidental poem?), our inventory of what rewards literary-critical attention multiplies as well, to include writing not usually considered literary: polemics in favor of plain speaking, sociological studies, the close readings of literary critics themselves.

Ricks's train of thought sometimes has the momentum of a runaway locomotive, plowing through language via its own internal combustion. "Bob Dylan's art does not traffic in clichés, but it travels far and near by the vehicle of cliché," he says of the musician's lyrics, where metaphorical *trafficking* in cliché, in the sense of *engaging in* or *dealing with*, shifts gears into a different metaphor, where cliché becomes a "vehicle"—not the vehicle of a metaphor but rather a metaphorical motor vehicle, one that's cruising easily along, having left all the traffic in its dust (365). Quoting a quatrain of Dylan's song "I Shall Be Free" that ends with the line "I see better days and I do better things," Ricks quips, "The phrase *seen better days* has itself seen better days—that would do as the definition of a cliché. But Dylan brings it from its past into his and our present, by turning it into the present tense, 'I see better days,' and by marrying it to 'and I do better things,' he does a far better thing with it than usual" (366). Dylan refurbishes a worn-out cliché to make it as good as new, but we might not appreciate the force of this fast-forward into the present tense if Ricks didn't also insist on backtracking into the past and rehashing old ground: "better things . . . better thing"; "better days . . . better days."

"The phrase *seen better days* has itself seen better days—that would do as the definition of a cliché." What Ricks does with that cliché would do as a definition of close reading: recycling language to give it a second life, noticing Dylan's reanimation of a cliché and then using his own turn of phrase to reanimate it yet once more. Turning cliché on itself like this works almost homeopathically: repeating "seen better days" back to *seen better days* is like forcing the beaten-up cliché to look in the mirror, recognize what bad shape it's in, and snap out of its stupor. The only difference in the repeated version of the phrase is self-consciousness, but that's enough to make it better than usual. His attention to language's self-animating resources allows Ricks to notice and thereby awaken clichés not only in the writing of others, but also in his own. In this way, Ricks models for us how to weave what we discover in a text into our own writing, to manage the co-operation between our language and another's.

My metaphor of close reading as interweaving is barely a metaphor at all: it's a dead metaphor, a kind of cliché, such a common way of describing the integration of textual evidence in an analytic essay that the picture of strands of fiber interlaced at right angles on a loom is hardly present in our minds. This uninspired image is inspired by another essay of Ricks's, a study of the seventeenth-century poet Andrew Marvell called "Andrew Marvell: 'Its Own Resemblance.'" Marvell was famous for a stylistic technique that another critic, William Empson, called the "self-inwoven simile," which Ricks modifies, fabricating a different cloth-based term, to "self-enfolded simile." Picking up Empson's thread, Ricks develops a reading of self-enfolded similes in Marvell's poetry, where "something finds itself compared to both of the terms within a comparison," like a dewdrop that looks "like its own tear": this almost incestuous simile "invites us to see the dew drop as a tear wept by itself; to see it therefore both as eye and tear."[6]

In his essay, Ricks not only analyzes Marvell's habit of enfolding the active subject (e.g., an eye) of a figurative relation into its passive object (e.g., a tear): in his Ricksian way, he imitates it. As he enfolds a quotation from a Marvell poem within his rendition of a comment from T. S. Eliot, he coins his own self-enfolded metaphor:

> It is grist to my mill—indeed, is itself both grist and mill—that T. S. Eliot, when he wished to deplore the related (though not strictly reflexive) images which finally close "Upon Appleton House" within their Chinese boxes or their Russian dolls:
>> But now the *Salmon-Fishers* moist
>> Their *Leathern Boats* begin to hoist;
>> And, like *Antipodes* in Shoes,

6. Christopher Ricks, "Andrew Marvell: 'Its Own Resemblance,'" in *The Force of Poetry*, 34, 37. Ricks then fluidly transitions into a similarly liquid passage from Proust where a character looks like she's literally about to cry her eyes out; they "seemed on the verge of breaking from her face and rolling down her cheeks like two great tears" (37).

> Have shod their *Heads* in their *Canoos*.
> How *Tortoise like*, but not so slow,
> These rational *Amphibii* go?
> Let's in: for the dark *Hemisphere*
> Does now like one of them appear.
>
> —that Eliot, deploring these lines, should find himself to have succumbed to this very Marvellian image: "images . . . which support nothing but their own misshapen bodies."[7]

"Grist to my mill": a phrase so overused as to have been ground down to almost nothing. Does this cliché, like "seen better days," offer us an image of the manufacture of cliché: an unthinking machine taking the fresh raw material of language and overworking it into a homogenous slurry? Or is the proverbial mill's grinding of grist analogous to what Ricks and the authors he analyzes in "Clichés" do with clichés, when they process unremarkable material into a refined final product?

Before we can quite decide which, Ricks interrupts himself by correcting himself, and in so doing both removes himself (by removing the personal pronoun "my") and, by creating a strange new phrase, leaves the mark of his personal style: "It is grist to my mill—indeed, is itself both grist and mill." The metaphorical mill is no longer Ricks's, and the grinding work has been reassigned to Eliot's own language, the co-operative labor of close reading reallocated. The cliché has been remodeled to accommodate the phenomenon of the self-enfolded simile: Eliot describing a Marvellian image with his own Marvellian image is "itself both grist and mill," both descriptive and described, both a critical analysis of Marvell's self-enfolded language and a complicit refolding of it.

Let's unpack that. Eliot's description of "images . . . which support nothing but their own misshapen bodies" is supposed to shore up his claim that Marvell has a weakness for nonsensical images that are "over-developed or distracting."[8] What, Eliot complains, are these random fishermen doing with canoes on their heads, like weird tortoises whose shells are also, somehow, shoes? But Eliot's gloss of this passage from "Upon Appleton House," like Orwell's of his series of clichés, is underwritten by a co-operative subconscious;

---

7. Ricks, "Andrew Marvell," 42–43.

8. *The Complete Prose of T. S. Eliot: The Critical Edition*, eds. Anthony Cuda and Ronald Schuchard (Johns Hopkins University Press, 2014), 2:313.

he's co-opted the very Marvellian tic that ticks him off. His own phrase has morphed into a kind of tortoise with a shell-shoe: an image supporting its own body—supporting it how, exactly? What does it even mean for an image to have a body?—is as impossible to visualize as Marvell's mutant turtles, and it's as if the misshapen bodies have been somehow spawned by the images that are also the same thing as those bodies, like eyes that are their own tears. Ricks's Marvellian treatment of the Eliot quotation is, by contrast, conscious—and yet there's something almost mechanical about its motions, so much does Ricks give the impression that writing is about using language as a self-enfolding machine, as both grist and mill. The passage practically writes itself, packaging itself into "Chinese boxes" and "Russian dolls" and tying itself up with a bow: "that T. S. Eliot, when he wished to deplore . . . that Eliot, deploring," all that traffic leading back to a standstill, like a tear swallowed up by its own eye.

Thinking of language as a self-writing machine might seem like uninspired and uninspiring advice for students, particularly at a time when it is easier than ever to outsource writing to artificially intelligent content mills. As Orwell warns, cliché, a kind of proto-ChatGPT, makes it easy to avoid the hard work of thinking original thoughts: "You can shirk it by simply throwing your mind open and letting the ready-made phrases come crowding in. They will construct your sentences for you—even think your thoughts for you, to a certain extent."[9] But what Ricks is doing, and what the art of noticing in close reading does, is not so much let ready-made language do his thinking for him as coax language into doing its own thinking for itself—and then very carefully regulate its operation, co-operating with it, intervening with a thousand invisible micro-adjustments.[10] Part of what gives Ricks his own personal, idiosyncratic style is, counterintuitively, the prestidigitation by which language seems to be operating entirely impersonally, automatically, milling its own grist, *Achilles' heel* hot on the heels of *jackboot*, tenors traveling far and near by the vehicles of their own metaphors, the critic showing his hand by playing the one he's dealt. "The only way to speak of a cliché is with a cliché," Ricks says in "Clichés," just as words are the only way to speak of words. Still, there's more than one way to grind grist, and some may find Ricks's readings a bit too

9. Orwell, "Politics and the English Language," 362.
10. This is, coincidentally, how Ricks elsewhere describes the grandness of Milton's "grand style": a "strength manifesting itself in innumerable tiny, significant, internal movements." Christopher Ricks, *Milton's Grand Style* (Oxford University Press, 1963), 150.

fine-grained, overly implicated in language's self-enfolding folds. There's a risk of getting gummed up in the noticing stage, too taken with the complicated pleasures of textual closeness to move on to the necessary next analytical steps. But such self-co-opting close reading can sometimes allow us to see the tear in our own eye, to find the spark of life that gives the lie to exaggerated claims of language's death and the key to the ignition of interpretation. One man's trash talk is another's close reading.

8

An Odd Way of Listening to Men

BARBARA JOHNSON ON JANE CAMPION

Summer Kim Lee

In the 1970s and 1980s, deconstruction was revolutionary: it turned New Criticism, the status quo, on its head. New Critics saw literature as harmonious, its elements ideally working in unity; deconstructionists argued that such harmony was fantasy, a projection, that literature is inevitably riven with difference in a world structured by socially constructed binaries. Barbara Johnson (1947–2009) was a giant of deconstruction who, as a feminist, plied the gender binary to reveal what its unjust logic means for art. Here, Summer Kim Lee notices that for Johnson, noticing afforded a feminist reading practice. Johnson notices the details of difference in film reviews, in passing conversations with friends, in everyday life. She notices how men in literature envy feminine muteness but can't keep quiet about it. And she teaches us that when women notice and collect irreconcilable details—with ambivalence and the refusal to resolve them—they can build a foundation from which women can reclaim power that men have seized from them.—DS + JW

IN HER essay "Muteness Envy," Barbara Johnson has noticed something odd in poetry written by men. In John Keats's "Ode on a Grecian Urn," for instance, the urn is not glorified for what it holds inside, but for its outside, as a silent, impervious surface. "The ego ideal of the poetic would seem, then, to reside in the muteness of things," Johnson writes.[1] Keats praises his urn as a "still

---

1. Barbara Johnson, "Muteness Envy," *The Feminist Difference: Literature, Psychoanalysis, Race, and Gender* (Harvard University Press, 1998), 129. All subsequent citations given in text.

unravished bride of quietness," the "foster child of silence and slow time," and a "Sylvan historian, who canst thus express" (129). "Heard melodies are sweet, but those unheard / Are sweeter" (129). For Keats, the muteness of the urn is an aesthetic ideal he covets for his own poetic voice. And yet, while men tend to write poetry idealizing muteness—the muteness of, if not women, then feminized things like Keats's urn—they seem unable to commit to such muteness themselves. Johnson gathers evidence of this tendency in men's writing as a pattern of behavior that speaks more broadly to the gendered logics of Western aesthetics. For however sweet that unheard melody might be, Johnson notices that many male poets—Keats, Archibald MacLeish, Wallace Stevens, Francis Ponge, Stéphane Mallarmé among them—cannot help but sing one of their own, eager to be heard.

By following Johnson's close reading practice in "Muteness Envy," this chapter asks: What might we hear if we listen to men? I do not mean a passive kind of listening as a form of assent, deference, or obedience—the kind that would lead us to do a man's bidding. I mean the kind that gathers evidence of particular patterns of behavior and, from it, gains intel and accrues leverage and authority in a wordless grasp for power. In this way, listening is not so dissimilar from the act of noticing, as the grounds for a close reading practice that shuttles between a loose receptivity and an exacting scrutiny, where something odd is discovered, then given context and structure, and as such, becomes not so odd after all. The task of noticing seems of a piece with femininized social etiquette, except rather than make ourselves adaptable to appropriately attentive forms of sociality, we make ourselves adaptable to a text. This can provoke anxiety: we wonder if we have overlooked some important feature that will read as careless, negligent, or ill-mannered, or that will now cause us to fail to see the larger picture, to get the reading right.

Noticing might also stir up feelings of paranoia in the attempt and failure to grasp the totality of a system, or a text. For feminist scholars, such paranoia need not be dispelled and instead can be retooled as a mode of feminist inquiry—a means of wrapping one's mind around a dauntingly vast, pervasive system like, for instance, patriarchy.[2] This paranoia might emerge alternatively from being *on* notice—to be cautioned and warned, to receive and respond to something ominous, not yet within comprehension, language, or narrative.

---

2. See Naomi Schor, "Female Paranoia: The Case for Psychoanalytic Feminist Criticism," *Yale French Studies* no. 62, (1981): 204–19; Sianne Ngai, *Ugly Feelings* (Harvard University Press, 2005).

Johnson's way of listening to men, as a close reading practice, blurs distinctions between noticing and being on notice, between the politeness and the paranoia of a feminized position that must learn to navigate the larger structures in which it finds itself.

In her essay, Johnson reads men's poetry, theory, and literary analysis, moving from that general sense of an odd something, to a more keenly felt understanding of a "recurrent poetic condition" she calls "muteness envy" (131). Johnson plays off of Freud's writing on "penis envy," insofar as she proposes that muteness envy, like penis envy, can be a marker of what differentiates women from men (131–32). Whereas penis envy speaks to the psychic, sexual development of women, muteness envy speaks to the development of men, and for Johnson, such development is not only psychic and sexual, but canonically poetic, too.

Johnson reminds us of Keats's description of his urn as a "still unravished bride" (134). This "still" makes evident the inevitability of ravishment that by definition can mean either rape or ecstasy. The double-sidedness and ambiguity of ravishment's meaning, when it could "still" go either way, when muteness has not yet spoiled as an ideal, is where Keats situates his ode. In wondering what surrounds the urn, Johnson quotes Keats,

> What men or gods are these? What maidens loth?
> What mad pursuit? What struggle to escape?
> What pipes and timbrels? What wild ecstasy? (134)

Question met with question leaves open what kind of ravishment has yet to happen, holding out a moment prior to mad pursuits, pipes, and timbrels. Therefore Johnson writes, "The privileged aesthetic moment is a freeze frame just prior to ravishment. But how does pressing the pause button here make us sublate the scene of male sexual violence into a scene of general ecstasy? How does the maidens' struggle to escape congeal into an aesthetic triumph?" (135). Put differently, how does the freeze frame that threatens or holds out the possibility of rape or ecstasy become the site of an aesthetic ideal, akin to what Keats described as the height of beauty and truth? What Johnson first noticed about men's noncommittal preoccupation with a muteness bestowed upon urns and women speaks to the silent unknowability of women's pleasure and pain, which Keats, among other men, transforms into art.

On this matter, Johnson broadens her inquiry further by turning to "one of the primal scenes of Western literature": Apollo's pursuit of the nymph Daphne, who, in her attempts to escape Apollo's capture and protect herself from rape, transforms into a laurel tree, "still unravished." But as Johnson points out, Apollo is not wholly at a loss, for he does claim something of her muteness as his own. "He enters a whole new dimension of symbolization," Johnson writes, "plucking off a laurel branch and using it as a sign of artist achievement" (135). The moment before Daphne's rape becomes Apollo's own "aesthetic triumph," where his thwarted desire turns into the source of his art, as that which he honors because he did not get to "ravish" it and her, yet and still.

Johnson quotes literary scholar Peter Sacks's reading of the Greek myth, who describes Daphne's transformation not as an escape from Apollo, but the act of becoming Apollo's "consolation prize—a prize that becomes *the* prize and sign of poethood." He writes, "Daphne's 'turning' into a tree matches Apollo's 'turning' from the object of his love to a sign of her. It is this substitutive turn or act of troping that any mourner must perform" (135). Mirroring Sacks's own analysis, Johnson "turns" to what the freeze frame of the moment prior affords men like Sacks, stating:

> Thus, "any mourner" must identify with Apollo, not Daphne, and the fact that Apollo does not carry out the intended rape is coded as "loss"—a loss that becomes a model for the aesthetic as such. The rapist is bought off with the aesthetic. And the aesthetic is inextricably tied to a silence in the place of rape. (136)

Daphne's escape from rape is understood as Apollo's sorrowful loss, and in his mourning, poetry is his consolation. According to Sacks, Daphne's "turn" away from Apollo nevertheless "turns" her into his prize. In her sharp reading of Sacks, Johnson notes how his wording places the poet, and additionally the critic and scholar, in a masculinist position, aligned with Apollo as "any mourner," who, as such, becomes the universal figure of the artist, while Daphne remains that figure's prized art object. Johnson shows how we as readers are subsequently made to side with the artist as mourner (and hence, attempted rapist), bought off with a laurel wreath as an "aesthetic trophy" that attests to an artist's ability to make loss into something beautiful, like an ode (136).

In all this, Daphne says silent. "There seem, then, to be two things women are silent about," Johnson writes, "their pleasure and their violation. The work performed by the idealization of this silence is that *it helps culture not to be able to tell the difference between the two*" (137). As a result, sexual violence against women—whether through their objectification into a bride or an urn, or through rape—is rendered unknowable if not impossible. For how can we read the silence of such ravishment when it can mean different, contradictory things? Johnson puts emphasis on the canon—on Keats's "Ode on a Grecian Urn," as one of the "best known poems in the English language," and Apollo and Daphne as "one of the primal scenes of Western literature"—to show how a recurring condition of muteness envy is not anomalous but in fact foundational to Western aesthetics. Such envy is not particularly all that odd, and instead quite usual, banal, and to be expected.

Men have provided Johnson with examples of their tendencies in turning women's muteness—as a sign of the nondistinction between women's pleasure and pain—into art. While Johnson has given sufficient attention to Sacks's "any mourner," which is to say, the male artist, she then considers Daphne's point of view, or that of Keats's urn. How might they speak? To try to answer, Johnson leaves men to play with their laurel wreaths and begins to listen to women's muteness. She does not believe that if women break their silence they will become empowered, their agency restored, nor that reclaiming silence is a feminist form of resistance, for that, too, idealizes muteness. She does, however, understand the difficult position the aesthetic tradition of muteness puts women in, for once women speak, their words are either discounted as ignorant or as "guilty speech." "It is as though women were constantly subject to the Miranda warning," she writes (137). What can women say about their muteness, since it can or will be used against them?

In her attempts to hear the urn and Daphne, Johnson turns to Jane Campion's then-recent 1993 film, *The Piano*. Here, her close readings primarily focus on the fraught reception of the film, culled from conversations with acquaintances and friends, film reviews, letters to editors, as well as published interviews with Campion and the actors in the film. Anecdotes of friends' opinions about the film comingle with articles by film critics, adding variation and texture to the voices of men we have been introduced to thus far. What Johnson notices about the film has then as much to do with her own experience of viewing it as much as the experiences of others who, like her, are trying to make sense of the film's aestheticization of women's muteness, beyond the scope of a myth or a poem.

Through these various sources, Johnson addresses the debates around whether or not its story about a mute woman named Ada, caught between the desires of two men—her husband, Stewart, and her husband's neighbor, Baines—is a narrative of romance or of rape. For while Baines coerces her into sexual encounters that ambiguously turn into something more meaningful, Stewart, upon discovering these encounters, cuts off one of her fingers out of jealousy and rage. As a romance, Ada's muteness is the sign and source of her strength as she experiences her pleasure in relation to two men who are enthralled with her. Alternatively, Ada's muteness is about her victimization at the hands of two men, whose desire prompts the violence they enact upon her.

Tracking the overlapping discussions of the film becomes "a political game of 'muteness, muteness, who's got the muteness,'" and trying to answer leads to an exasperating ambivalence around the film (150). Close reading practices can generally leave room for ambivalence to breathe. To notice and gather small details requires an acknowledgment of disagreement, difference, multiplicity, and the gaps in between. In the introduction to *The Feminist Difference*, Johnson's essay collection that includes a reprinting of "Muteness Envy," Johnson wonders if "there is something healthy about claiming the right to ambivalence. [...] If resistance is always the sign of a counter-story, ambivalence is perhaps the state of holding on to more than one story at a time."[3] Silence could be a sign of ambivalence, where more than one story—of romance and rape—exist at the same time. But, to close read like a paranoiac, what is the larger system in which these stories are taking place? What broader context holds these stories together?

Johnson's ambivalence is palpable in the way she bristles at those who would want to wholly insist on Ada's silence as a source of resistance and empowerment. For although Ada's actions could be read as empowering, this reading cannot account for her disempowered position within preexisting social structures, or for the possible transformation or destruction of such structures themselves. Ada might find pleasure in her day-to-day life, nevertheless such pleasure must fit into Ada's conditions of existence as a woman, as a wife "traded between men like land, ebony, and ivory" (147). In the film, Johnson writes,

> Women may be angry, but as soon as men show any restraint, sensitivity, or need, women will abandon their anger, fall in love, and adapt happily to society as it is. Nothing, therefore, needs to be changed in the social *structure*. But in that *structure*, Ada does *not* have power. Stewart and Baines may both be responding to a *sexual* power that Ada does have over them (and there is nothing new in seeing women's power as sexual), but Baines, not Ada, can decide to go away, and Stewart has the power to either mutilate her body or give her to another man. (147–48)

Culture's investment in not being able to tell the difference between women's violation and women's pleasure, in the freeze frame of the "still unravished,"

---

3. Johnson, "Introduction," *The Feminist Difference*, 2.

keeps patriarchal structures of power in place that simultaneously withhold women's interiority and readily give space and sympathy to the interiority of men, as mourners suffering the loss of their loved object. What is "healthy" about ambivalence is not the ability to accept the fact of sexual violence, but rather the ability to notice what is structural to that sexual violence—to hold on to the anxiety that tugs at one's reading practice when something keeps repeating itself as "nothing new" yet no less cruel, no less urgent.

While Johnson initially wanted to consider how women might speak in the face of their idealized muteness, she finds that men still, even with regard to a contemporary film like *The Piano*, cannot help but loudly profess their pain and suffering, their loss and longing. Men like Stewart, Baines, and all the rest are represented as mourners and moreover victims of their loss. After all, Campion and Sam Neill, the actor who plays Stewart, describe Ada's husband as "vulnerable," while Baines's "wretchedness" is that of a poor man "sick with longing" (152–53). Johnson notices that in much of the critical discussion of the film, a lot of attention is given to the men and their choices, to their helplessness and violence when confronted with their desire for a silent Ada. Meanwhile, Ada need only make a choice between two men—for her, there is no escape from the structures she is bound within. The game of "muteness, muteness, who's got the muteness," becomes a game of who gets to play—and speak—as the victim, and according to reactions to *The Piano*, it seems like the victims who do get to speak do not include Ada, and instead, are the men around her. "It is in this male two-step—the axe wielder plus the manipulative sufferer, both of whom see themselves as powerless—that patriarchal power lies," Johnson crucially argues (153).

What might seem odd and suspicious about men's muteness envy gradually starts to make some kind of sense. Victimhood is framed as a position of power, rather than one of powerlessness. Men's muteness envy is the desire to attain the authority of speaking as the victim contingent upon the omission of women's pleasure and violation. "It is not that the victim always gets to speak—far from it," Johnson writes, "but that the most highly valued speaker gets to claim victimhood" (153). She is careful here to clarify that she is not saying all victims of sexual violence or of other forms of violence and abuse have this power. Rather, she is underlining the ways that "the most highly valued speaker"—for instance, men writing their poetry—have sought to construct and claim victimhood for themselves, wielding it as an insidious form of power.

Johnson notes that "feminism seems to have become reduced, in the public mind, to complaints about sexual victimization" (151). However, throughout

Johnson's essay, it becomes clear that given the long aesthetic tradition of men who have been eager to claim such victimization, convinced of their powerlessness, this is "nothing new" and also not the provenance of feminism but of patriarchy. In closing, while noticing silences and their ambivalence, she squarely positions her essay within a feminist politics, afforded by what she has noticed in her reading practice, by the evidence she has gathered, where what was odd has been fleshed out as the structural norm, and what seemed suspicious has been found out and exposed.

If Johnson is asking, "are you hearing what I'm hearing?" by the essay's end, for me, the answer is yes, but not without countless, slow, obsessive misreadings and rereadings. This is where the anxiety of close reading comes in, again and again—am I reading it right? I have noticed that whenever I read this essay, as I did numerous times in order to write this one, I repeatedly read the last sentence: "If feminism is so hotly resisted, it is perhaps less because it substitutes women's speech for women's silence than because, in doing so, it interferes with the official structures of self-pity that keep patriarchal power in place, and, in the process, tells the truth behind the beauty of muteness envy" (153).

Allow me to risk another reading: Johnson suggests that feminism is resisted not because women are speaking out against their silence as victims, which they are in fact doing. Johnson does not deny the personal, political force of speaking out—it is just that her argument does not end there. Instead, she asserts that feminism is met with such resistance because when women speak, they ruin the workings of patriarchal power contingent upon an envious relation to women's muteness. Without women's silence, there is no ideal for men to covet, to suffer over, to long for in anguish that excuses the brutal exercise of power purportedly in service to something higher, like art. Johnson's close reading practice, as one of listening, noticing, and being *on* notice, unfreezes the privileged aesthetic moment prior to women's pleasure and violation. Johnson jump-starts a scene, enabling us to move past the "still unravished," on to the next frame. To push past that moment is to push past the ideal of muteness, to disrupt the beauty it makes possible and the uglier "official structures" that beauty hides. Johnson listens and takes notice of who, in their silence, is powerless to speak, and who, in their *want* for silence, is emboldened to speak of their powerlessness. But read it again, because it's likely you'll notice something that I haven't.

PART III
Local Claiming

9

The Apple of Experience

ERICH AUERBACH ON ADAM AND EVE

Julie Orlemanski

How can you make a historical claim about a passage from a literary text? After all, words change their meaning over time; social norms change; we have information that comes later that past authors lacked. We have to begin with the assumption that different conventions were operative. Orlemanski distills from Erich Auerbach (1893–1957)—discussed in the third part of this volume's introduction and in chapter 1—two strategies: the hermeneutic circle and performative audacity. You notice a detail in Homer or Shakespeare or even Toni Morrison. You might use that detail as the occasion for research relevant to that detail from its historical moment. You might, in fact, toggle between the text, historical research, and the construction of your close reading. Such toggling—the hermeneutic circle—is normal procedure but is usually occluded by the final close reading; as Orlemanski notes, the process is messy. Once you know enough about a text's historical context and the relevant background for your chosen detail, you might—licensed by Orlemanski's reading of Auerbach; grounded by research—use your imagination. How would the text have felt to its contemporaries? You might boldly, provocatively, vividly bring the text's world to life again for your reader. A local claim can be an opportunity to reveal a detail's historical plenitude.—DS + JW

LIKE MOST chapters in Erich Auerbach's *Mimesis*, this one begins with a fragment of literary text. Some thirty-odd lines of *Le Jeu d'Adam* (*The Play of Adam*) appear first in their original language—in this case, Old French for the dialogue, Latin for the stage directions—and then in translation. Textual fragments like this are essential to the interpretive practice that Auerbach developed, and he called these pieces of language *Ansatzpunkte*, or "points of departure." The present chapter explores how Auerbach's starting point is already shaped by the local claiming he goes on to perform—and what this tells us about the process of close reading.

In this instance the kickoff text revolves around Adam and Eve at a fateful turning point in sacred history, the moment when Eve persuades Adam to eat from the Tree of Knowledge. In the text of Genesis, the account of these events is brief: Eve "took the fruit thereof, and did eat, and gave to her husband who did eat" (3:6). But the medieval playwright, whose identity is unknown, freely expands the canonical narrative, turning it into a lively disagreement between husband and wife. Having seen Eve talking to the Devil, Adam chastises her:

ADAM Don't you believe that traitor. He is a traitor, I well know.
EVE   But how do you know?
ADAM I have tried it out.
EVE   Why should I care about that and not see him again? He will make you change your mind.
ADAM He won't, for I won't believe him in anything I have not tried out. Don't let him come near you again, for he is a fellow of very bad faith.[1]

Stage directions tell us that at this point a "skillfully fashioned serpent" whispers in Eve's ear, and after listening, she plucks an apple from the forbidden tree. "Eat, Adam," she urges him. When he hesitates, she takes a bite herself, crowing, "I have tasted it. God, what a savor! Never have I tasted such sweetness." Adam finally takes the fruit from her hand, telling her, "I shall believe you. You are my equal." He eats.

Mimesis has long been considered a masterpiece of close reading. Written between 1942 and 1945, when the German-Jewish Auerbach was teaching in Istanbul after he fled the Nazis, it was translated into English in 1953, six years after Auerbach immigrated to the United States and at a time when the New Critics were at the height of their institutional power. Auerbach's magisterial

---

1. Originally in French; quoted from Erich Auerbach, *Mimesis*, translated by Willard R. Trask (Princeton University Press, 1953), 144. All subsequent citations given in text.

study was a cosmopolitan complement to the New Criticism, a tour de force of stylistic analysis that could evoke a whole historical lifeworld from a page or two of a literary work. Together with figures like Leo Spitzer and René Wellek, Auerbach helped establish close reading and literary criticism in departments of comparative literature in the United States. Auerbach read at least eight languages, which he drew on freely in the course of *Mimesis*, to tell a story about the arc of the European literary tradition from Homer's *Odyssey* and the Hebrew Bible to Virginia Woolf's *To the Lighthouse* (discussed by Oren Izenberg in chapter 1 of this volume).

As mentioned above, nearly all of Auerbach's twenty chapters begin with an excerpt from a literary work. From there, each chapter follows a sequence very like the five steps of close reading identified in this collection: Auerbach *sets the scene*, paraphrasing the preceding piece of text and contextualizing it, and his description is already an act of *noticing*, highlighting aspects of style, structure, and circumstance that will be significant in the account to come; he then seizes on a puzzling or surprising aspect of the passage and begins to unfold his explanation (*local claiming*), which gradually expands to the literary ethos embodied in the larger text (*regional argumentation*) and the encompassing horizon of the text's historical moment (*global theorizing*). As readers of *Mimesis* can attest, the dazzlement of Auerbach's method lies in just how vividly it conjures a historically specific way of sensing and knowing, feeling and understanding, from an isolated fragment of writing.

In the case of *Le Jeu d'Adam*, that isolated fragment turns out to embody an interpretive claim even before any reading is offered. Auerbach has already made choices in how he presents the text that he then goes on to interpret for us. We realize this when he begins his exposition by zeroing in on a sequence of dialogue where, as he says, "the text of the manuscript is somewhat confused in respect to the distribution of lines between the two speakers" (148). Another scholar, he explains, has proposed a different version of the lines, an alternative that runs as follows:

ADAM   Don't you believe that traitor. He is a traitor.
EVE   I well know.
ADAM   But how do you know?
EVE   I have tried it out. Why should I care about that and not see him again?
ADAM   He will make you change your mind.

EVE   He won't, for I won't believe him in anything I have not tried out.
ADAM   Don't let him come near you again, for he is a fellow of very bad faith.
(quoted from Auerbach, *Mimesis*, 148, although there the lines are in Old French; I have repurposed the earlier translation to make this one.)

In this alternative edition, it is Eve who has learned by experience and who promises not to trust what she hasn't tried. "I consider this impossible," Auerbach tells us. "It is not possible for Eve to say *bien le sai* [I well know], nor for Adam to ask how she knows, nor for Eve to refer to her previous experience" (148).

Well, why not? *Le Jeu d'Adam* survives in just a single handwritten copy, parts of which are confused or difficult to construe. In this passage, one or more speaker labels seem to be missing. Since Auerbach was a professor of Romance philology (the historical study of languages descended from Latin, including French, Italian, and Spanish), we might expect him to reach for philological tools to settle this argument, like codicology (the technical study of manuscripts), paleography (the study of historic systems of handwriting), or the linguistic development of the French language. The *Jeu* is the oldest known European drama scripted in the vernacular, or the regional language of spoken discourse. The play is thought to have been composed in the mid-twelfth century in a form of French associated with the Norman rule of England, though the surviving manuscript was copied almost a century later, in southeast France. No one knows how many performances or how many copies of the text intervened between the play's origins and the rough-and-ready copy that survives and enables it to be read today.

Strikingly, Auerbach's rebuttal of this other scholar's assignation of lines rests not on technical grounds but on what he sees as the motivations and personalities of the play's characters. To persuade us of these, Auerbach re-narrates the scene's action, telling us how to imagine the lines being delivered and the sentiments that lie behind them: Adam "calls his wife to account as a French farmer or burgher might have done when, upon returning home, he saw something that he did not like"; Eve "answers in a way that is meant to impress him"; "her playful curiosity has failed to grasp the ethical problem. Even now she does not grasp it, for she does not want to"; Adam grows angry, and "with the authority of a man who knows himself master of his house and fully in the right as to the facts, he now clearly states the reasons for his view and forbids Eve to have dealings with the Devil"; and so on (147–48). Like many dramatic scripts, the language of the *Jeu* comes alive in performance, and Auerbach tries to evoke the expressive tones of speech to animate the meaning he wants us to perceive. Regarding the line "I have tried it out [*Car l'esaiai*]," he insists, "These words cannot be Eve's . . . it is the tone of *his* voice which we hear in his energetic reply" (147, emphasis original).

At first glance, this train of local claiming may seem odd. After all, Adam and Eve are not real people, or certainly not ones whose intentions can be readily recovered. But it soon becomes clear that Auerbach's descriptive restaging relies not on what Adam and Eve must have been thinking there in the Garden of Eden, back at the dawn of human history, but on what the medieval playwright, actors, and audience must have had in mind. "Adam is a good man, a French peasant or burgher," Auerbach declares; he "talks and acts in a manner any member of the audience is accustomed to from his own or his neighbor's house; things would go exactly the same in any townsman's home" (151). Auerbach thinks he knows how this audience thinks, and, so, how Adam thinks: "In the normal course of life [Adam] is reliable and sure of himself. . . . He also knows that he has his wife under his thumb. He is not afraid of her occasional whims, which he regards as childish and not at all dangerous." Auerbach's interpretation is assured of the uncomplicated misogyny of medieval commoners. A touch of modernity's condescension toward what has come before inflects this ventriloquism of the townsmen Adams in their modest homes. At the same time, the ennobling fusion of biblical history and everyday medieval life is crucial to *Mimesis*'s larger interpretation: "The dialogue between Adam and Eve—the first man-woman dialogue of universal historical import—is turned into a scene of simplest everyday reality. Sublime as it is, it becomes a scene in lowly, simple style" (151). The meeting of "high" and "low" registers, profound mysteries and quotidian details, is necessary to Auerbach's narrative of how literary representation develops. Medieval Christian drama "falls perfectly within this tradition" by opening church ritual "to receive the simple and untutored and to lead them from the concrete, the everyday, to the hidden and the true" (155).

Let us step back from Auerbach's account of *Le Jeu d'Adam* to hazard two large-scale observations about close reading that can be gleaned from his reading practice. First: *close reading may appear linear but is circular*. As I mentioned, the chapters of *Mimesis* all follow a similar sequence of steps, beginning with an excerpt of text, the *Ansatzpunkt*, that is described and contextualized, followed by the interpretation of a stylistic detail, which expands gradually into a wider historical argument. For readers, this sequence offers the seductive impression that we are ascending steadily from specificity to generality and from the concrete to the speculative. We are learning by experience, tasting these historically distant texts for ourselves. But as this particular chapter of *Mimesis* makes clear, that tidy sequentiality is rhetorical, not investigatory; it is the form of communication, not of discovery. After all, Auerbach makes explicit that the text of *Le Jeu d'Adam* is not simply a starting point for interpretation but interpretation's outcome. It is because Adam and Eve are *like* French farmers or burghers, and French farmers and burghers are a rather predictable bunch (on Auerbach's account), that he has made the editorial decision of who says what in the medieval playtext he presents us. In other words, Auerbach's establishment of the textual object, the thing to be read, depends already on *global theorizing*, on a sweeping characterization of how medieval commonfolk perceived reality. (Incidentally, later editors have not preferred Auerbach's solution. For instance, Paul Aebischer's 1963 edition and Véronique Dominguez's of 2012 both adopt the assignment of speakers against which Auerbach pitches his argument.[2])

The toggle between textual details and the larger whole, or between literary design and the greater culture for which a work is made, constitutes what is known as the "hermeneutic circle," or the iterative process by which different scales and sites of interpretation inform one another in the process of textual understanding. Auerbach brings his knowledge of twelfth-century French society to bear on *Le Jeu d'Adam*, and the *Jeu* also teaches him something about medieval men and women, about what they sought from the theatrical animation of sacred history in the language of everyday speech. Close reading operates by a recursive rather than linear logic in other chapters of *Mimesis* as well. Certainly, most literary works that Auerbach presents to his readers are more textually stable; they do not feature a corrupt passage or a hotly debated crux. But they do need to be excerpted. Snipping a passage from a larger whole creates a representative sample, in which certain elements are present and visible while others are absent and accordingly obscured. Decisions of what to excerpt, or how to constitute the text to be read, are made in light of a larger idea, a bigger picture. Microcosm mirrors macrocosm. To observe such

---

2. See Paul Aebischer, ed., *Le Mystère d'Adam* (Minard, 1963), 52, and Véronique Dominguez, ed., *Le Jeu D'Adam: Édition bilingue* (Champion Classiques, 2012), 230 with further discussion at 100–2).

circularity is not to debunk Auerbach's readings. After all, their circularity is obvious. Instead, it invites us to reflect on just how we come to know texts historically, by tacking back and forth among our various sources of evidence—linguistic and stylistic details, their role in the totality of a narrative form, and the work's place in a broader cultural system. The hermeneutic circle also asks us to distinguish between how we *write* literary arguments, often with artful linearity, and how we come up with them in the first place, in a messier process of turning again and again to the text, recalibrating our sense of how its components signify in light of one another and within the wider world.

The second large-scale observation that might be made on the basis of Auerbach's chapter is that *close reading is performative*. Reading is fruitfully considered action, an activity executed with the aid of the text. Different readers generate different understandings. This is obvious in the case of the scholar with whom Auerbach disagrees: that editor read the *Jeu* differently. But we might also think of the long history of the *Jeu* being performed. Various actors in the twelfth and thirteenth centuries would have staged the dialogue of Adam and Eve on the steps of different churches in the French-speaking world, to different audiences, in different weather, with different copies of the play, to different effects. A single play gives rise to a wide range of performance possibilities. Scribes, patrons, performers, and spectators would all contribute to the generation of distinctive versions of the play.

Indeed, Auerbach's desire to make *Le Jeu d'Adam* a synecdoche for a whole historical period, bolstered by a totalizing sense of medieval people, leads him to gloss over differences and even conflicts that would have run through the enactment and interpretation of the playtext. The elaborate Latin stage directions, for instance, suggest that the play's original author was a medieval cleric, a priest or other Church official comfortable reading and writing Latin. Few people outside the clergy could understand Latin, whether on the page or spoken aloud. The playscript shows a certain amount of anxiety about the relation between its Latin and French parts, for instance by offering meticulous (and unusual) instructions for how the French dialogue should be delivered:

> And let this Adam be well instructed as to when he ought to make his replies, so that he doesn't respond either too quickly or too slowly. Nor does this apply only to him, but let all the characters be instructed similarly, so that they should speak correctly and make gestures appropriate to the things about which they are speaking. And in their observance of the verse

let them neither add nor subtract a syllable, but pronounce everything confidently and say those things that ought to be said in the right order.[3]

In these and other stage directions, we might discern a certain anxiety from the playwright about the freedom of textual performance and the readily understood French language. How will he control the vernacular voices of actors? Auerbach, in insisting on Adam's direct equivalence to French burgher or peasant, misses some of the ways that the playtext is itself uneasily divided, between Latin and French, clergy and laity, man and woman. The play may not speak on behalf of a harmonious medieval collective, but might instead be crosscut with different voices and appeals to oppositional parties. These divisions may have shaped scenes of performance, which would have taken place outside in front of the church, where priests and laypeople both had claims to authority.

When Auerbach declares other construals, other vocalizations, of the *Jeu* "impossible," this is surely overstating the case. Priests and commoners, men and women across different scenes of reception could have interpreted the script and its performance differently. The textual confusion in the sole surviving copy suggests that scribe and performer both had to struggle with the logic of speech in this rapid-fire exchange. Like Auerbach, they might have weighed factors of narrative character, theology, and gender in deciding how the lines should be played. And let us not forget that the play itself was created by refashioning the text of Genesis. The playwright rewrote a paradigmatically authoritative text, the Bible, to create a script that would be revoiced, reembodied, and rewritten in turn.

Auerbach, of course, is not ignorant of this. Nonetheless, his close reading gains some of its rhetorical power by arguing what the text *must* mean. The theatrical performance context nonetheless usefully highlights what we might call the under-determination of *Le Jeu d'Adam*, or the rather straightforward fact that it would have signified differently for different people, depending on who they were, what they believed, how the play was performed, and other circumstances of reception. If words are prompts to speak and imagine, to think and feel, they can work only probabilistically, by seeking to steer the enactment of speech and thought, but incapable of generating those acts

---

3. Translation from Carol Symes, *The Play of Adam*, in *The Broadview Anthology of Medieval Drama*, eds. Christina M. Fitzgerald and John T. Sebastian (Broadview Press, 2013), originally in Latin.

mechanistically. The effort to read historically, or to reconstruct some sense of what the *Jeu* meant for medieval audiences, makes this especially clear. We learn about the play's language, its manuscript and context, its audience and authors, and then we read again—running repeatable experiments in which variables are shifted and new elements of historical understanding are introduced, to track the experience to which the text gives rise. It is part of criticism's negative capability—or our readerly capacity to suspend self-insistence and be open to uncertainty and possibility—that we read in attempted alignment with the past, in sympathy with and under the influence of models of textual reception different from our own.[4] Hermeneutic playacting is part of what we do as students of literary history, putting on "period ears" as best we can.

Auerbach reads *Le Jeu d'Adam* and in the process enacts yet another performance. Like the Latin stage directions, or some erstwhile medieval theater director, he tells us how lines are to be delivered and fits the scene into a theological structure and a historical moment. Like other accomplished close readers, he promises his audience the chance to learn by experience, to read along with him and watch his conclusions unfurl from textual details with graceful but illusory inevitability. This is Auerbach's apple, as it were, or the promise of close reading—that of tasting a literary work and experiencing its savor become knowledge, just as the apple did for Eve and Adam. The lure of direct experience—"I have tried it out"; "I have tasted it. God, what a savor!"—is why an excellent reading does not obviate future interpretations or displace past ones. Instead, readers enter anew and for themselves the recurrent, looping processes of interpretation—saying the lines aloud in our heads, playing out the possibilities of delivery, stabilizing text and its context, and discerning the layered possibilities of voice, meaning, and experience.

---

4. The British Romantic poet John Keats coined "negative capability" in an 1817 letter to his brother; it has since become an important literary-critical term. For an overview, see E. Rohrbach, "Negative Capability," in *The Princeton Encyclopedia of Poetry and Poetics*, 4th edition, eds. Roland Greene, Stephen Cushman, et al. (Princeton University Press, 2012), 925–26.

10

Local Claiming, Capacious Life

KEVIN QUASHIE ON LUCILLE CLIFTON

Lindsay Reckson

Kevin Quashie (1971–) calls our attention to quiet moments in a loud world. When scholars were focused on the politics and spectacle of Black resistance, he invited us, in The Sovereignty of Quiet, *to recognize the power of Black silence and vulnerability. In the 2020s, with the ascendance of Afropessimism—a philosophy that foregrounds the ongoing connection between Black being, slavery, and death—he wrote a book to envision* Black Aliveness. *Quashie reveals Black aliveness in his acts of local claiming, his movement from noticing a feature in a text to saying what it means. Lucille Clifton's repetition of "they," a they who do so much with so many different verbs, evokes a Black world marked by capaciousness, care, multiplicity, radiance. Keeping Black imagination in view, Quashie licenses us to behold in Black literature how Black life exceeds, even as it remains ineluctably marked by, Black death.—DS + JW*

A LONG parenthetical interrupts Kevin Quashie's introduction to his 2021 book *Black Aliveness, or a Poetics of Being*. Writing in the summer of 2020, in the aftermath of the murder of George Floyd by white police officer Derek Chauvin, Quashie uses the parenthetical to register the conditions of antiblackness in and through which he writes: "(Today I am sad, mad, wild, full of rage in and out. Today is a day in June 2020, summer of racism's recurring pandemic . . . Today there is no reconciling the facts of our lives, which seem tethered to death, and the case for black aliveness. Both have to be true at the same time.)"[1] A close reading of this parenthetical might attend to the way Quashie's anaphora "Today"—its incantatory repetition—situates us in time and place inseparable from the grief and rage and cumulative daily onslaught of antiblack violence. But it might also note that Quashie's use of the parenthetical (a kind of holding place or aside, a crucial interjection that nevertheless remains necessarily—grammatically—ancillary to the primary clause) enacts his insistence that while black poetics contend with antiblackness, antiblack violence does not begin to encompass the poetics of black life. The parenthetical sustains the contradiction at its heart, holds us in time and place, allows us to sit with both the felt impossibility and the radical urgency of imagining a world undelimited by antiblackness. This, for Quashie, is the work of black aliveness.

Black Aliveness is an intervention in the fields of poetics, phenomenology, and black pessimist philosophy; it is also a poetic invocation, a critical practice that enacts the very world-making it describes. This is another way of saying that as Quashie reads for black aliveness—a poetics of Black being in its most capacious, radiant plurality—in the work of Lucille Clifton, Amiri Baraka, Audre Lorde, June Jordan, and others, he also models a critical practice that figuratively builds a world; one that exceeds the totalizing and pervasive repetitions of black death.

"Imagine a black world," Quashie proposes, in the book's opening lines (1). This invitation or instruction insists on the primacy of black aliveness. In what follows, I will try to follow the sentence-level work of Quashie's invocations—his simultaneous description and summoning of black aliveness—through the close reading of Lucille Clifton's 1991 poem "reply" that opens *Black Aliveness*. In theorizing black aliveness locally, at the level of the poetic line, Quashie's language offers its own poetic ode to the expansiveness of black life and living. In doing so, Quashie reminds us that close reading can be itself a form of world-making, a practice of care that builds new worlds of critical (and lived) possibility.

"Imagine a black world," Quashie insists, "where blackness exists in the tussle of being, in reverie and terribleness, in exception and in ordinariness" (1). Clifton's poem "reply," for Quashie, is a practice of world-making; it imagines— and by imagining calls into being—a black world, "where every human question and possibility is of people who are black." In a sense, "reply" is an

---

1. Kevin Quashie, *Black Aliveness, or a Poetics of Being* (Duke University Press, 2021), 12–13. All subsequent citations given in text.

unexpected place to make this claim, insofar as the poem takes shape ostensibly as a response to its racist epigraph "from a letter written to Dr. W.E.B. Du Bois by Alvin Borgquist of Clark University in Massachusetts and dated April 3, 1905," which inquires with a violently detached empiricism "whether the Negro sheds tears." As Quashie notes, what makes the invitation to "'imagine a black world' so necessary is the exemption of black humanity from our commonsense understanding, the world's lack of imagination for black being that is also its brutal enactments against such being."

Amid this lack of imagination, Clifton's "reply" offers a dynamic, abundant, (un)commonsense of blackness and black life. The poem unfolds as a deceptively simple series of two-word lines, each a pronoun and a verb: "he do/she do/they live/they love/they try/they tire/they flee/they fight/they bleed/they break/they moan/they mourn/they weep/they die/they do/they do/they do." Quashie begins his close reading by inviting the reader to *notice*: "Notice first the dancing waltz of the anaphora, as if this is a drum- or heartbeat of paired stressed syllables . . . Notice, too, how the poem's speaker directs us where to look and assumes that we can and will know how to look rightly . . ." You can also notice, here, how Quashie's own anaphora—his repeated call to notice—waltzes to Clifton's beat. Notice, from the Latin *noticia*, meaning knowledge, information. But how does one notice language as it waltzes? As it dances, as it moves, as it refuses stillness and static forms of looking and knowing? A waltz takes practice before it becomes intuitive. (Anaphora, maybe, is the literary shape of this practice, a way of building through repetition.) It requires us to know without knowing the form, the steps, the pace: all the ways the dance moves. Arguably, it also requires *being* moved, collectively. The waltz is intimate and relational—it takes at least two. Notice: Quashie instructs us, gently, with repetition. Notice, meaning: slow down. Pay heed to this. Practice. Here are the steps.

It matters that Quashie begins his close reading with a call to notice Clifton's anaphora, that incantatory and embodied effect of repetition, of each line's two beats. This is a key moment of local claiming, as Quashie uses the details of sound—the "drum- or heartbeat of paired stressed syllables," the "rich, deep vowel echoes" of assonance—to show how the poem's rhythmic waltz underscores its assertion of a black collectivity. Notice, too, that noticing is not the same as looking. The anaphora, alliteration, and assonance at work in Clifton's syllabic pairs ("they flee/they fight/they bleed/they break/they moan/they mourn") demand that we also listen—that we hear the relations between them (for example, the long *e* in flee and bleed, words that precede and give needful context to the line that might otherwise function as a flat admission: "they weep"). The sonic force of these pairs as they spill or bleed down the page "creates," in Quashie's terms, "a deliberate formation in what might otherwise *look* like a random gathering of actions" (3; my emphasis). Here is a critical act of local claiming: to listen to the waltz of these lines is to recognize that this is not a catalog or a dataset (black aliveness, notes Quashie, "eludes quantification and qualification"—black life is not an object to be known but a poetics, a vital rhythm) (16). Nor is it something we can register simply by looking at static words on the page. Quashie instead enables us to hear a series of (sonic) relations—and through them, a world of black aliveness embedded in relationality, threaded through sound and action.

Notice, too: this is about scale. Local claiming is how we move from the seemingly small work of a rhetorical figure like anaphora to the poem's world-making, what Quashie calls its "cosmological arc of being." Part of Quashie's point is that the arc of being, the radiant multiplicity of black aliveness as it flees, fights, bleeds, breaks is right there in the repetition, in the gorgeous play of sonic sameness and difference (3). "They do/they do/they do." Through repetition, blackness multiplies and radiates: a black world in every word, in every breath, in every locale, in every instance of "they" and "do," in each long *u*—each of which invokes a world, a whole black world. Which is why we have to listen for the details.[2] As Quashie suggests, Clifton's speaker inhabits the detachment of the third person ("he do/she do/they do") in order "to relish in distance and plurality." In the place of looking, and as a refusal of the epigraph's racist "investigation," Clifton "invites the reader to *behold* the other" (3; emphasis original). To behold as an act of care, of being beholden to another.[3] To behold the manifold plurality of blackness and thereby to interrupt the violence of looking deployed to possess and secure difference, a form of racial surveillance and objectification.

Notice, now, how Quashie's close reading shifts us—readers of Clifton as well as of Quashie—from a practice of noticing to one of beholding, where

---

2. On radical methodological cues embedded in the details, see Alexandra Vazquez, *Listening in Detail: Performances of Cuban Music* (Duke University Press, 2013).

3. Here and throughout *Black Aliveness*, Quashie is thinking with Christina Sharpe's account of beholding in the wake of the slave ship's hold as an act of beholden-ness: "In what ways might we enact a beholden-ness to each other, laterally? . . . How are we beholden to and beholders of each other in ways that change across time and place and space and yet remain?" Christina Sharpe, *In the Wake: On Blackness and Being* (Duke University Press, 2016), 100–1. See also Ross Gay's extended reply (of sorts) to Sharpe in *Be Holding* (University of Pittsburgh Press, 2020): "how do we be / holding each other" (74).

the latter signals an ongoing and relational act. Beholding as a way of keeping something close, *holding* it in view, being beholden—which implies a responsibility on the part of the beholder. This is active work. For Quashie, the pronoun "they" is crucial for how Clifton's poem "negotiates the politics of looking . . . casting the speaker awry from and as observant of black collectivity" (3). As Quashie argues, it is absolutely crucial that the poem's speaker never says "we," as in "we do." The use of the collective "we," he notes, "would cement the poem's stance as being against the hateful question," consolidating its posture of address—and its imagining of black aliveness—only or primarily as a response to antiblackness. "We," that is, would invoke collective black identity only as a "reply" to the epigraph's racism. In the use of the pronoun "they," the speaker "*witnesses*, such that the reply is not toward white violence but instead recognizes the capaciousness of being: *here the speaker stands not on a side but in the midst of the whole world of black being*" (4, emphasis original). If "we" consolidates sameness, "they" opens up multiplicity within ("in the midst"); the speaker can be among *and* awry *and* beholding. This is a subtle but absolutely urgent distinction; in their use of the pronoun "they," Clifton's speaker does not practice a form of surveillance, looking from the outside toward a "they" deemed less than human from the start (as in the logic of Alvin Borgquist's question, "whether the Negro sheds tears"). Instead, in "reply," the speaker's use of "they" bears witness to plurality and difference *within* black collectivity, refusing to reduce "the whole world of black being" to a "we" formed solely in response to white violence. Instead of "we do," Clifton's speaker suggests "they do," where "they" signals a whole world of relational possibility. "They do," such that the poem "unfurls as a text of black world relationality where the difference between the (black) one saying 'they' and the (black) ones indicated by 'they' reflects the breadth of our humanity" (4).[4]

Quashie reads Clifton's poem as "a world of *us* told in a reply" (5). Set against Clifton's omission of the "we," Quashie's use of "we" and "us" is worth lingering over. Quashie writes to—and thereby invokes—a world where every question and possibility and address is of and to people who are black. In his own reply to Clifton, and in the close reading he performs as a kind of care work, Quashie importantly assumes a black readership, even as the audience

---

4. A breadth we might also understand as fundamentally gender queer, as "they" elongates and expands the possibilities of the poem's opening "he/she" while also signaling the plurality of Quashie's "one." In each instance, "they" is potentially both one and many, is indeed an undelimited set of relations between the singular (one) and the plural (they).

for his work is undelimited (I am a white reader, and while Quashie's book continually teaches and transforms me, his work is not primarily *for* or addressed *to* me).

Writing at the intersection of black studies and literary studies (and against the presumptive and often too real whiteness of the latter), Quashie's close reading of Clifton at once theorizes and enacts an aesthetics of black world-making rooted in black feminist practices of intimacy and relationality. These are distinctly local practices, rooted as much in care and community as in the specificity of poetic repetition and sonic play. And from the details they open onto expansive new worlds of being and possibility. ("Black feminist thinking," Quashie notes, "might be specific in naming black women, but its ambition has always been the breadth of being alive") (11). This interplay between the local and the global—indeed the cosmological, the very breath and breadth of being—suggests a close relationship between poetry as a creative practice, close reading as a critical practice, and black world-making as both an aesthetic and a political tool. Local claiming might be rooted in the details, in other words, but it requires that we demonstrate how those details are central to the poetic and political work of imagining. And this is, as Quashie reminds us, imperative work.

Notably, Quashie positions himself at once within and awry from the field of black pessimism, which theorizes blackness in the wake of slavery's "social death"; a lineage of thought that Quashie treats with an abiding care.[5] "The thinking on black being always has to countenance death, as the field of black pessimism makes clear" (8). Quashie does not so much depart from Afro- or black pessimisms as he excavates the aliveness that has gone under-recognized in the field's emphasis on death and nonbeing as the ontological condition of blackness under the colonial and antiblack regimes of Western humanism. Reading Christina Sharpe's crucial articulation of Black life in the ongoing wake of colonialism and chattel slavery—now a core text in Afropessimist thought and black studies more broadly—Quashie underscores that Sharpe's field-shifting account of "wake work" is itself a practice of black aliveness. Sharpe asks: "In the midst of so much death and the fact of Black life as proximate to death, how do we attend to the physical, social, and figurative death

---

5. See Orlando Patterson, *Slavery and Social Death: A Comparative Study* (Harvard University Press, 2018). See also Quashie's insistence on reading for vitality across the diverse theoretical works that he gathers around black pessimisms; Quashie, *Black Aliveness*, 164–164n20.

and also to the largeness that is Black life, Black life insisted from death?"[6] As Quashie's attention to this moment in Sharpe suggests, black aliveness is both a poetics and a reading practice; to attend to black aliveness in the context of an antiblack world is to find it "in the midst and aftermath of those interminable conditions" (8).[7]

(Notice, I often tell my students, Quashie's textually registered "sigh," repeated at key moments throughout the introduction: an embodied inhalation and exhalation that is at once mournful and insistent. The sigh—registered in the context of a summer when George Floyd's three words "I can't breathe" propelled the Black Lives Matter movement—insists on breath, on life, on movement. It breathes black worlds into being, or breathes into the expansiveness of black worlds, which is also what Clifton's poems do.)

In a line I return to over and over, Quashie reminds us that "antiblackness is total in the world, but it is not total in the black world" (5). The plurality of worlds here is crucial. Despite the title and epigraph of Clifton's poem, which we might read as underscoring its function as a "reply" to the "racist happening" that surrounds it (textually and materially), Quashie holds that "Clifton's poem proper is a scene of aliveness" (5). If the epigraph functions as acknowledgment that antiblackness is "total in the world"—is what Sharpe describes as "the weather," the "totality of our environments"—Quashie maintains that the aesthetic details of the poem itself are world-making.[8] In this sense, Quashie's theorizing of black aliveness is also an urgent practice of, most critically, imagining: "Since blackness cannot exist fully, humanly, in the world, we will imagine a world where the condition of being alive is of us. In a black world, the case of our lives is aliveness; not death, not even death's vitality, but aliveness" (12).

Local claiming binds the word to the world; it shows us how intimately the two are enmeshed, and thus how imagining can be a critical methodology, a

---

6. Sharpe, *In the Wake*, 17.

7. Through this reading, Quashie also importantly refuses what literary and performance studies scholar Koritha Mitchell identifies as a "false dichotomy" in the cultural criticism of black texts; as Mitchell notes, critics have often "approached black art as if African Americans either protest injustice or ignore the forces arrayed against them, but this is a mistake because racial self-affirmation so often takes place in the midst of acknowledging the violence perpetrated against black families and communities." Koritha Mitchell, "Identifying White Mediocrity and Know-Your-Place Aggression: A Form of Self-Care," *African American Review* 51, no. 4 (Winter 2018): 253.

8. Sharpe, *In the Wake*, 21.

form of black world-making. "Imagine a black world" is a call to read (and thus imagine) alongside Clifton, alongside Quashie. To behold the dancing waltz of the poem's anaphora as its refusal to be still, to be caught, to be seen, to be known. To behold black aliveness assumed and asserted in every space and movement of the poem. To move with it. To breathe into it. And then, maybe, to dance.

11

Exquisite, Golden, Fragrant, Flaunting

JUDITH BUTLER ON NELLA LARSEN

Natalia Cecire

Judith Butler (1956–) changed how we think about—and experience—gender. They argue that gender is not something essential about one's identity but rather exists through its enactment under socially coercive pressures. Gender is the performance of the accoutrements of gender. Critics, as Cecire explains here, asked them about the relationship between gender and the body. As part of their response, Butler turns to close reading. Cecire shows us how Butler studies a scene from a novel for its representations of bodies in action, governed by the social demands of race and sex. We learn about the power of a technique called free indirect discourse, *and how we can train ourselves, like Butler, to notice it and suss out the implications of its use to assemble provocative local claims.—DS + JW*

JUDITH BUTLER's landmark book *Gender Trouble: Feminism and the Subversion of Identity* (1990) contains little close reading; in contrast, their subsequent book, *Bodies that Matter: On the Discursive Limits of "Sex"* (1993),

---

I am grateful to my colleague Ronan McKinney, whose request that I prepare a lecture on Nella Larsen's *Passing* occasioned my revisiting *Bodies that Matter*, and to my former PhD supervisee Katherine Parker-Hay, whose thesis on the affects of queer theory includes a brilliant discussion of the affective dynamics of Butler's preface to *Bodies that Matter*. See Katherine Parker-Hay, "Queer's Late Style: Shifting Mood in the Late and Minor Texts" (PhD thesis, University of Sussex, 2021), 142–46, http://sro.sussex.ac.uk/id/eprint/97121/.

contains a lot. Why? *Bodies that Matter* undertakes several tasks, but one of the most important is that it answers critics of *Gender Trouble*'s polarizing account of gender performativity, which builds on the philosopher J. L. Austin's influential account of performative language.[1] Implicit in these objections was the suggestion that language is something apart from or even antithetical to material (physical) reality. As Butler writes in the preface to *Bodies that Matter*, "the question was repeatedly formulated to me in this way: 'What about the materiality of the body, Judy?'"[2]

Butler's practice of close reading, I will suggest, allows them to reaffirm the centrality of "the body" in their theory of gender while maintaining their theoretical investment in the register of language, because an understanding of what language can do is always at stake in the practice of close reading. Butler uses close reading to insist that bodies matter, but not because bodies are some ultimate reality where philosophy and language must stop. On the contrary, they matter because social power dynamics imbue them with significance. In this chapter, I examine Butler's close reading of Nella Larsen's *Passing* (1929) in the sixth chapter of *Bodies that Matter*, "Passing, Queering: Nella Larsen's Psychoanalytic Challenge," to show how Butler uses close reading on two levels at once. First, Butler's close reading supports a chapter-level argument about the roles of race and sex in psychoanalysis. In order to explain this chapter-level argument, I will provide some historical context for the literature of racial passing, of which Larsen's novel is a prominent example. Second, as a method, close reading also supports a book-level retort to critics of *Gender Trouble* who argue that understanding gender through philosophy of language is incompatible with taking physical bodies seriously. I'll conclude by explaining how Butler takes direction from the Black feminist critic Barbara Christian to suggest that, on the contrary, language can be one of the most direct ways of understanding how bodies interface with the social world.

As its title suggests, *Passing* is a narrative of racial passing, a genre that was particularly prominent during the period of Jim Crow segregation in the United States (approximately 1877–1964). Jim Crow laws presumed that bodies could reliably furnish proof of their own racial classification—for example,

---

1. J. L. Austin, *How to Do Things with Words*, The William James Lectures 1955 (Clarendon Press, 1962).

2. Judith Butler, *Bodies That Matter: On the Discursive Limits of "Sex"* (Routledge, 1993), viii. All subsequent citations given in text.

that it would always be clear who should go in the "white" or "colored" train car. But race is not biological; although bodily markers such as skin colors, hair textures, and facial shapes are invested with racial meaning, they do not always emerge in predictable combinations. Passing narratives tell stories of people who appear "racially ambiguous" and can "pass," or be socially received, as belonging to more than one racial classification. Passing narratives thematize the fact that we can't reliably determine "race" from a body's appearance; rather, race is defined by social contexts: whether you are let in the door in certain places, how you are treated, who associates with you. Race is not *in you*; it emerges in how you and others are treated, over and over, through time.[3] This repeated social norm *becomes* the meaning of the body, which is then understood as constituting its materiality (race). Passing narratives are thus centrally concerned with how bodies are "materialized" through the reiteration of social norms (xviii).

Passing focuses on the relationship between two light-skinned Black women who were once childhood friends. One, Irene, whose perspective the narrator adopts throughout the novel, occasionally passes for white in order to enter whites-only spaces such as shops and tea rooms.[4] However, in her daily life she identifies as Black and is married to a darker Black man, Brian. More than that, Irene is a pillar of bourgeois Black race activism, forwarding projects of what was then known as "racial uplift" through respectable women's channels such as fundraising and volunteering on committees. Her counterpart Clare, in contrast, passes permanently, having been raised by white aunts, and her husband John is a proudly racist white man who frequently mentions his hatred of Black people. Although Clare enjoys wealth and status, she longs for Black community and must constantly accommodate her husband's racist comments.

---

3. Scholars of race understand race to be a product of racism (rather than racism targeting preexisting, well-defined "races," which don't exist). The geographer Ruth Wilson Gilmore defines racism as the "production and exploitation of group-differentiated vulnerability to death." In other words, different segments of a population are treated in ways that afford them different life chances, and this treatment is then justified by being attributed to—materialized as—people's bodies. See Ruth Wilson Gilmore, *Golden Gulag: Prisons, Surplus, Crisis, and Opposition in Globalizing California* (University of California Press, 2007), 28.

4. When a narrator adopts the perspective of a character, this is called *internal focalization*. Free indirect discourse, discussed below, is one narrative technique that contributes to internal focalization. See Gérard Genette, *Narrative Discourse: An Essay in Method*, trans. Jane E. Lewin (Cornell University Press, 1980), 189–94.

Butler's chapter-level intervention is to read *Passing* for the ways that its racial critique extends to sex. Psychoanalytic feminist critics have usually understood sex to be less subject to social contextualization than race; Butler's chapter argues against this. "It is this assertion of the priority of sexual difference over racial difference that has marked so much psychoanalytic feminism as white," Butler remarks, "for the assumption here is not only that sexual difference is more fundamental, but that there is a relationship called 'sexual difference' that is itself unmarked by race" (135).[5] For Butler, *Passing* provides evidence that, contrary to dominant accounts, not only is sex *not* more psychically fundamental than race, but in fact they shape one another (123).[6]

Butler introduces the opening close reading in chapter 6 of *Bodies that Matter* abruptly: "Consider, if you will, the following scene:"

> She [Irene] remembered her own little choked exclamation of admiration, when, on coming downstairs a few minutes later than she had intended, she had rushed into the living room where Brian was waiting and had found Clare there too. Clare, exquisite, golden, fragrant, flaunting, in a stately gown of shining black taffeta, whose long, full skirt lay in graceful folds about her slim golden feet; her glistening hair drawn smoothly back into a small twist at the nape of her neck; her eyes sparkling like dark jewels. (123)[7]

Butler surrounds this quotation with scene setting and noticing that helps us understand why the quoted passage is relevant. Butler then points out a dense interplay of desiring gazes in the scene: Irene sees Clare, Brian sees Clare, Irene sees Brian seeing Clare. Amid this thicket of gazes, Butler notes, the narrator creates grammatical ambiguity about *who*—Irene or Brian—"had found Clare there too." Finally, Butler points out Irene's "choked exclamation," and the key

---

5. For a more recent and historically inflected account of how race constitutes sexual difference, see Kyla Schuller, *The Biopolitics of Feeling: Race, Sex, and Science in the Nineteenth Century* (Duke University Press, 2018).

6. Michel Foucault's concept of "biopower" is the classic framework analyzing how sex, sexuality, and race are co-articulated. See Michel Foucault, *The History of Sexuality: An Introduction*, trans. Robert Hurley (Vintage, 1990), 1:133–59; Michel Foucault, "17 March 1976," in *"Society Must Be Defended": Lectures at the Collège de France, 1975–76*, eds. Mauro Bertani and Alessandro Fontana, trans. David Macey (Picador, 2003), 239–63. Butler is also concerned with how psychoanalysis might help account for this interrelation, on which see also Anne Anlin Cheng, *The Melancholy of Race: Psychoanalysis, Assimilation, and Hidden Grief* (Oxford University Press, 2000).

7. Nella Larsen, *The Complete Fiction of Nella Larsen: Passing, Quicksand, and the Stories* (Random House, 2001), 233.

point for which this passage stands as evidence: the way that free indirect discourse in the novel takes over just at the points where Irene's voice is lost.

Free indirect discourse is a narrative technique in which the narrator's voice merges seamlessly with that of a character, so that, although the character is not literally speaking, the narrator seems to speak on the character's behalf. The technique is often used to give readers access to thoughts and feelings that a character cannot express verbally. Because those thoughts and feelings are spoken by the narrator rather than by the character, however, they take on an authoritative and quasi-objective character. Thus, as Butler says of this passage, "the narrator emerges to speak the words Irene might have spoken: 'exquisite, golden, fragrant, flaunting,'" taking on the role of "exposing more than Irene can herself risk" (124). Here, Butler points out that *the narrator* gives us an expression of Irene's desire precisely where *Irene's body* suppresses it by choking it back. As Butler reads Larsen presenting it, choked-back admiration is not just a silence; instead, the act of choking back admiration is something to be noticed; moreover, through the narrator's free indirect discourse, we also learn exactly what is being choked back, an intimate and desiring description of Clare's "flaunting" body. This is then an occasion for local claiming: Butler concludes from noticing this narrative technique at work that silence and transgressive desire are conjoined in this novel.

Butler's noticing operates at a relatively sophisticated level; undergraduates have often been trained in the first instance to notice *words*, and here words like "golden," "shining," "glistening," "sparkling," and "jewels" certainly present Clare as a rare and shiny treasure. An attentive reader of this vocabulary might even notice that what is "golden" (the color of Clare's hair and body, the reason she can pass) and what is "black" in this vision (the dress covering her golden body for this occasion, a return to Black society) are equally light-reflecting. Butler, however, sails past vocabulary to examine narrative voice, drawing attention to both Clare's embodiment and Irene's. This is the most prized form of noticing: it rests on what is indisputably and concretely manifested in the text, yet not everyone would notice it. It seems obvious only after being pointed out, and bespeaks Butler's literary training. Butler's reading foregrounds the interarticulation of psychological interiority, language, and physical bodies in Larsen's prose. What is being noticed, in this case, is the way that literary form at the sentence level makes bodily and psychological dispositions available to readers, the way that the materiality of text constitutes the materiality of a body (*Judy*).

Butler's noticing thus brings attention to textual bodies (Irene's and Clare's), but also, in the act of noticing, dwells in the sensory register of language, tarrying with vision dazzled by sparkles and shine, the smelling of fragrance, and the haptic and auditory qualities of a "choked" cry. Importantly, this sensory register remains present across every level of their close reading, creating a bridge from noticing to local claiming and global theorizing. Irene's "choked," desiring cry, first noticed early in the chapter, later becomes just one entry in a catalog of choked, muted, or silenced expressions that are called "queer"—expressions of forbidden desire that are, in the first instance, homosexual, but which also extend to moments of impropriety, including crossing the color line. For example, convinced that Brian is having an affair with Clare, Irene cuts off her own angry speech. Again using free indirect discourse, the narrator channels Irene's silent realization: "her voice, she realized *had* gone queer"—all too nearly revealing her jealousy (but of Clare, or the man who gets to have her?) (130).[8]

Here, Butler shifts scale: rather than focusing on a single passage, they begin to track the words *queer* and *queering*—terms that could, but did not necessarily, refer to nonnormative sexuality in the period—across the entire novel (130). This move opens up the relevance of that earlier close reading and lets us see how narrative technique makes bodies matter throughout the novel, enabling their global theorizing. Butler's noticing at this new, novel-wide scale reveals that the term "queer" arises in moments of eruption or crossing, as when Irene, in the company of a Black friend, Felise, meets Clare's husband on the street, revealing her own racial crossing. "Been 'passing,' have you?" Felise says. "Well, I've queered that" (130).[9] Felise *queers* Irene's passing by acting as a visibly Black social context for Irene, one that changes the meaning of Irene's own body and renders it newly legible as Black. Larsen's usage of the word *queer* places such racial transgressions in the same category as choked cries of transgressive sexual desire. Butler shows how Larsen's overlapping uses of "queer" leave no space between racial and sexual desires, between having Clare and being her. "To the extent that Irene desires Clare," Butler theorizes, "she desires the [racial] trespass that Clare performs" (132). By connecting noticing at the scale of the whole novel to specific scenes of racial and sexual crossing, Butler establishes Larsen as a theorist of the psychic interarticulation of race and sex.

In proposing Larsen as a theorist of race and sex, Butler uses close reading in a way that goes beyond the chapter-level argument. Close reading provides a way for Butler to reply to critics of *Gender Trouble* who argue that its language-inflected account of gender ignores "the materiality of the body."

8. Larsen, *The Complete Fiction of Nella Larsen*, 249.
9. Larsen, *The Complete Fiction of Nella Larsen*, 259.

Butler does this by taking "Barbara Christian's advice to consider literary narrative"—such as *Passing*—"as a place where theory takes place" (135). Butler refers, here, to Christian's classic 1987 essay "The Race for Theory," which argues that the newly prestigious theory of the period operates as a covert backlash against, and system for devaluing, a then-recent bloom of attention to "the literature of peoples of color, of black women, of Latin Americans, of Africans."[10] In Christian, Butler finds a productive antagonist, for in many ways *Gender Trouble* exemplifies exactly the kind of theory that Christian sees as trampling the hard work of Black and ethnic literary studies, and which Christian glosses as producing "texts as disembodied as the angels."[11] But by turning to literary language, Christian also shows that language need not be "disembodied" at all, giving Butler a way forward. Against theory, Christian sets two alternatives that she presents as linked: embodied experience and literary narrative. "Because I went to a Catholic Mission school in the West Indies," Christian writes, "I must confess that I cannot hear the word 'canon' without smelling incense ... 'discourse' reeks for me of metaphysics forced down my throat in those courses that traced world philosophy from Aristotle through Thomas Aquinas to Heidegger."[12] Theoretical keywords appear in Christian's artfully crafted account as attacks on her body, assaulting her with the unwanted smells and force-feeding of hierarchy and domination. Such a description suggests that language is not only a site of abstraction; language can be the medium of institutional power, with visceral effects. In particular, Christian writes that in contrast to the arid language of theory, literature "seemed to me to have the possibilities of rendering the world as large and complicated as I experienced it, as sensual as I knew it was."[13] For Christian, it is not language as such that drifts away from the body, but rather the kind of abstract language that dominates *Gender Trouble*. Literary language, in contrast, is, she suggests, both adequate to experience and "sensual." Literary texts and the literary method of close reading thus hold out the promise of a language that, far from seeming "disembodied," keeps faith with bodily experience.

Christian's call to value literary language thus makes Butler's point through the back door: to understand gender through ideas about language need not

---

10. Barbara Christian, "The Race for Theory," *Cultural Critique*, no. 6 (1987): 55.
11. Christian, "The Race for Theory," 56.
12. Christian, "The Race for Theory," 55.
13. Christian, "The Race for Theory," 56.

leave the body behind. The sensory act of noticing necessarily grounds and warrants any theorizing work that close reading is capable of doing; thus close reading's relay between noticing, local claiming, regional theorizing, and global theorizing ensures that something of the sensory must remain even at the most theoretical level. Bodies matter in Larsen, Butler's close reading shows, but not because they offer up forensic proofs that resolve inquiry or foreclose ambiguity. Quite the reverse: it is the body's social construction, the way that Irene and Clare are white on the rooftop of the Drayton hotel and Black at a party in Harlem, that makes it matter so very much, because it is in social acts that power makes itself felt. "Exquisite, golden, fragrant, flaunting": by drawing textual detail up through every register of their theorizing, Butler's close reading demonstrates, as much as it argues, what it means for a body to matter.

12

A Matter of Perspective

ELENI COUNDOURIOTIS
ON YAMBO OUOLOGUEM

Farah Bakaari

Who is speaking? Who is watching whom? These are questions about perspective and they merit careful attention. Narrators not only speak, they also have the power to slip into the minds of characters and narrate the world through their perception. One of the most common causes of error in criticism is the misrecognition of perspective. Perspective is, conversely, a great resource when explaining what a noticed detail means—when making a local claim. How, to give an example from Eleni Coundouriotis (1964–) discussed by Bakaari here, are readers to understand the dissonance in a rape scene where the woman's experience is described as if she were seduced? Coundouriotis posits that the woman's perspective itself has been colonized by her rapist; we are seeing her experience through his mind. That local claim builds, for Coundouriotis, to a global theory about how African novelists respond to a tricky situation: how to evade the trap set by imperialists who defined Africans as Other, outside of history, outside of time; how to claim agency on their own terms; how to reject the colonial gaze.—DS + JW

IN HER landmark monograph *Claiming History: Colonialism, Ethnography, and the Novel*, Eleni Coundouriotis traces the intricate genealogy that connects the rise of anthropology as a discipline and the birth of the African novel. Examining the vexed relationship among ethnography, history, and fiction, she begins the book with an account of the large and influential body of ethnography, travelogues, and other nonfiction writings that conceive of the African as an ahistorical eternal Other who occupies a time different from the ethnographer's present. Paradigmatic for Coundouriotis are the Victorian travel narratives that purported to document and report on the ubiquity of human sacrifice in nineteenth-century Dahomey (present-day Benin). The European narratives consistently ignored and misrepresented the historical origins and communal meanings of the practice in order to produce an image of Dahomey as a "sacrificial landscape" where "money and human beings are interchangeable signs of wealth that are wasted in an act of communal transgression."[1] In addition to suppressing the historical link between the human sacrifices and the transatlantic slave trade, the ethnographic invention of Dahomey propagated a colonial discourse about the debased wasteful African, which sought to justify the imperialist project. In other words, ethnography supplants history and effaces the subjectivity of the African.

How, then, do African novelists respond to the violence of ethnography and wrest history away from the colonial gaze that seeks to locate them outside of time? Well, for one, they write ambitious historical novels that thematize the African political past and reassert themselves as historical subjects. In the effort to contest and correct the European invention of Africa, however, the African novelist must confront what Coundouriotis terms the "ethnographic impulse." In response to European ethnography, which sought to fix Africans in time, early African novelists like Chinua Achebe and Paul Hazoumé appropriated ethnographic description to narrate historical change in the realist novel. And yet, for the African novelist a question remains: how to subvert the ethnographic paradigm without falling into the confines of the "native informant" whose resistance can only be registered within the narrow Manichean binary of colonized vs. colonizer. In what follows, I show how Coundouriotis attends to the nuanced treatment of the gaze in the African novelist's "practice of history." In particular, I focus on her close reading of *point of view* (the perspective from which the action of the story is narrated) in Yambo Ouologuem's controversial novel *Le Devoir de violence*.

Published in 1968, *Le Devoir de violence* narrates the eight-hundred-year history of a fictitious West African republic called Nakem from the founding of its empire by tyrannical Arab Saifs who invaded the region in the eleventh century to the advent of French rule in the nineteenth century and concluding

---

1. Eleni Coundouriotis, *Claiming History Colonialism, Ethnography, and the Novel* (Columbia University Press, 1999). All subsequent citations given in text.

in the mid-twentieth with anticolonial struggle in full swing. Responding to its portrayals of extreme violence and erotic content, the reception of the novel has generally fallen into two camps: the European reading public praised the novel for its "authenticity," thereby revealing and reinscribing the "conventional tendency to identify an authentic Africa with an excessively sexualized and violent place" (124). African critics, on the other hand, tended to disavow the novel largely because of its potential to elicit such damaging interpretations. Coundouriotis, however, contests both sides of this critical consensus. Equipped with the exacting tools of narratology—a structuralist method of literary analysis that is concerned with the formal techniques of storytelling—she explains how critics have failed to properly read Ouologuem's text and continue to miss his historiographical intervention because they have read him too *literally*. Instead, she suggests that if we pay close attention to the volatility and fluidity of point of view in the novel, especially in these charged sexualized scenes, we can grasp Ouologuem's ironic treatment of fiction's ethnographic inheritance.

To build her argument, Coundouriotis begins with an instance of *noticing*. The scene in question regards the violent rape of a female character named Awa, an African woman sent by the Saif (the Chief) to spy on Chevalier, a colonial administrator. But to theorize the function of violent sexual scenes in "Ouologuem's historical thesis," Coundouriotis first must demonstrate that Awa's encounter with Chevalier is in fact rape, even though "the scene is narrated as a scene of seduction" (128). She begins with a classic *scene setting*, reminding us of what we already know: the Saif orders Awa to offer herself to Chevalier, and the colonial administrator knows this because he regularly receives women from the chief. In short, Awa's consent is null. Given this dynamic, Coundouriotis, then, registers her surprise that "the scene is narrated as a scene of seduction." She reproduces striking fragments from the text, noticing how Awa is "breathless with delight at the pink hangings, the semicircular bed, and the silk counterpane which seemed to be strewn with rose petals" (qtd. in Coundouriotis 128). Coundouriotis, then, interprets this dissonance as evidence that although the scene is presented as if from Awa's point of view, it is actually Chevalier's perspective that controls the narrative. The narrative technique whereby the subjective experience of one character orients the third-person narration is called focalization, as if the narrator is seeing through that character's eyes. Coundouriotis summarizes her *local claiming* as follows:

> Awa's consent is not won through the action but is established narratologically by co-opting her point of view in the telling of the story. Awa's

experience is increasingly absorbed into Chevalier's point of view as his fantasy of her seduction. This violence constitutes a second order of action that is an extension and completion of the physical molestation of Awa. (128)

In other words, Chevalier assaults Awa *twice*. First, physically. Second, by coercively assuming her point of view and therefore alienating her from her own experience. But, if you as a reader were not entirely or immediately convinced by this argument, which comes after swift succession of scene setting, noticing, and local claiming in a short paragraph, Coundouriotis repeats the steps once more with the same scene. She turns to a moment that comes a bit later in the scene when, as part of his "seduction," Chevalier orders his dogs to attack Awa. Afterward he inquires about her experience to which she responds: "Oh! I've never seen anything like it" (qtd. in Coundouriotis 128). Coundouriotis quotes this line, but she also reproduces the original French alongside the English translation—"*Oh! Jamais je n'avais encore vu ça.*" Awa *sees* her assault rather than *experiences* it, corroborating Coundouriotis's local claim that she is not herself. Given her second reading of the scene hinges on a single word—*seen*—she offers the French alongside the English to prove that it is not just a fluke of translation. "This is an odd answer," she then tells us.

> Awa stands outside her own experience, observing it rather than feeling it. Already objectified, she views herself from outside herself, serving Chevalier's pleasure, which is extended through the recognition that Awa now sees herself as he has invented her. (128)

For Coundouriotis this single word decidedly alters how we read the long ensuing passage where the narrator's indirect discourse excessively expounds on Awa's sexual pleasure. Indirect discourse refers to a style of narration where the speech or thought of a character is reproduced without quotation marks. "A slap from him made [Awa] bark," the third-person narrator tells us, "she coiled up with pleasure, panting under his cruel caress, manipulating him like a queen or a skillful whore" (128). But if we recognize Awa's relationship to her point of view as one of alienation, then we can understand that "the excitement reflects Chevalier's understanding of 'his black girl' and not Awa's consciousness" (128). Coundouriotis is once again reminding us that a third-person narration is not always neutral, that it can adopt or align with the point of view of a specific character, and that this has consequences. What is more, appropriately identifying this focalization as Chevalier's fantasy enables Coundouriotis to recognize the mood of the passage. She proposes that the "excessive language, the parody of the pornographic" indexes the ironic quality of the scene through which Ouologuem seeks to implicate the reader.

In contradistinction to the critic who reads the scene literally, Coundouriotis is cognizant that Awa is not herself. And yet, she can only arrive at this knowledge by being present for, guided by, and risk being engulfed by the colonizer's invasive point of view. In other words, Ouologuem implicates his reader in the violence he thematizes. Because the reader's initial entry into the scene is through Chevalier's point of view, the text forces the reader to adopt, at least momentarily, the perspective of the perpetrator. By appropriating Africanist discourse's predilection for "aesthetics of spectacle," Ouologuem constructs what Coundouriotis names in her *regional argumentation* a "molesting text," defined as an "invasive text that involves the reader intimately in the violence perpetrated" (123). That is, more than simply unlocking the text, close reading here stages a confrontation between reader and text by laying bare how the text anticipates and constructs its own readers. For Coundouriotis, the rape scene calls into being two kinds of readers: the "masterful reader" exemplified by Chevalier's colonizing gaze and the "molested reader," whose consciousness, like Awa's, is attacked by what she sees but who still maintains a keen awareness of its otherness. We will soon explore what happens when the two kinds of readers confront one another.

The reader who accepts the rape of Awa as erotic spectacle is not only complicit in Chevalier's violence but is consequently locked out of the text's historical thesis. The instability of point of view instantiates a discursive gap between the narrator and what is being narrated as well as between reader and text to make explicit the distance between who sees and who speaks that founds the ethnographic paradigm. Ouologuem wants to thematize the violent dispossession enacted by the anthropological gaze that positions the African not as a speaking subject but as an object of study. But for the close reader to grasp this historical thesis, she must open herself up to the attack mounted by the text against and on Awa's behalf. Coundouriotis is interested in the parallel Ouologuem draws between seeing and reading through which she explores the distinction between "an act of witness that yields testimony and an act of voyeurism that yields fantasy" (125). If the discordant focalization of Awa's rape is the pivotal scene for Coundouriotis to illustrate how Ouologuem's text elicits the very reader it seeks to undermine, it is with the scene concerning Awa's death that she most fully reckons with the stakes of her argument.

Once more challenging the critical tendency to assign an affinity between eroticism and violence in Ouologuem's novel, Coundouriotis illustrates how the competing points of view in the scene of Awa's death refute the alleged pleasure of her murderer, her African fiancé Sankolo. But more than an enumeration of these discrete points of view, she frames the scene as a clash between the "molested reader" and the "masterful reader." She begins at the end of the scene when Sankolo stabs and buries Awa, quoting:

> Sankolo seized Awa by the throat. His knife whirled, twice he planted it in her left breast, slitted her belly from top to bottom. Suddenly expelled, her pink viscera crackled. He didn't even know whether the woman had screamed. He licked the blade, put the knife away in his belt. Covered the corpse with a wall of mud. (qtd. in Coundouriotis 131)

It is Coundouriotis's contention that to address the pleasure Sankolo experiences in his brutality, we first must detach it from the "aesthetic of spectacle" and locate it in narrative. Here, she flips the order of her close reading steps, starting with local claiming. "Sankolo's barbarism," she reasons, "is induced by a profound sense of powerlessness and self-hate that stems from his subjugation to both African and European oppressors" (131). He kills Awa because she stumbles upon him in a state of humiliation and he mistakes her sympathetic gaze for confirmation of his debasement. In support of this local claim, Coundouriotis submits a detail she notices in the preceding page, where "the narrative contradicts Sankolo's assumption about Awa's feelings" because, "throughout his violent attack on her, we are told that she loves him" (133). In other words, she wants us to notice how Ouologuem offers two distinct but parallel narratives for the same scene, each focalized from a different character's point of view. This prompts Coundouriotis to frame Awa's death as a catastrophic outcome of the incommensurable clash between the "masterful reader" and the "molested reader." While Awa feels implicated by Sankolo's pain, he receives her forlorn expression as an extension of his own mood. He misreads her care for him because he is unable to make room for an external autonomous point of view. Only after this does Coundouriotis set the scene.

Awa discovers Sankolo masturbating as he hatefully surveys Madoubo, the chief's son, having sex with Sonia, the daughter of a white ethnologist. Jealous and furious, Sankolo intends to humiliate his boss's son with his gaze while at the same time desiring to occupy Madoubo's position. "It is Madoubo's privilege that he desires," Coundouriotis suggests. "Sankolo, too, wants to master and conquer" (133). Coundouriotis alerts the reader to the exaggerated and pathetic scene where Sankolo imagines himself directing the couple's lovemaking with his own penis. "Tell me, my member, have you seen the two white pigeons in the dovecote" (90, qtd. in Coundouriotis, 133). It is while Sankolo is in a frenzy of tortured excitement that Awa discovers him and inadvertently thwarts his orgasm. Therefore, for Coundouriotis, "the pleasure he derives in the killing of Awa (cutting her with a knife, licking the blade) is displaced from the frustrations of the earlier scene of masturbation. Sankolo is humiliated by Awa's gaze, which catches him unawares" (131). Moreover, it is her close reading of Awa's encounter with Chevalier that allows Coundouriotis to grasp Sankolo's disproportionate reaction to Awa's gaze, the threat of being absorbed into another's imagination, of being made into a spectacle. "Reading the erotics of spectacle in continuum with the previous scene between Chevalier and Awa," she writes, "we understand that Awa's gaze emasculates Sankolo" (132). The castration he fears in and attributes to Awa's gaze, in turn, "reveals the intent of his own gaze on Madoubo and Sonia." It is precisely because he wants to humiliate the privileged son with his invasive unidirectional gaze that he receives Awa's look in the same register. Coundouriotis shows that Sankolo's pleasure in the murder of his fiancée is not just intended to satiate his orgasmic frustration but to expunge the humiliation of his arousal.

But what interests Coundouriotis the most is how narratologically the scene of Awa's death concurrently represents and contests Sankolo's pursuit to fully subsume Awa's point of view into his fantasy. She quotes a long passage relaying their physical struggle:

> He struck Awa a light blow on the cheek. She raised her hand in defense. He struck her full in the mouth, looking away one eye, at the couple disporting in the truck. That gave him a terrible air of detachment, as though to destroy Awa he needed only half his will.
>
> He went on striking her haphazardly, absently—less interested in punishing her than in making blood flow and inflicting pain. Awa's hands were of no use to her; she made no attempt to return the blows, she loved him, she was tortured by the horror and degradation of this physical struggle. (qtd. in Coundouriotis 132)

Noticing the "simultaneity of the two actions (he watches the lovemaking and beats Awa)," Coundouriotis confirms that in this instance for Sankolo, Awa appears "only as an instrument for his anger" with no autonomous perspective of her own. But, she maintains, "Awa's subjectivity is preserved, however, by the narrator's indirect discourse." Here, she turns our attention to the last line of the paragraph: "she was tortured by the horror and degradation of this physical struggle." The tragedy lies not necessarily in the fact that Awa and

Sankolo have a different experience of the struggle, but that Awa "falls prey" to the pain of his humiliation while "Sankolo is oblivious to her suffering" (132). But there is yet a third point of view in the scene: the narrator's. Coundouriotis makes the case that the sentence, "That gave him a terrible air of detachment, as though to destroy Awa he needed only half his will" belongs to neither Awa nor to Sankolo, but to the narrator who alone perceives this dispassion in Sankolo. For Coundouriotis, the narrator's perspective "indicates Sankolo's repression of his conscience, his own dehumanization in the violence that, when narrated from his own point of view (for example, the description of Sankolo's licking the blade), he enjoys" (133). The interjection of this third perspective suggests that, in the end, Sankolo fails to perceive the full extent of his own alienation.

Coundouriotis's deft and precise use of narratology allows us to appreciate Ouologuem's text anew. It is through her refusal to take for granted the neutrality of third-person narration and her diligence to attend to the subtlety of language that betrays itself that Coundouriotis identifies perspective as a site of both dispossession and contestation. If the violence of ethnography lies, at least partially, in the appropriation and erasure of the African's point of view, then for the African novelist the task becomes how to imagine "a history from the point of view of the dispossessed without reenacting a further dispossession by taking over their point view" (122). Coundouriotis's close reading of focalization unveils Ouologuem's attentiveness to these political questions. What might initially seem like a sensationalist spectacle, reveals itself upon a closer read to be a ruse to make the reader aware, skeptical, even complicit in the gaze of the other. As this short chapter illustrates, Coundouriotis is a difficult thinker, her prose dense, her analysis acute. But she is also, at her core, a narratologist who thinks systematically and structurally about how language makes meaning. This makes her an inviting thinker.

13

What, What to Do with All This Black Feminine Life?

HORTENSE SPILLERS ON
GWENDOLYN BROOKS

Omari Weekes

Hortense Spillers (1942–) is a foundational scholar of Black studies. Her 1987 essay, "Mama's Baby, Papa's Maybe: An American Grammar Book," is a touchstone for the field and beyond with its theorization of the long legacies of slavery. Here, Weekes shows us Spillers at work on this book's third step: local claiming. In an overlooked essay, Spillers reads Gwendolyn Brooks's only novel, Maud Martha, *to study how Black women inhabit femininity, a category from which they were long denied. In a crucial moment, Spillers must decide what to make of apparent contradictions in Maud Martha's—the novel's protagonist's—desires. Spillers notices that these desires are incongruous. Some might say they show Maud is naive; but in her leap to a claim, Spillers recognizes Maud's incongruities as her genius, an incandescence, an essayistic imagination that marks her as feminine over and above her gender. Spillers show us what Black women can teach us about femininity, and what femininity can teach us about Blackness.—DS + JW*

1.

Maud Martha, the poet Gwendolyn Brooks's only published work of prose fiction, first released in 1953, reads with a deceptive simplicity. The novel, which consists of thirty-four relatively short chapters, chronologically charts the life of its titular character from childhood through courtships, marriage, pregnancy, birth, and early motherhood in Jim Crow-era Chicago. While Maud Martha's vibrant inner life and Black female interiority anchor the text, the actual events of her life are unextraordinary. From *Maud Martha*'s opening chapter, with its sharp attention paid to the undistinguished beauty of dandelions, a common weed, to its conclusion, in which a protagonist expecting her second child anxiously wonders "What, *what* am I to do with all this life?," Brooks considers what the poetics of a typical Black woman's life tells us about midcentury America.

If *Maud Martha* is deceptively simple, "'An Order of Constancy': Notes on Brooks and the Feminine," the Black feminist literary critic Hortense Spillers's virtuosic article on Brooks's singular novel, reads with a deceptive complexity. This is not to suggest that Spillers's language or ideas are easy to parse; the essay, much like the rest of Spillers's corpus, builds on a number of interventions in feminist theory and Black study, using the technical language of these fields to make sense of something many purport to know when they see it: the "feminine." As Spillers notes, the "feminine," an inconstant category traditionally understood to encompass characteristics, traits, social behaviors, desires, and attitudes that are primarily associated with women and girls, makes for a designation "whose elusive claims escape not only precise definition but also decided terrain."[1]

But even if the "feminine" could simply hold a strict correlation with what women are or do, who counts as women? This serves as a more complicated question to answer than one might think! For reasons that Spillers unpacks here and in other well-read essays, Blackness modifies gender itself. The "feminine" has consistently been shaped by the historical exclusion of Black women from its purview. In effect, as Spillers argues, chattel slavery rendered Black women as "a special instance of the 'ungendered' female, as a vestibular subject of culture, and as an instance of the 'flesh' as a primary or first-level 'body'" (149). The flesh—in some sense, what Spillers calls the biological stuff of the body before that body gets read as "subject" or "individual" or even "human"—has been routinely violated physically and discursively. These violences, but especially the denial of Black women's access to their children during slavery, have produced regimes of social and cultural meaning under which

---

1. Hortense Spillers, "'An Order of Constancy': Notes on Brooks and the Feminine," in *Black, White, and In Color: Essays on American Literature and Culture* (University of Chicago Press, 2003), 131. All subsequent citations given in text.

Black women continue to live. Black women have been meticulously pushed out of what both the "feminine" and even "gender" refer to and Maud Martha's thoughts reflect those of a subject who refuses to merely reflect a "universal" consideration of either of those categories. Her existence is particular but also human, so Brooks takes the particular positionality of a working-class Black woman as a point of departure for extending what the "feminine" makes possible.

2.

To be feminine is not necessarily to be female, if Taylor Swift's sizeable crossgender appeal demonstrates anything. But, if one need not be female to be feminine, what might the "feminine" denote? Though Spillers carefully but swiftly explores how feminist theory expounds upon the relationship between the "feminine" and the "female body," perhaps her clearest articulation of how she is deploying the former term can be found in her claim that Gwendolyn Brooks's feminine resonates closely with what Virginia Woolf calls "incandescence" in the much-revered essay "A Room of One's Own." For Woolf, incandescence exceeds gender specificity *and* neutrality; in essence, it requires an androgynous mind.[2] Only the best creative geniuses can incorporate the "masculine" and the "feminine" in their worldview in ways that crosshatch and refuse to privilege one gender over the other. Consider how many men win Bad Sex in Fiction Awards narrating sex scenes from women's perspectives, for instance. No incandescence there.

For Spillers, the "feminine" holds a close association with the female body but is not exclusive to it. Rather than close ranks around the former term, pushing it into a territory that denies access to those who identify as men, Spillers explores how Maud Martha's decidedly feminine consciousness takes a piercing look at that which falls outside of her own racialized and gendered experience, such as her husband's lustful feelings and intentions, to which we will return. All across Brooks's novel, her protagonist exudes an incandescent genius. To show how, Spillers focuses on a series of events that take place just before and after Maud Martha gives birth to her first child. Once the baby has been born, Maud Martha reaches backward and forward through time, closely and deeply, searching for the stability that historical convention can offer amid the uncertain chaos of love after birth:

---

2. For more on incandescence, see Virginia Woolf, *A Room of One's Own* (Penguin, 1972), 97–112.

Could be nature, which had a seed, or root, or an element (what do you call it) of constancy, under all that system of change. Of course, to say "system" at all implied arrangement, and therefore some order of constancy.[3]

What she had wanted was a solid. She had wanted shimmering form; warm, but hard as a stone and as difficult to break. She wanted to found—tradition. She had wanted to shape, for their use, for hers, for his, for little Paulette's a set of falterless customs. She had wanted stone.[4]

In these passages, Spillers notices subtle incongruities between Maud Martha's stated desires. Though both "stone" and "solid" evoke a stability that withstands time, only the former refers to an actual physical object while the latter more abstractly describes a fundamental state of matter. Taken alongside Maud Martha's yearning for "shimmering form" and "tradition"—two conceptual terms possessing a softer malleability than stone or solids—Spillers locates Maud Martha's vision of "some order of constancy" in the character's inconstancy, in her possessing an "intelligence that tries things" by placing the ordinary stuff of everyday life into "whimsical combination" (138, 139). Rather than attribute this potentially discordant thought pattern to naiveté or ignorance, Spillers locally claims—offering us a path toward deeper understanding—that these desires amount to a "capable imagination," an artistry spun out of bringing diverse, perhaps competing elements of the quotidian together and lusting after the resulting collage of ideas (139). In the face of an anti-Black, misogynist world, Maud Martha is not content with bare survival; instead, she plays a spirited game with the cards that she has been dealt, conjuring up new poker hands along the way.

We most deeply feel this whimsical combination in *Maud Martha* in what the poet-scholar Elizabeth Alexander has coined as the Black interior, a term that encompasses both the domestic spaces that Black people fashion for themselves and an "inner space in which black artists have found selves that go far, far beyond the limited expectations and definitions of what black is, isn't, or should be."[5] In "Characteristics of Negro Expression," the Black writer and anthropologist Zora Neale Hurston gestures toward both Black interiors when she speaks to how the garish, often charming mishmash of stuff that one can find in many Black homes, what she calls our "will to adorn," is a direct

---

3. Gwendolyn Brooks, *Maud Martha* (Third World Press, 1993), 101.
4. Brooks, *Maud Martha*, 102.
5. Elizabeth Alexander, "The Black Interior," in *The Black Interior* (Graywolf Press, 2004), 5.

reflection of our understanding "that there could never be enough beauty, let alone too much."[6] It is our imaginative potential and our attention to beauty in all of its diverse, sometimes competing forms that inform the Black aesthetics we bring to bear on our homes and thoughts, especially when beauty has been so systematically denied to us throughout modern history.

Maud Martha radiates this desire for beauty in ways that her husband cannot. Paul lives a stoic masculine life concerned with the satiation of need rather than the exuberance of want. Before she is pregnant, Maud Martha reads literary fiction while her husband reads didactic pamphlets on sex after marriage. As Maud Martha contemplates how handsome her newborn is, Paul focuses on the gray fleshiness of what he mistakes as a stillborn child. Once the baby arrives and begins to need things, Paul concentrates on his job and takes offense about being asked for what he considers to be trifling eccentricities like "a velvet-lined buggy with white-walled wheels," an extravagance that he swears Maud Martha would think their baby deserves.[7] Whereas Maud Martha wants to be involved in the mess that forges traditions out of the rhythms of the everyday, Paul desires a submissive wife carved out of patriarchal traditions that preceded him, patriarchal traditions he has no hand in shaping. His creative vision, which clings cloyingly to masculinity, stretches little further than this.

It is within what Spillers calls a "capacity to draw the outer into itself, retranslating it into an altered exterior, as though fields of force magnetized by an abiding centrality" that the "feminine" may be found (139). Whereas Brooks's masculine can only envisage a social world that capitulates to and approximates white standards of human value (for instance, men over women and lighter-skinned people over darker-skinned people), Brooks's feminine takes chances, makes mistakes, and gets messy despite the oppressive conditions of midcentury America. As we will see in the next section, such an incandescent, feminine genius takes in new information, imagines otherwise, and refuses limitations even in the moment of their imposition. If fine art is inaccessible to a working-class Black woman, then that working-class Black woman treats holiday decorating like the curation of a museum exhibition. When Maud Martha sees the phrase "New York" while living in Chicago, her mind's eye immediately whisks her away to the Empire State. Hers is a complex

---

6. Zora Neale Hurston, "The Characteristics of Negro Expression," in *The Negro: An Anthology*, ed. Nancy Cunard (Wishart, 1934), 25.

7. Brooks, *Maud Martha*, 103.

subjectivity, affected by her station in life but not penned in by it. Instead, she uses her thoughts as a pen to write against those who insist her world must be small *because* she is a dark-skinned Black woman.

3.

For Spillers, the chasm between a wife who dreams kaleidoscopically about a freer world and a husband who dreams of little more than social climbing reaches its widest point in a chapter set at the Foxy Cats Dance Ball, an annual gala put on by a private club for upwardly mobile African Americans. In her reading, Spillers demonstrates how the difference in imagination rather than a mere difference in gender explains why Maud Martha and her partner react so divergently to the orthodoxies of upper middle class Black life that they witness and participate in at the event. Or, to be more accurate, Maud Martha witnesses and participates in the ball as Paul loses himself to the currents of historical narrative and American myth that surge through the scene.

When the couple arrives at the ball, Paul quickly leaves a pregnant Maud Martha on the sidelines to dance with Maella, a Black woman who is described by Brooks as "red-haired and curved, and white as a white."[8] Spillers notices the similarity between the words "Maella" and "mulatta," a now obsolete term that was popularized in an American context during slavery and used to describe people of mixed racial ancestry, especially those who were half Black and half-white (142). She also observes that this light-skinned Black woman who could be mistaken for white has a "gold-spangled bosom," a description that resonates with "star-spangled," a term closely associated with the national anthem of the United States (142). If white women have historically been projected as symbols for the nation that must be adored and protected, with the absence of any white women in the Black world of this chapter, and without saying a word, Maella dutifully steps into the role of American ideal of feminine beauty as white women's understudy. Colorism, a form of discrimination in which light skin is seen as preferable to darker skin, aligns Maella with whiteness, making her all the more desirable to Paul, who cannot register how his desire for a Black woman who can pass for white has been determined by slavery, colonialism, and other structural instantiations of anti-Black racism that have propped up the United States since well before its founding.

8. Brooks, *Maud Martha*, 85.

Paul's sudden, unquenchable thirst for Maella, driven principally by social phenomena spawned from racist histories that he did not shape and will not challenge, seems paltry in comparison to Maud Martha's shrewd accounting of her husband's actions and her own place in his desires: ". . . not that they love each other. It oughta be that simple. Then I could lick it. It oughta be that easy. But it's my color that makes him mad. I try to shut my eyes to that, but it's no good. What I am inside, what is really me, he likes okay. But he keeps looking at my color, which is like a wall. He has to jump over it in order to meet and touch what I've got for him."[9] Though Paul's dancing with Maella might read as a spectacular instance of colorism and a stunning matrimonial betrayal, Spillers argues that the form of the novel and Brooks's focus on Maud Martha's consciousness transform this into little more than a common event for her. She does not linger on Paul's thoughts or feelings precisely because they have already been processed in the sequence of events readers see in the novel, in events that readers do not see occurring in the interstices of the novel's chapters, and in the broader racist and misogynist world of which Maud Martha's milieu is a microcosm. This capacity to draw the elements of the world into oneself, to transfigure these elements from within via imagination, behind closed doors, under concealment, and the ability to find comfort and hope within uncertainty, Spillers goes on to argue, is the work of the "feminine."

The "feminine" performs all of this work not by eschewing the possibility of gender difference or resolving contradictions across gendered lines but by leaning into the quotidian complexities of gender in poetic fashion—and Spillers insists that readers should see this as the sign of an incandescent genius. The novel's disjunctive form, which narrates Maud Martha's life as a series of thirty-four discrete episodes, and its stream-of-consciousness style, which emphasizes Maud Martha's instantaneous reactions to external stimuli, can read like a poem that freely plays with the "masculine" and the "feminine" without resolving incongruities between the two categories. As Spillers suggests, the loose attachments between chapters and the novel's dogged insistence on reflecting the polyvalence contained within the everyday life of Black women "create an aesthetic surface without 'bulges'—the 'peaks' and 'valleys' of a schematic plot structure—or syntactic elements that do not adhere in a relationship of subordination and coordination" (144). Brooks turns to the poetics of everyday life and the free associations we make in every moment rather than the traditional structure of a novel, which would force the

---

9. Brooks, *Maud Martha*, 87.

trajectory of Maud Martha's life into a predictable sequence: exposition leads to rising action leads to climax leads to falling action leads to resolution. Brooks neglects to show how exactly Maud Martha comes to understand that being a woman in Western society is to occupy a subjugated position, for instance, because the recognition of such a gendered status requires no dramatic event or attempt at resolution—it simply is what it is.

In this way, Maud Martha's nondescript life reflects the ordinary and ubiquitous character of race, gender, and class oppression in the United States. The familiar disappointments that Maud Martha experiences over the course of her life, ones outside of but in relation to the most spectacular violences enacted upon Black people over the last four centuries, culminate not only in a durable self-awareness that flashes up in the face of her husband's unfortunate desires, but also into what Spillers calls "a profoundly active poetic sensibility, happily unbound in a world of marvelous color, of infinite allure" (143). This sensibility is impressionistic, recalling the nineteenth-century artistic movement that emphasized small brushstrokes composed together into scenes of the everyday, and, in *Maud Martha*, we can see many of the disparate strokes of unadorned labor that go into living through the "feminine" while Black.

4.

The sculpting of an interiority replete with subtlety, discordance, stillness, zeal, and other shimmering forms in a world that diminishes women and femininity is the domain of the "feminine." As Spillers shows, Maud Martha's private responses to the events of her life demonstrate a "woman-freedom" that "fixes herself as subject and object of deeply embedded public and private motives" (146, 149). Black women have historically been silenced and talked about rather than allowed to speak for themselves and to gain access to Maud Martha's interiority is to see how a Black woman who utters very little still contains a vibrant subjectivity, a resplendent inner life. Though racism, sexism, and economic precarity have limited her life chances, Maud Martha cultivates an imagination so vivid that it collates the complicated beauty of the world and its most common objects—the sky, a mouse, a snake plant, an iron, war, the sun—into the small living quarters of a kitchenette. In this way, Maud Martha is, perhaps, every feminine; it's all in her.

PART IV
Regional Argumentation

14

The Drama of Comparison

ALEX WOLOCH ON JANE AUSTEN

Elaine Auyoung

Why do some characters get to be central while others remain peripheral? What makes a main character? One of the twenty-first century's major works of narrative theory, Alex Woloch's (1970–) The One vs. the Many taught us to notice how characters compete for narrative attention. In doing so, he achieved a great feat of literary criticism, transforming the way we understand an established classic, Jane Austen's Pride and Prejudice. Narrative theory is the systematic study of narrative. Narrative theorists examine techniques such as perspective (who's seeing? who's speaking?) and chronology (is there a difference between the order things happened and the order the narrator presents them?) to make arguments about how narratives achieve their effects and to reveal how stories create meaning. Here, Auyoung demonstrates how Woloch builds to his analysis of a character-system through side-by-side analyses of brief passages. She demystifies the sometimes-obscured work of inductive reasoning by which critics achieve regional argumentation, inviting us to participate in the perceptual transformation that is its reward. —DS + JW

SOMETHING THAT published works of literary criticism occlude is the messy process by which their authors determine what they want to say. If a close-reading essay is organized around a regional argument supported by intricate analysis of multiple local examples, how does one discover that argument in the first place? How do you know when a feature you have noticed about a specific passage is not just random but actually "a thing," part of a higher order pattern, concept, structure, or technique that recurs across the text? This chapter aims to recover the inductive process by which literary critics discover the underlying regularities and relationships that can support a compelling regional argument. A practice that will turn out to be central to this process is side-by-side comparison or examining two or more examples in juxtaposition.

Side-by-side comparison operates on multiple levels in Alex Woloch's virtuosic, eighty-two-page close reading of Jane Austen's *Pride and Prejudice*, which forms the opening chapter of his 2003 book, *The One vs. the Many: Minor Characters and the Space of the Protagonist in the Novel*. This introductory chapter challenges the tendency for critics to take literary characters at face value—to accept that some characters just happen to possess great depth and complexity while others just happen to be shallow. Woloch's groundbreaking insight is that, in fictional narratives, the qualities that an individual character comes to have inside the story are shaped by the constraints of storytelling itself—by the need to distribute narrative attention across many different characters. As *Pride and Prejudice* unfolds, the narrator increasingly devotes disproportionate attention to a single protagonist while devoting less attention to everyone else. This asymmetry contributes to the distortion and flattening of minor characters like Mary Bennet and Mr. Hurst while rendering Elizabeth Bennet more complex, interesting, and worthy of attention by comparison.

The chapter is striking because of how fully it succeeds in realizing the methodological potential of close reading. To a greater extent than most critics, Woloch develops his regional argument by means of incremental, intensive examination of many examples from a single text. Because he shows his work so thoroughly, his analysis doubles as a justification of close reading itself. It proves that literary critics can inductively discover a powerful argument by means of intricate attention to local details. Woloch's success is made possible not only by his critical ingenuity but also by the ingenious construction of *Pride and Prejudice*. In this novel, no detail is random or careless. Fine distinctions matter. Jane Austen's neoclassical commitment to order and consistency means that her narrative really is governed by abstract, regional principles waiting to be discovered. In other words, there is an uncommonly happy marriage between Austen's method of representing her characters, the regional argument that Woloch develops in relation to it, and the procedures of literary criticism. This fortuitous match between text, critic, and method in turn makes it easier to see the features that many instances of close reading have in common.

Krinein, the Greek root of "criticism," means to separate or discern. While this suggests that critics are more discriminating in general, they especially prize two types of critical acuity: (1) the ability to discover abstract structures or regularities that multiple examples share, and (2) the ability to detect qualitative differences that make individual examples distinct. Being able to perceive both abstract structures and qualitative distinctions is fundamental to expertise in many domains. Conductors recognize the structural components of symphonic form *and* discern the qualities that differentiate Mozart's late symphonies from earlier ones. Pastry chefs recognize the components that many cake recipes have in common *and* discern the qualitative differences associated with batter that has been overmixed or underbaked. Literary critics recognize the dramatic elements of Greek tragedy *and* discern the qualities that make Oedipus's tragic flaw distinct from Antigone's.[1]

A surprisingly effective strategy for facilitating both types of noticing is to consider two or more examples side by side. While this may seem too simple and prosaic, too much like a schoolroom exercise in comparing and contrasting to spot differences and similarities, side-by-side comparison facilitates the inductive processes involved in learning (and distinguishing between) categories. These processes of abstraction and differentiation are central to developing literary critical expertise.[2] Looking at multiple examples side by side makes it easier to see past individual differences to identify abstract underlying patterns, as when critics notice that several poems use the same rhyme scheme or that films that belong to the same genre have shared narrative components. Side-by-side comparison also makes it easier to detect subtle differences in gradation, as when critics notice that one couplet ends with a stronger stress than another or that a narrator's tone is slightly rather than heavily ironic.

In short, considering several examples in relation to each other makes it easier to notice which of their local features have regional or global significance. Because critics seek to discover these higher-order forms of significance and to help others perceive what they have found, side-by-side comparison is embedded in written works of literary criticism at every stage of literary study. From a five- or six-page undergraduate essay to a thirty-page dissertation

---

1. Elaine Auyoung, "A Language for Literary Expertise: Epistemic Resources and Perceptual Transformation," *New Literary History* 55, no. 3–4 (2024): 515–42.

2. For more on how comparison facilitates learning, see Jonathan T. Shemwell, Catherine Chase, and Daniel L. Schwartz, "Seeking the General Explanation: A Test of Inductive Activities for Learning and Transfer," *Journal of Research in Science Teaching* 52, no. 1 (2014): 58–83.

chapter, to a published scholarly book, close readers routinely consider multiple passages, texts, authors, or genres in tacit or explicit juxtaposition.

Side-by-side comparison is everywhere in Woloch's close reading of Jane Austen. It is central not only to his method and argument, but also to Austen's technique of characterization. To be one of Jane Austen's characters, Woloch observes, is to be "continually contrasted, juxtaposed, related to others"[3] (43). In *Pride and Prejudice*, the first chapter ends with a juxtaposition of Mr. and Mrs. Bennet. Whereas Mr. Bennet is characterized by an odd "mixture of quick parts, sarcastic humour, and caprice," the narrator says of Mrs. Bennet: "*Her* mind was less difficult to develop. She was a woman of mean understanding, little information, and uncertain temper." Woloch calls attention to the narrator's abrupt shift from husband to wife because it marks the first of many similar juxtapositions throughout the text. In this local moment, Austen contrasts "complexity and superficiality in a way that will be repeated throughout the novel" (52). Woloch then shifts to another example that juxtaposes characters in a similar way: "In understanding Darcy was the superior. Bingley was by no means deficient, but Darcy was clever." When presented side by side, the juxtaposition of Mr. Bennet with his wife and of Mr. Darcy with Mr. Bingley highlights Austen's tendency to differentiate between her characters' intelligence.

After establishing Austen's habit of presenting two characters side by side, Woloch goes on to show that these juxtapositions frequently have the same underlying structure. He presents several examples side by side to facilitate *our* process of analogical induction, of discovering deeper underlying regularities across multiple examples. Although each example involves different characters and is drawn from a different part of the narrative, they all have two components in common: (1) They rank characters in competitive relation to each other. Whenever Austen juxtaposes characters in *Pride and Prejudice*, one always comes out ahead. Her reliance on this technique, Woloch argues, forces readers "to see characters in a comparative context and to get used to judging characters in a hierarchical framework" (70). (2) Characters are ranked according to their inner qualities. Although the characters themselves engage in social comparisons based on beauty, wealth, or height, "understanding" is the quality that matters most to Austen.

---

3. Alex Woloch, *The One vs. the Many: Minor Characters and the Space of the Protagonist in the Novel* (Princeton University Press, 2003), 43. All subsequent citations given in text.

Thus far Woloch performs a familiar form of regional argumentation: he positions several different passages side by side to bring out their shared components. This provides support for Austen's tendency to consider two characters in juxtaposition and to rank them based on their inner qualities. It is here that his analysis takes on an additional, revelatory dimension of complexity. Whereas his opening move has been to look beyond surface differences to identify the structural components that multiple juxtapositions have in common, he proceeds to show that some of these differences have regional significance, too. Considering so many of Austen's juxtapositions in relation to each other has enabled him to discover systemic variation *between* them.

To help us notice these recurrent differences in gradation, Woloch juxtaposes two of Austen's juxtapositions in a single block quotation. Whereas one passage "subtly" juxtaposes Elizabeth and Jane, the other "more harshly" juxtaposes Mr. Darcy and Mr. Hurst. Woloch highlights a shift in the narrator's tone: "The irony that is so clearly emphasized in the second passage is almost imperceptible in the first." By presenting these examples side by side, Woloch brings out a difference in gradation that is not random but that reflects another dimension of regularity in the text. Whereas Hurst is consistently presented as a "reduced and flattened caricature," Jane is "the one sister who is not harshly juxtaposed with Elizabeth" (70). The difference in tone that Woloch notices between the two passages corresponds to the disparate positions that Hurst and Jane occupy "within the asymmetrical character structure of the narrative as a whole." In effect, the relationship between "a character's specific position" in the text and "the narrator's mode of presentation" is governed by a principle of stylistic decorum that Austen has inherited from classical drama and poetry. The marginalized Hurst is handled in a heavily ironic, satirical manner that further justifies his delimited role, while the narrator's gentle, discreet treatment of Jane reflects and reinforces her more central position.

For Woloch, Austen's tactic of positioning two characters side by side has an even more important payoff: one character can seem to possess greater depth and complexity simply by being presented in juxtaposition with another who is simple and flat. When the narrator notes that Hurst is "thinking only of his breakfast," this detail not only cements Hurst's status as a "quintessentially reduced and flattened caricature," but also doubles as "an extension and an elaboration" of *Darcy's* comparative "depth of character" (53). When considered alongside the extremely limited range of topics that interests Hurst (eating, drinking, and playing cards), the mere fact that Darcy's consciousness is "divided" (between admiration of Elizabeth's brilliant complexion and doubt about the propriety of her behavior) becomes more than enough to indicate his complex interiority.

By arguing that a novelist can endow her characters with inner depth by positioning them in relation to characters that are comparatively flat, Woloch advances a global theory of narrative representation that has a familiar analogue in visual art. To produce the illusion of three-dimensional depth, painters replicate the visual effects of linear and atmospheric perspective by creating perceptual contrasts between objects in the same plane. These contrasts involve multiple, tightly correlated parameters that vary along a gradient: whereas objects in the foreground have a larger relative size, greater density of detail, darker value, and higher color temperature and saturation, objects in the distance have a smaller relative size, lower density of detail, lighter value, and lower color temperature and saturation.

Just as a figure appears to be in the foreground of a painting when it is positioned in relation to smaller, less detailed, less saturated, less shaded figures in the background, a protagonist can seem to have greater depth when she is positioned in relation to characters who are comparatively less central and less complex. In a sequence of chronological examples, Woloch alerts us to the minute gradations by which Elizabeth is gradually singled out as "the center of the narrative" and revealed to be a "character with more and more depth" (77–78). An early moment in this process takes place after the Meryton assembly, where Jane has been "distinguished" by Mr. Bingley and his sisters:

> Jane was as much gratified by this, as her mother could be, though in a quieter way. Elizabeth felt Jane's pleasure. Mary had heard herself mentioned to Miss Bingley as the most accomplished girl in the neighbourhood; and Catherine and Lydia had been fortunate enough to be never without partners, which was all that they had yet learnt to care for at a ball.

Again, Woloch notices a detail that is not arbitrary but reflects a consistent difference in Austen's treatment of her protagonist: the narrator's description of Elizabeth is already "qualitatively distinct" from that of the other sisters. Whereas Jane is "gratified," Mary "hears" herself mentioned, and Catherine and Lydia "dance," Elizabeth's "sensation is on a second order of apprehension, the consciousness of someone else's consciousness." She "feels" *Jane's* "pleasure" (66). As the narrative unfolds, Elizabeth's depth will continue to be developed by means of comparisons to her sisters' delimited qualities. Woloch notes that, when we consider *these* comparisons side by side, they display consistent fluidity: "Sometimes the contrast is between Elizabeth and the two youngest sisters; sometimes between Elizabeth and Jane against the two youngest sisters; sometimes the two oldest are contrasted with all the three younger ones." Once we look beyond the superficial variation between examples, however, we discern their underlying function: to ensure that Elizabeth always comes out ahead (70). Whereas Mary is pedantic, Elizabeth has real intelligence. Whereas Lydia is reckless, Elizabeth is spirited. Whereas Jane is kind to a fault, Elizabeth is discriminating. And whereas her sisters are limited to a single trait, Elizabeth becomes multifaceted by means of comparisons to each of them.

But why does Austen need to privilege one sister in the first place? Why must one character receive more attention than the rest? Since protagonists have existed long before novels, there are many ways to approach this question. For Woloch, the unequal distribution of narrative attention in Austen's fiction is motivated by its subject matter: a marriage system that produces socioeconomic inequality. As the narrator of *Mansfield Park* observes, "there certainly are not so many men of large fortune in the world, as there are pretty women to deserve them." In the face of this grim social reality, *Pride and Prejudice* distinguishes itself from many other novels by delivering "the most exemplary of happy endings" (45). Austen produces a narrative that "seems to hover on a border between novel and fairy tale" by ensuring that the young woman who ends up with the best marriage is also the one who incontestably deserves it the most. In Elizabeth Bennet, the most desirable marriage, the most central narrative position, and the most deserving personal qualities miraculously converge on a single character.

To fully account for Elizabeth's singularity, however, Woloch emphasizes the extent to which her many virtues become apparent to us only by means of continual comparisons between her and her sisters. Austen's reliance on juxtaposition is exemplified by her handling of Mary Bennet, the sister who "fits into a simple opposition with Elizabeth" (71). Whereas "the former has artificial knowledge, the latter has real intelligence; while Mary is learned, Elizabeth is both clever and thoughtful." Mary's "single-minded pedantry" serves both to "valorize" Elizabeth's quickness and to justify her own delimited position in the narrative. Moreover, her "remaining at home, which seems to have arisen so naturally out of her personality and the configuration of descriptive strategies that converge around her, is also the necessary result for 'some one or other' of the daughters who cannot marry into the limited property available" (75). The same positive feedback loop that singles out Elizabeth confines Mary "even more firmly into a cramped corner of the narrative" (74).

Woloch's account of the systematic process by which *Pride and Prejudice* "contains and flattens, or compresses, minor characters" to strengthen its protagonist satisfies many of the unspoken aesthetic ideals associated with close reading. Literary criticism is a means by which critics transform the way others see a text. Especially dramatic, aesthetically satisfying instances of perceptual transformation reveal how a local detail that has been overlooked, ignored, or taken for granted turns out to have profound regional or global significance. Because minor characters permit us to pay less attention to them by design, recovering the significance of why and how these characters have been made to seem less interesting performs precisely the kind of perceptual transformation that critics admire.

A related form of perceptual transformation that literary critics value is to discover that local, seemingly disparate parts of a text fit together as part of an interdependent whole. When the New Critics established the protocols of close reading in the mid-twentieth century, they wanted to explore how parts of a poem that seemed contradictory ultimately fit together in a unified way. Woloch transposes this part-to-whole structure to the scale of a novel, enabling us to perceive every character in *Pride and Prejudice,* from the most central to the most marginal, as an interdependent part of a "unified character-system" (68).

This system's asymmetric structure also helps to ensure that the experience of reading Woloch's chapter is continually surprising and interesting. A close reading focused on demonstrating that many examples contain the identical structure or pattern can become repetitive and predictable. Eagerness to apply a regional argument to as many examples as possible carries the danger of becoming overly general, reductive, or indiscriminate. The beauty of narrative asymmetry, however, is that individual differences between characters retain the potential to be significant—to constitute meaningful instances of systematic variation. All of Austen's characters are subject to the same governing principles, but the critic still needs to discover the distinctive way in which each character has been positioned in asymmetric relation to the others. The result is a close reading that, like *Pride and Prejudice* itself, produces a pleasurable "mixture of suspense and certainty" (45). We know that Lydia, Kitty, Mr. Wickham, Mr. Collins, Charlotte Lucas, Lady Catherine de Bourgh, and Mr. and Mrs. Gardiner will fit into the character system, but we don't know precisely how.

Since its publication in the early twenty-first century, *The One vs. the Many* has been applied and adapted by many critics working on many different narrative traditions, genres, and media forms. Its outsize scholarly impact is due not just to the explanatory potential of Woloch's global theory, but also to the intricate way in which he traces, again and again, the inductive process by which a local detail has regional significance. His meticulous approach to close reading helps us see that literary critics' fascination with "the transition from the concrete to the abstract" is ultimately a fascination with the experience of perceptual transformation at the heart of inductive discovery.[4] But inductive discovery is not something critics perform merely to display their ingenuity. It is fundamental to perceptual and conceptual learning in many areas of study. Enabling others to perceive how concrete, local details fit into more abstract regional or global concepts and structures is both a method of pedagogy and a performance that gives pleasure. By means of close reading, literary critics seek to produce the same effects they have long attributed to literature: instruction and delight.

4. Sharon Marcus, "Erich Auerbach's *Mimesis* and the Value of Scale," *MLQ* 77, no. 3 (2016): 297–319, 311.

15

Befriending Poems

ROBERT PENN WARREN ON
JOHN CROWE RANSOM

Emily Ogden

Robert Penn Warren (1905–1989) is the only person to have won a Pulitzer Prize for both poetry and fiction. As Ogden notes here, he also coauthored an influential New Critical textbook, Understanding Poetry, *first published in 1938 and reissued in new editions through the fourth in 1976. For Warren and his fellow New Critics, close reading is distinctly social because literature is experiential. Close reading's sociality sets literary studies apart from science. We learn from literature about the human world, ineluctably perfused by human aims and human values. For Ogden, channeling Warren, the sociality of close reading means we are most astute as readers if we encounter literature as we would a person and bring what we know about people to the text. Just as it can be misleading to take someone's words out of their social context, it can be misleading to interpret one passage apart from its relation to the full text. New Critics called this relationship between part and whole* irony *and it is, for Ogden, a key to regional argumentation.—DS + JW*

READING A poem is more like talking to a person than it is like solving a math problem. Poems give us knowledge—this is the view of the critics Robert Penn Warren and Cleanth Brooks in their influential early-twentieth-century college textbook *Understanding Poetry*—but not by conveying messages that will be revealed if only we plug the words into the right decoding formula. They give us knowledge of "the world of experience, and . . . that world considered, not statistically, but in terms of human purposes and values." Such knowledge is "dramatic," Brooks and Warren say, by which they mean that it is like a play: it is given in terms of a version of everyday (or sometimes extraordinary) interaction with other human beings.[1] No doubt the poem, like the play, is a highly specialized version of such interactions. But the important point is that when we read poems, we must find a way to bring our ordinary social capacities into play—even though many of the features of situations that usually activate those capacities are not present. I mean that there is no human being in front of us (save in the exceptional case of a live poetry reading) and thus there are no gestures; there is no tone of voice; and there is not much of a context. All of the information we might normally get from context, tone, gesture, we must get from the words alone.

Close reading is the art of activating our capacities to read other people—to infer, by complex cues, that they are angry, or sad—in the face of a text, in spite of the absence of the ordinary features that would trigger us to use these capacities. As a thing to learn, then, close reading can seem both strange and familiar: it is hardly obvious that you should treat a text like a friend (or enemy); but treating-like-an-enemy (or friend) is a thing you already know how to do. A close reader learns to find in a text's semantic features—its word choice, its pacing, its figures of speech, its odd decisions about word order, and an indeterminate list of other qualities—something like the same information that a guest at a cocktail party might take from tone, gesture, body position, clothing, facial expression, and an indeterminate list of other qualities. Close reading, like gleaning social information, is so complex that all its possible techniques cannot be listed. But this indeterminacy does not prevent it from being learned, any more than a child is prevented from learning how to interact with other children by the fact that no one can list the rules for these engagements. Close reading is a specialization of a social capacity that every human being begins to learn in the first year of life. You started learning it a long time ago.

Something like the view I have been articulating here—of close reading as the specialization of a social capacity—is the position of the New Critics in general, and of Brooks's and Warren's textbook in particular. The book went through four editions and its influence continues, not least in that it was probably used to teach some of the people who taught some of the people who now

---

1. Cleanth Brooks and Robert Penn Warren, *Understanding Poetry*, 3rd edition (Holt, Rinehart, and Winston, 1960), xiii.

teach you.² These things linger. The New Critics, early- to mid-twentieth-century American poets and academics who included Brooks, Warren, Allen Tate, John Crowe Ransom, and William K. Wimsatt, focused the study of poetry not on history nor on the intentions of the writer nor on the reactions of the reader, but on the words of the poems themselves. Poems, they thought, were best compared to organic wholes, meaning that all the parts were interrelated and mutually modifying. "Irony" was their name for these internal relations—for the way the whole modified the meaning of each part.³ Because of the theoretical importance of irony to the New Critics, they were especially focused on, and especially good at practicing, what this collection calls *regional argumentation*: the analysis of how parts of a poem relate to each other and to a whole. The relationship between New Critical irony and our ordinary social judgment is not far to seek, either: what we constantly do, as we interpret other people's actions, gestures, expressions, and speech, is to relate these fleeting bits of information to the social contexts in which we observe them. Your narrowed eyes will change in meaning for me depending on any number of contextual factors: Do I know you to make this gesture when you are joking, or suspicious? Which of these attitudes could make sense in context? Is it sunny?

Regional argumentation, in the hands of Robert Penn Warren, has a sociability about it: Warren is good at understanding how details of tone modulate major statements, as an effective poker player might be good at understanding how a tell modulates, or transforms, the meaning of an opponent's spoken bet. In his essay "Pure and Impure Poetry," he reads his friend John Crowe Ransom's poem "Bells for John Whiteside's Daughter," which is an elegy for a child who died. It is one of those cases where the reading mysteriously manages to be better than the poem itself—or manages to *make* the poem better somehow. Here is the poem:

> There was such speed in her little body,
> And such lightness in her footfall,
> It is no wonder that her brown study
> Astonishes us all.

---

2. Naomi Levine, "*Understanding Poetry* Otherwise: New Criticism and Historical Poetics," *Literature Compass* 17, no. 7 (July 2020): np. The first edition of *Understanding Poetry* appears in 1938.

3. Cleanth Brooks, "Irony as a Principle of Structure" (1949), in *Critical Theory since Plato*, ed. Hazard Adams (Harcourt Brace Jovanovich, 1971), 1041–48.

Her wars were bruited in our high window.
We looked among orchard trees and beyond
Where she took arms against her shadow,
Or harried unto the pond

The lazy geese, like a snow cloud
Dripping their snow on the green grass,
Tricking and stopping, sleepy and proud,
Who cried in goose, Alas,

For the tireless heart within the little
Lady with rod that made them rise
From their noon apple dreams, and scuttle
Goose-fashion under the skies!

But now go the bells, and we are ready;
In one house we are sternly stopped
To say we are vexed at her brown study,
Lying so primly propped.[4]

The poem stages a war between two clichés, Warren points out: the one, "won't that child ever be still, she is driving me distracted," and the other, how could such a vigorous child die? There is something "savage" in the way the second cliché answers the first, as Warren notes: "the child you wished would be still *is* still" (985).

But to point out the bitterness with which these two clichés answer each other is, for Warren, to have said almost nothing about the quality of the poem, because a poem is an experience, not a box for carrying a message. To have noted these clichés is at best to have a thesis of sorts—tenable but tiresome, and not at all revealing of the poem's textures, of what it is like to experience it. Such a simple reading, as Warren notes, "is not the game here" (985). The scant value Warren places on having a thesis, or finding a thesis in the poem, is an exact illustration of the New Critical tenet, expressed in *Understanding Poetry*, that poems are not message boxes but things to be experienced. His thesis-indifference is also what makes Warren a great close reader. He simply doesn't care about making a defensible and tidy point about the poem; what he wants, instead, is to experience the particular way this speaker handles his point-making.

4. Robert Penn Warren, "Pure and Impure Poetry" (1943), in *Critical Theory since Plato*, 985. All subsequent citations given in text.

Most of Warren's reading of Ransom's poem has to do with this handling—with the "modifications and modulations" of a savage experience, "modulations and modifications contingent upon an attitude taken toward it by a responsible human being" (985). The brutality of death is what, in a sense, the speaker and the New Critic will modulate together, by their attention to the kind of New Critical irony where the parts delicately modulate the whole. In the end, we'll have a brutish fact of life—that children die, including when we have been annoyed with them for making too much noise—but this fact will be tempered so that it is somewhat more tolerable to us. "Form," Warren and Brooks say in their textbook, "is the recognition of fate made joyful, because made comprehensible."[5]

What Ransom does, on Warren's reading, is to put a scrim between us and the ghastly tableau of a dead child with whom we have been annoyed. None of us were personally annoyed with John Whiteside's daughter, of course, but who does not recognize this possibility, of having been annoyed with, or even cruel to, a mortal being, as if that human being were eternal, and then realizing that they could die? Who has not oscillated between irritation at a loved one, and prospective grief at their mortality? And thus in a sense we are included among the "we" who are "sternly stopped" at the house where the wake is being held. Many of the features of the poem that seem unfocused or peculiar on first reading become, in Warren's hands, merciful acts toward we guilty mourners. The poem has, as Warren notes, a "wavering rhythm," which can seem like Ransom's shaky prosody. Why is the last line of the first stanza too short? Why is the first line of the second stanza end-stopped? Why the amateurish rhyme between "window" and "shadow"? But these aren't failures of craft on Ransom's part; instead, they gently restore the rhythm of the child's tripping gait.

The poem exercises its mercy, too, in the way the living child is seen: at a distance, in the charming but not especially heartrending (rather, comical) activity of bothering the geese. Rather than representing Ransom's failure to find an image sufficiently lofty or iconic, this choice represents the way his speaker spares us, or himself, from bursting into yet another storm of tears. (The poem is spoken well after the first realization of death—a few days later, to be exact, at the moment when everyone is bracing themselves to get through the funeral.) Above all, Warren's reading solves the strange diction of us being "vexed" at her "brown study"—an archaic term for a childish sulk that, here,

---

5. Brooks and Warren, *Understanding Poetry*, xiv.

stands in for her death, as being "vexed" (annoyed) stands in for grieving. Why these anticlimactic terms for death and mourning? To spare us. At the wake, the crescendo of grief, Ransom pulls focus. Her death and our former irritation at her are best touched softly.

The poem's achievement, then, is a decidedly human achievement, one fit for ordinary social occasions (albeit somber ones): it makes life a little more bearable, as we make grief more bearable for each other by choosing a phrase of consolation that touches the fact of death at an oblique angle. We call the death a friend is grieving a "loss"; we think carefully about whether we even use the word *death*. We weigh whether or not to bring it up. Even the use of stock phrases in a condolence card can be a form of tact: we might speak this way if we don't want to require the aggrieved to spend any time thinking about, or reacting to, our own reactions. The poem has its own forms of tact, to be sure, that are not necessarily closely related to these examples. But the point is that its obliquity in relation to death is something we might already understand, and instinctively expect, at a time of grief. Thus like us, when we are in the company of a grieving friend, the poem comes, Warren writes, to "some kind of terms, perhaps not the best terms possible but some kind," with the death it describes (986). To help us come to terms with the hard facts and the joyful possibilities of experience is what poems do for us, Brooks and Warren argue in their textbook. In the case of this particular reading, the human work of the poem and its reader and the theoretical concept of New Critical irony—the parts modified by the whole—are closely related to each other. It is only by noting the "savage irony" of the poem's reigning clichés on the one hand, and the mercy of its pulled focus, non-iconic images, and wavering rhythms on the other, that all these elements of the poem are saved from being what, otherwise, we'd probably call each of them individually: bad poetry.

I still can't quite decide whether the poem itself *is* good, or whether that's an impression Warren manages to give. To treat a poem as a whole has a friendliness about it, friendliness that approaches bias in favor: a reader proceeding in this way wants to help the poem be what it is, to shore it up, to assume that the poem works as it should and is made as it should. One might object that such a critical bent is unscientific. The New Critics would have conceded, indeed insisted on, the point. Back in 1938, when Brooks and Warren first published *Understanding Poetry*, they already felt that the humanities were embattled; that literary study was being falsely measured by a yardstick imported from what we would today call the STEM disciplines; and that it was necessary to respond by forcefully articulating an alternate way of knowing. "Poetry gives us knowledge" are the first words of *Understanding Poetry* in the third edition.[6] Brooks and Warren find themselves articulating the notion that this knowledge is social and experiential because they want to explain that it is not, and can never be, value- and judgment-neutral in the way that the hard sciences might require. Nor can it involve us leaving our social capacities at the door and applying a neutral, one-size-fits-all method. If we have one thing above all others to learn from the New Critical mode of regional argumentation, it's an implication of their friendliness to poems: the axiom that poems teach us how to read them, and each one has to be read on its own terms. Close reading is, as Roland Barthes wrote, a "science of a single object."[7] It must be developed anew for each object—which is just another way of saying that we would do well to attend to how the parts are modified by the whole to which they belong. Every friend teaches us a new lexicon of word and gesture—a new way of modulating and finding joy among life's hard realities. With that friend, often with that friend alone, we speak the language the two of us have developed together. Poems and their readers speak together in much the same way.

---

6. Brooks and Warren, *Understanding Poetry*, xiii.

7. Roland Barthes, *Camera Lucida: Reflections on Photography*, trans. Richard Howard (Farrar, Strauss, Giroux, 1981), 8.

16

Close Reading and the General

QOLAMHOSSEIN YOUSEFI ON
AHMAD SHAMLU

Pardis Dabashi

Be specific! We often find ourselves giving this note to students. Attention to details can stave off banal generalizations that evacuate the text of meaning. We find ourselves in league with the Iranian critic Qolamhossein Yousefi (1928–1990) who takes this practice further than us—so far as to reject global theorizing altogether, to refuse to extend his analysis beyond regional argumentation because of his commitment to specificity. Like Christopher Ricks and Helen Vendler in this volume, Yousefi sustains the tight New Critical focus to the words on the page—coupled, for Yousefi, with Arabic, Persian, and Aristotelian traditions—into a period when most Anglo-American critics had become preoccupied with history and theory. But, as Dabashi shows here, neither Yousefi nor any of us can escape generalizations, even in starkly specified readings. We use concepts in which we can claim, or at least aspire toward, expertise. We use those concepts to organize our thoughts. An inescapable challenge of close reading, then, is not hewing with perfect discipline to specificity, but finding that right ratio of specificity and generality for our purposes—in this particular case.—DS + JW

[T]hought would be impossible if it did not misjudge the nature of being from the very start: it has to posit substance and identity, because a knowledge of total flux is impossible; it has to impose made-up qualities upon appearance in order to exist itself.

—FRIEDRICH NIETZSCHE, *UNPUBLISHED FRAGMENTS*

1.

In the introduction to his 1990 collection of essays titled *Bright Fountain* (*Cheshme-ye roshan*), prominent twentieth- and twenty-first-century Iranian literary critic Qolamhossein Yousefi specifies that each chapter of his book is dedicated to reading "one good piece" (*yek assar-e khoob*), and one piece only, from each of the multiple poets he examines.[1] There is a pedagogical bent to this approach, in that *Bright Fountain* reproduces in book form what you might expect to encounter in a detailed survey of Persian poetry. But this acute attention to one piece from each poet also extends from a methodological ethos. "I believe that in this way," Yousefi writes, "the reader is going to encounter" a more "precise [*daghightar*] discussion than if one were to discuss the entire body of the poet's work in general terms [*be tor-e koli*]."[2] "The best and most specific" literary criticism, Yousefi writes, quoting from Scottish literary historian and critic David Daiches's *Critical Approaches to Literature* (1956), "'prefers to deal with one single literary work rather than with the whole body of work of a writer. Even when [T. S.] Eliot makes a general judgment, he almost always has a specific poem in mind.'"[3]

Each of *Bright Fountain*'s seventy-one chapters indeed presents one poem from a Persian poet, starting with the canonical figures of classical Persian poetry Yousefi had long been known for dedicating his attention to, such as Hafez, Sa'adi, Rumi, and Abolqasem Ferdowsi, and moving through what by 1990 were recognized as prominent figures of modern and modernist Persian poetry such as Nima Yushij, Forugh Farrokhzad, and Ahmad Shamlu. But even as the breadth of *Bright Fountain* is vast, encompassing close readings of poems from the tenth century all the way to the twentieth, the book's primary commitment is to the particular over the general. Each poem, Yousefi tells us, is taken not as indicative of a broader trend—within a genre, an era, a poet's oeuvre, and so on—but as indicative of itself and itself alone. The turn toward the broad would risk imprecision. Yousefi in *Bright Fountain* is a consummate theorizer of localized precision in that he rejects the notion that the single

---

1. Many thanks to Azita Hamedani Kamkar for her close collaboration with me in translating the Persian to English.

2. Qolamhossein Yousefi, *Bright Fountain* (*Cheshme-ye roshan*), (Entesharat-e elmi, 1990), 11–12.

3. David Daiches, *Critical Approaches to Literature* (Longman, 1956), quoted by Yousefi, *Bright Fountain*, 12.

poem could be representative of a more general tendency within a poet's work or a poem's genre or form.

To illuminate this point, let's consider his reading of modernist poet Ahmad Shamlu's 1957 poem "Dust." Yousefi resists drawing conclusions about what Shamlu generally does, and instead limits his argument to what Shamlu does *here*. Drawing inspiration from the Anglo-American New Criticism (*naqd-e jadid*), classical Arabic and Persian "criticism of eloquence" (*naqd-e balaqat*), and Aristotelian poetics, Yousefi is invested in the principle of the unity and wholeness of the single text.[4] "The author," he writes of himself in the introduction, "has considered each literary work as a whole [*be envahn-e koli*], the form [*surat*] and content [*mohtavah*] informing each other."[5] But here's the rub: while Yousefi keeps his focus limited to the single text for the sake of what he calls "precision," he nevertheless relies on heuristic categories of genre and mode that seem analytically less precise, though, as we will see, unavoidably so. By way of a vocabulary of "hardness" and "softness," Yousefi relies on the categories of *epic* and what a Western audience would characterize as *lyric* poetry to communicate what he sees as the fusion of these traditions and modes taking place in Shamlu's single poem.[6] These are categories that he knows are deeply complex but that he nevertheless distills into apparently simple terms to convey something more clearly about his object of study. In so doing, Yousefi teaches us something important about close reading, particularly the way that expertise influences the language we use to do it. He teaches us that theorization of a single poem often relies on some elements of general theories of poetry.

---

4. The "New Criticism" was an influential mid-twentieth-century movement within British and American literary criticism led by such critics as Cleanth Brooks, W. K. Wimsatt, and John Crowe Ransom; its central tenet was to close read literature (particularly poetry) as a self-contained, self-referential aesthetic object, without allowing historical or other contextual information to be considered in the process of interpretation. Arabic and Persian "criticism of eloquence" refers to literary criticism of classical Arabic and Persian poetry and the Quran (for a great resource on *naqd-e balaqat*, see Lara Harb, *Arabic Poetics: Aesthetic Experience in Classical Arabic Literature* [Cambridge University Press, 2020]). In his *Poetics*, Aristotle emphasized, among other things, the formal principle of unity that influenced both Arabic and Persian criticism of eloquence and the New Criticism.

5. Yousefi, *Bright Fountain*, 13.

6. Yousefi does not use the actual word *ghazal* in the essay, the word that would most accurately correspond to the word "lyric" in English. That is because the term *ghazal* has a very specific meaning in the history of classical Persian literature and corresponds to poets such as Hafez and Rumi—poets from whose classical style, as I mention later in this essay, Shamlu is decidedly breaking, particularly at the level of rhyme and meter. Also see note 8.

Through invocations of the categories of epic and modern lyric, Yousefi shows us that when you know *a lot* about something, you often find yourself relying on what might sound like overgeneralizations but are actually expressions of expertise. They are expressions of a world of knowledge whose particularities you must crystallize into generalizing terms if you are to say anything about the artwork and not get paralyzed by those particularities—what Nietzsche in my opening epigraph calls "total flux." Experts often know things are more complicated than how they're describing them, but they sometimes need to reach for shorthand in the process of making a claim. The first part of this chapter will address Yousefi's argument concerning the poem itself; the second will consider how he relies on general concepts to make that argument.

Before making any claims, Yousefi reproduces in full Shamlu's relatively brief poem, "Dust," published in his breakthrough 1957 collection, *Fresh Air*, of which the following lines are especially key for his argument:

> I do not fear the howl of the raging storm
> and I do not mourn the roar of the thunder;
> I do not take meager death for granted. [...]

> Tell the vine of destitution
> Not to wrap itself uselessly around my arms and legs. [...]

> But when seagulls fly over the sea [...]—
> I run after them barefoot.
> Tears well up in my eyes,
> Though I am strong as iron. [...]

> And [though] my conviction itself has become like steel—
> If a bird were to sing in the heart of the night
> Tears of compassion would flow from my eyes.[7]

Yousefi's first analytical move, through a dance of noticing and local claiming, is to identify the two poetic moods he sees at work: the hardness of epic and the softness of modern lyric. "There are two important points and states of mind in the poem," he notices. "[O]ne is endurance, stability, masculinity and recklessness," which belongs, he writes, to the world of "epic" (*hemasi*), while the other is "the pathos of emotions and poetic feeling, which requires tenderness" (*narmi*), an affective repertoire he associates with modernist Persian

---

7. Ahmad Shamlu, "Dust," quoted by Yousefi, *Bright Fountain*, 728.

revisions of classical lyric (a movement of which Shamlu is considered one of the founding architects).[8] Yousefi locates the epic tone in the first part of the poem, notably through an observation about how Shamlu creates combinations, or concatenations of phrases: "The first part," Yousefi writes, "has an epic tone: not only do the combinations of 'the howl of the raging storm,' 'the roar of the thunder,'" and the expression of "'no fear'" or "'sorrow'" in regard to death, "fit that tone." But also, he writes, to describe "'death'" with "the adjective 'meager'" and to liken "'destitution'" to a "vine"—as well as to express "indifference" to "poverty"—"strengthens this [epic] meaning." "The sum of these and the appropriate words and rhymes," Yousefi writes, "have given this part a toughness and solidity [*koobandegee va salahbatee*]."[9] In form and in content, then, the opening four stanzas of "Dust" belong to the world of epic.

Yousefi then reads the second and third parts of the poem, which, by contrast, move into a different "state of being," where the cold indifference of what he reads as the epic masculinity articulated in the first four stanzas yields to "tenderness, compassion, and kindness." In the fifth and sixth stanzas, he writes, "the images and compositions are soft," such as "the flight of birds from the sea over the bridges, roofs, and swamps," and the poet-speaker "running barefoot after them."[10] These softer, more wistful images, Yousefi suggests, introduce the gentler, more supple register of modern lyric.

Or more precisely, for Yousefi, the encroachment of lyrical vulnerability into the steely fortitude of the terrain of epic suggests the way that the poem in fact entangles these two modes with one another, not so much reconciling them as making them increasingly mutually dependent. It is the "contrast

---

8. Yousefi, *Bright Fountain*, 729–30. The epic and lyric traditions Yousefi is thinking of here are Persian; for him, this would mean the *ghazals* (short lyric poems) of Hafez, for instance, or Ferdowsi's epic *Book of Kings* (*Shahnameh*). These Persian literary traditions neither can nor should be conflated with those of Europe, but epics more familiar to Euro-American audiences include *Beowulf*, for instance, the *Epic of Gilgamesh*, or Homer's *The Iliad*, works that foreground heroic action and that predate the Romantic concept of the individual with a unique and expressive subjectivity central to the lyric poetry of such authors as William Wordsworth, John Keats, and Charles Baudelaire. For helpful sources on Persian lyric and epic, see *Persian Lyric Poetry in the Classical Era*, ed. Ehsan Yarshater (Columbia University Press, 2019); Kumiko Yamomoto, *The Oral Background of Persian Epics: Storytelling and Poetry* (Brill, 2003). For definitions of Euro-American epic and lyric, see *The Princeton Encyclopedia of Poetry and Poetics*, 4th edition, eds. Roland Greene, Stephen Cushman, Clare Cavanagh, Jahan Ramazani, and Paul Rouzer (Princeton University Press, 2012), 439–48, 826–34.
9. Yousefi, *Bright Fountain*, 730.
10. Yousefi, *Bright Fountain*, 731.

between these two images," Yousefi writes—the poet-speaker running barefoot after the birds and returning to the hut dragging his feet—as well as the sharp distinction between the "tears" in the poet-speaker's "eyes" and his description of himself as "strong as iron," that starts to throw that entanglement into relief. These contrasting combinations of images, Yousefi writes, provide "suitable grounds for comparing" the poet-speaker's "vigor with regret and sadness, and this tenderness with strength and steadfastness." This imbrication of the emotive and the withdrawn, the tender and the unfeeling, is mirrored in the rhythm of these two stanzas, which Yousefi describes, tellingly, as at once "soft and coarse" (*narm va dorosht*).[11] Principal to Yousefi's argument about "Dust"—the particular case he makes about this particular poem—is indeed this pairing gesture, culminating here in the phrase "soft and coarse." What yields the poem's internal "unity," or "harmony," as he alternately calls it, is the way it comprehensively fuses epic form and states of feeling with those of modern lyric. The final stanza fully fuses the lyric and epic registers that the earlier parts of the poem have lain out in more separated terms. "In the last part," he writes,

> there is first a return to the epic aspect of the poem with the same powerful tone and images. It is about the indifference and attitude of recklessness toward "the roar of the storms" and "the hurling of the winds," as well as "steel" and "war." And then he [the poet-speaker] refers to a softer song, with the line "[i]f a bird were to sing in the heart of the night" and "the tears of sympathy." That contrast is noticeable, too, between the two lines: "And my conviction itself has become like steel/The tears of compassion fall from my eyes."[12]

The juxtaposition of epic and modern lyric finally collapses, in other words, into synonymity, Yousefi suggests. And it is here where we finally get his summation of the poem's "essence," what he reads as its central accomplishment: "These last few stanzas contain, in fact, the essence of the whole poem [*asl-e hame-ye shehr*], with the same two tones and two different qualities [of lyric and epic]." Shamlu's piece, Yousefi concludes, "has done well in combining two poetic worlds."[13]

---

11. Yousefi, *Bright Fountain*, 731.
12. Yousefi, *Bright Fountain*, 732.
13. Yousefi, *Bright Fountain*, 732.

2.

But notice how Yousefi has a problem. To arrive at what he calls a "precise" assessment of the single poem, he relies on unavoidably less precise concepts drawn from *bodies of other texts*: the epic and lyric traditions. Yes, Yousefi restricts his claims to a single poem from each poet, arguing, in this case, that the central accomplishment of *this* work is the merging of formal effects of and thematic concerns with hardness and softness. But he can't make this claim without relying on very big categories—in this case, the genres and modes of epic and lyric. These categories (and others like them) have long formed the foundation of the professional institution of literary criticism. And we—professors, but also students—rely on them to make conclusions about works of art. A key takeaway here is that one of the challenges of remaining focused on the particular, perhaps ironically, is expertise. Yousefi was a consummate classicist; *Bright Fountain* was one of the very few instances in which he ever turned his attention to modern literature. In other words, he absolutely knows that it's not entirely fair to characterize epic in terms solely of iron reserve. (To take just one example with which Yousefi would have been intimately familiar: there is a famous scene in Ferdowsi's *Book of Kings* where the character Rostam, a divinely strong warrior, discovers with earthshattering horror that he has unknowingly killed his own son, Sohrab, in battle. The scene is marked by extreme tenderness and pathos.) Nor would it be fair to assume that Yousefi wasn't familiar, albeit less intimately, with modern poetry. He would have known, for instance, about the strategically steely restraint of some of Forugh Farrokhzad's verses, many of which complicate the view of modern lyric as associated exclusively with the expression of gentleness and vulnerability. Indeed, his chapters on epic and modern poets in *Bright Fountain* (including Ferdowsi and Farrokhzad themselves) demonstrate the nuance of Yousefi's expertise in what he calls these "two poetic worlds." And zooming out even further, Yousefi was also undoubtedly aware of how skeptical Shamlu himself was of the category of lyric—the *ghazals* of the classical period—which he named, alongside the *qasida* (ode) and the *ruba'i* (quatrain), the "dingy prison" of the classical tradition from which modern poets, including himself, were breaking free.[14] The very fact that Yousefi relies on the language of the *tender* and the *soft* in opposition to epic, as opposed to the explicit language of the

---

14. Ahmad Shamlu, *Hamchun kucha-yi bi entehā* (Like an Endless Street), (1973. Tehran: Negah, 2005), 21.

ghazal (or the ode or quatrain, for that matter) suggests his own resistance to overgeneralize. It is *I* (the close reader of the close reader) who has relied more on the language of the *lyric* as a rhetorical shorthand in drawing out for an audience potentially less familiar with the history of Persian lyric poetry than they are with that of Europe, what Yousefi means when he refers to the poetic alternative to epic masculinity by drawing together the various terms he uses—softness, vulnerability, etc.—under one, more economical but inevitably less precise, shorthand.

Indeed, the point of mentioning these counterexamples is not to suggest that Yousefi is being careless or sloppy (nor, hopefully, that I am). The point, rather, is to show something counterintuitive about how expertise can make itself apparent in close reading. Yousefi is relying on certain words, certain concepts, that he knows are more complicated than he is making them seem, but that he nevertheless uses for the sake of making his argument, or what in his introduction he refers to as "ease of communication."[15] When we come across these invocations of such big categories, so big they may sound imprecise, what we are in fact witnessing is the accumulation of his training. We know he knows that epic and lyric cannot be distilled into a neat, mutual distinction (even if, in his further defense, what he shows throughout his close reading is indeed how Shamlu complicates that binarism). But, simply put, he has to rely on analytical shorthands in the process of making a claim.

It will of course take time and training before you will accrue the level of expertise necessary to generalize about epic and lyric literary traditions in the way that Yousefi does. However, we all have our version of what Yousefi is doing here. Yousefi's close reading practice showcases the inescapable tension we as close readers must negotiate between concepts and instances, categories and counterexamples. At this stage in your learning, your professors most probably have knowledge that you don't quite have yet, of what epic *tends* toward, for instance, of what lyric *tends* toward, etc. But you very often do depend on other, less generically broad references, such as Yousefi's own "soft" and "coarse," for instance, or even "action" and "emotion." But even these relatively simple concepts are quite complicated. The concept, or feeling, of softness can be argued to flirt with the coarse, the active with the emotive. What reading of a poem about familial love, for instance, would be convincing without some recognition on the part of the close reader of the callousness that can permeate the most seemingly safe and tender of amorous bonds; or,

---

15. Yousefi, *Bright Fountain*, 12.

for that matter, the often heightened capacity of emotions to have profound effects on the world and thus to constitute their own form of action? To put it simply, no matter what concepts or categories a close reader is working with, one could, more often than not, if one chose, find oneself saying *it's more complicated than that*, drawing, as a source of authority, on one's knowledge of the world beyond the region of the text. The search for "precision" can indeed take the form of a vertiginous, if not paralyzing, infinite regress. We cannot read purely particularly, even when we try, as this would involve a kind of unimaginable, even solipsistic, nominalism. As long as two of the basic tools of literary analysis are language and experience—be it the latter in the form of professional expertise, experience in the world, or some combination of the two—some measure of generalization is necessary for making claims about art and conveying those claims to others. It is against the background of the inevitable imprecisions of the general that the particular has any meaning at all.

Something to keep in mind about close reading, then, is that the close reader striving for precision has to manage the ratio of specificity to generalization while coming to peace with the inevitable idiosyncrasy of the point at which the person reading your analysis has deemed that ratio well managed. The inevitable pull of the imprecisions accompanying any general theory of poetry raises one of the thorny questions that literary critics have been asking recently with renewed urgency: What kind of expertise does one need in order to execute a close reading well?[16] Regardless of how we find ourselves answering that question, Yousefi's style of close reading shows us, counterintuitively, that at some point we must abandon precision—the obsession of the expert—for the sake of saying something, that we have the courage to, at some point, deem it precise *enough*. If we recognize this—the irreducible contestability of that point, its susceptibility to alternative judgments (maybe that point isn't the same for me as it is for you, or the same for either of us tomorrow what it was today)—then we might recognize, too, that close reading is far riskier and more vulnerable an act than it might initially appear. An appeal for my fragile threshold of precision to match up with yours, and for long enough that we have the opportunity to see something together.

16. For recent work addressing this question, see Elaine Auyoung, "Becoming Sensitive: Literary Study and Learning to Notice," *PMLA* 138, no. 1 (January 2023): 158–64; Robert Chodat, "Experts and Encounters," *PMLA* 135, no. 5 (October 2020): 989–1001; Michael W. Clune, *A Defense of Judgment* (University of Chicago Press, 2021); Jonathan Kramnick, "Criticism and Truth," *Critical Inquiry* 47, no. 2 (Winter 2021): 218–40.

17

Vibe Theory

LAUREN BERLANT ON JOHN ASHBERY

Brian Glavey

Few English professors are profiled in the New Yorker *and given obituaries by the* New York Times, *but Lauren Berlant (1957–2021) was extraordinary. They brought together feminism, Marxism, and psychoanalysis as a foundational thinker for affect theory, a field of study that Glavey describes here and that Kimberly Quiogue Andrews discusses in chapter 20. Most famously, Berlant coined the term "cruel optimism" to name "when something you desire is actually an obstacle to your flourishing." Glavey presents Berlant reading John Ashbery, an extraordinary poet. Regional argumentation, under Berlant's tutelage, can answer questions about desire and fantasy: What is the deepest desire in this poem, the guiding fantasy? We escape suburban ennui, in Ashbery's poem, by escaping into a lightly eroticized encounter, getting a little lost, inhabiting a hum, a vibe. Glavey teaches us how Berlant's regional argumentation finds a fantasy by making a vibe visible. But what happens when a reader as rigorous and skilled as Berlant makes a serious mistake? With compassion and clarity of vision, Glavey pursues Berlant's error and discovers a fuller truth about life in the middle, the regional.—DS + JW*

THE NEW Critics could get weird about feelings. In the middle of the twentieth century, when the New Criticism was still new, William Wimsatt and Monroe Beardsley published an essay titled "The Affective Fallacy" that outlined a position that many critics and teachers have taken to be one of the guiding principles of close reading ever since.[1] Our feelings, Wimsatt and Beardsley suggest, are too private. Close reading should be concerned, on the contrary, with things public and shared, with meanings that anyone can decipher from language that belongs to anyone who can read it.

But one problem with the affective fallacy is that it takes for granted that emotions are subjective and private. In fact, they can be every bit as public and shared as language. Everyone has had the experience of entering a room and feeling that the vibes are off. The euphoria of a concert or a dance party, the sense of meaningful sadness shared at a funeral, a feeling of hope or dread surrounding a historic election: collective feelings shape our lives all the time. Certain moods seem to circulate in particularly powerful ways in certain historical moments. For critics interested in feelings and emotions, art and literature are especially helpful for getting a sense of something like the tone or mood of these moments. The affect we access through literature is not limited to what a particular reader feels when she opens a book; we can also learn to recognize the sorts of ambient feelings that are in the air. This kind of feeling can be so pervasive that it is hard to see directly, and yet it is often possible to see evidence of it in the patterns that become visible in an aesthetic object when we know how to look for them. Close reading, in this regard, can be a kind of vibe check.

One of the most accomplished examples of this kind of vibe theory is Lauren Berlant's *Cruel Optimism* (2011). With the idea of cruel optimism, Berlant (who used they/them pronouns in their professional life) introduced a concept that made a rare leap from the province of academic theory into the wider culture. It's a straightforward idea announced in the book's opening sentence: "A relation of cruel optimism exists when something you desire is actually an obstacle to your flourishing."[2] Berlant was trying to answer a problem that has long troubled students of history: Why do people continue to participate in systems that oppress them? Berlant's answer has to do with the way our attachment to certain fantasies provides us with a sense of continuity and stability. These stabilizing fantasies might be about love: we might find ourselves choosing to be disappointed again and again by a relationship that never gives us what

---

1. W. K. Wimsatt Jr. and M. C. Beardsley, "The Affective Fallacy," *Sewanee Review* 57, no. 1 (Winter 1949), 31–55.
2. Lauren Berlant, *Cruel Optimism* (Duke University Press, 2011), 1. All subsequent citations given in text.

we need, thinking always that next time it will be different. They might be about politics: that a political system that is clearly not working for our interests will somehow come through this time. The tenacity of our attachment to such scenarios, even when on some level we know better, has to do with how much of our sense of self is wrapped up with them. We might recognize that these fantasies are bad for us, but we don't know who we would be if we let go of them. Appearing in the aftermath of the financial crisis of 2008, *Cruel Optimism* helped give form to feelings tied to the diminished expectations and accelerated forms of austerity that appeared in its wake. Berlant helped provide a vocabulary for the experience of working for a dream of prosperity no longer on offer, for buckling under student debt and side-hustling in the gig economy without ever getting ahead. All the old genres narrating what it would look like to flourish had lost their power and new ones had not yet taken shape.

Even though Berlant's book is about collective emotions on the one hand and political economy on the other, its insights into both are not drawn from studies of mass psychology or sociology but works of art: movies, novels, and, at the very beginning, a poem. The title chapter of *Cruel Optimism* begins with a close reading of a poem by the American poet John Ashbery (1927–2017). Berlant begins by quoting what they take to be the entirety of an untitled poem:

> We were warned about spiders, and the occasional famine.
> We drove downtown to see our neighbors. None of them were home.
> We nestled in yards the municipality had created,
> reminisced about other, different places—
> but were they? Hadn't we known it all before?
>
> In vineyards where the bee's hymn drowns the monotony,
> we slept for peace, joining in the great run.
> He came up to me.
> It was all as it had been,
> except for the weight of the present,
> that scuttled the pact we made with heaven.
> In truth there was no cause for rejoicing,
> nor need to turn around, either.
> We were lost just by standing,
> listening to the hum of wires overhead. (qtd. in Berlant 28–29)

The status quo that the poem disrupts is presented at the beginning of the poem as a slightly numbed version of the American dream, a monotonous municipal world of neighbors and their yards. In this world, nobody is at home but it hardly matters: we've known these places before and there are no real surprises. This account of the American dream as being tepid and uninspiring is itself uninspired. But that, for Berlant, is the point. The poem enacts the sleepwalking that is its subject not only in its argument but on the level of meter and diction as well: "the comforting sound and slightly dull rhythm of cliché," as Berlant notes, "performs exactly how much life on can bear to have there" (30). The beginning of the poem works, in other words, according to Berlant's local claim, because it is using clichés to think about what it feels like to live with them.

Berlant proceeds, regionally arguing, to read this poem as an example of an optimism potentially less cruel than most of the examples in their book. It represents a scene in which it becomes possible, if only for a brief moment, to loosen one's attachment to a fantasy of the good life that is no longer working for us, if it ever was. They are drawn to this poem, in other words, scaling up to the global, because it shows us what certain kinds of experiences—experiences with art, experiences with emotional or sexual intimacy—can sometimes make possible: they give us the kind of space and perspective to step away from our sense that the world has to be the way it is and to feel the possibility of something better.

Everything changes—space opens—with the third line of the second stanza: "He came up to me." Berlant argues that this moment represents a powerful interruption to the boredom and cliché that saturate the preceding lines. The disruption of the approach works in part, Berlant suggests, because the unexpected assertiveness of this "he" hints at a queer encounter with the presumptively male speaker of the poem. The queerness of this encounter seems to trouble the normativity of the rest of the poem. In noticing this potentiality, Berlant is no doubt drawing on their knowledge of the fact that Ashbery was himself gay. But they are also noting the way the shortest line in the poem shifts the dynamics throughout the poem in terms of both form and content. The subject of each sentence prior to this moment had been a repetitious first-person plural (*we*); the appearance of the third-person singular (*he*) shifts the sound and sense of all that follows: everything is almost as it had been, but the "weight of the present" "scuttles the pact we made with heaven." Berlant argues that this unplanned encounter with another person, an encounter vibrating with a kind of romantic or even sexual charge, shakes the poem out of the peaceful slumber of suburban anomie. The result is to transform the *we* from the beginning, a kind of generic general public, into the different, less defined *we* of two people working out a way to be lost together.

Berlant's reading of this drama is held together by a pattern they notice on the level of sound. At the beginning of their reading, they note that in first half of the poem, "home and hymn *almost* rhyme." This slant rhyme marks a shift from the first stanza, where none of the neighbors the speaker drives to see are home, to the second, where "the bee's hymn drowns the monotony," suggesting a kind of sacred and salvific music. In Berlant's reading, though, this music transforms further throughout the poem: "The event of the poem is the thing that happens when he comes up to me and reminds me that I am not the subject of a hymn but a hum, the thing that resonates around me, which might be heaven or bees or labor or desire or electric wires, but whatever it is involves getting lost in proximity to someone and in becoming lost there, in a lovely way." Berlant brings their reading to life by combining an attention to the formal details that they have noticed with an attention to the form of rhetorical address the poem enacts, thinking both about the echoes of assonance and alliteration and the scene that the poem is presenting. It might seem like a paradox, but close reading allows Berlant both to see the poem as if from a distance, noticing patterns that run across its lines, and from within: they take seriously the way the poem's first person invites the reader to step inside it.

Understanding the way the sound of the poem is part of the story it tells enables Berlant to recognize the way its narrative is transformed by a phoneme: "Moving from home to hymn to hum" (35). Once Berlant establishes this sonic pattern as the throughline of the poem, they then begin to elaborate upon it, introducing other terms not exactly present but suggested by the poem: him, *homme* (French for man), the nonsemantic um. In part, Berlant is being playful here, the pleasure that the poem takes in the sounds of words authorizes them to play along in the same spirit. This too is a feature of close reading that connects their method and the argument they are making: thinking along with another person's language can make it difficult to draw neat boundaries between one person's voice and another's. Our experience of art and literature might seem deeply private, but they also smudge the lines that keep the public and the private separate from one another. This smudging is what Ashbery's poem is up to according to Berlant. Replacing home with hum is literally about a kind of vibe, moving from a form of belonging tied to a discrete possession to a much more ambient vibration that surrounds but is invisible. The poem thus shows us a collective feeling that we might not otherwise have been able to see, something bigger than any one person's emotions. For Berlant, this feeling is a vague sense of potentiality, a sense that everything might change after.

There is only one problem with Berlant's account of the way this poem ends amid a kind of open-ended lostness—the poem does not in fact end with the humming wires. Berlant's reading is based on a strange and surprising mistake: the text that they quote is not a published but untitled poem. Instead, it is a quotation from a work in progress that was included in a biographical profile in the *New Yorker* magazine, a few lines from a poem that had already appeared under the title "Ignorance of the Law Is No Excuse," first in another magazine and then as the opening poem in Ashbery's 2005 collection *Where Shall I Wander?*[3] The lines appear in the profile as an example of what Ashbery was working on at the moment he was being interviewed, as if the author had taken a peek and scribbled down what was visible on the sheet rolled into his typewriter. The difference between this quoted fragment and the full poem is significant, especially because the published text includes a final, third stanza that potentially changes the way we read the other two:

> We mourned that meritocracy which, wildly vibrant,
> had kept food on the table and milk in the glass.
> In skid-row, slapdash style
> we walked back to the original rock crystal he had become,
> all concern, all fears for us.
> We went down gently
> to the bottom-most step. There you can grieve and breathe,
> rinse your possessions in the chilly spring.
> Only beware the bears and wolves that frequent it
> and the shadow that comes when you expect dawn.[4]

Ashbery's poem concludes not with a scene of the beautiful ambient hum of intimacy, but by returning to the more general and generic "we" of the first stanza. The "he" that Berlant reads as a kind of romantic partner has somehow mysteriously transformed into "rock crystal" and the emotional character of the poem shifts from reverie to mourning, to breathing and grieving in the

---

3. Larissa MacFarquhar, "Present Waking Life," *New Yorker*, November 7, 2005, 88. When this profile appeared, Ashbery's full poem had already been published as "Ignorance of the Law Is No Excuse," in *New York Review of Books* 51, no. 5 (March 25, 2004), and *Where Shall I Wander?* (Ecco, 2005). In a footnote added to the version of "Cruel Optimism" that appears in the book, Berlant notes that "the poem has since been revised into 'Ignorance of the Law Is No Excuse,'" but this too is inaccurate (*Cruel Optimism*, 272n14).

4. John Ashbery, "Ignorance of the Law Is No Excuse," *Notes from the Air: Selected Later Poems* (Ecco, 2007), 329.

aftermath of the loss of a way of life that had once seemed wildly vibrant. Most importantly, the poem's ending brings us back to a feature of the opening that Berlant, in their scene setting, had mostly ignored: the tone of ominous warning. Shifting from the first-person plural to the second person, the poem concludes by stepping into the position left out in the passive voice of the first line, not just telling us about a warning but actually warning us. Insisting on our need for vigilance, the poem is more like the disrupted scene of suburban blandness that Berlant describes than something rather more postapocalyptic. The bees seem less beatific when framed by the threat of spiders, bear, and wolves. And, most importantly, the phonemic pattern that organizes Berlant's reading—home, hymn, him, *homme*, um, hum—falls away in the third stanza. Can we still call it a pattern if it isn't there though the end?

How much does it matter that a profoundly useful concept—an idea that has influenced countless artists, critics, and general readers—is generated from a misreading? To return to the title that Berlant leaves out, we might genuinely wonder whether ignorance is or is not an excuse. It is possible to reasonably conclude that the answer is no: that Berlant is simply wrong and their initial misrecognition scuttles their interpretation of the poem and the cultural moment they take it to index. But we might also find that what Berlant says still makes a certain sense. Berlant takes Ashbery's poem to be about the lure of getting lost in the middle, to stay with a feeling before it settles down into something final or even fatal. The fact that, unbeknownst to them, the poem itself abandons this middle-ness to assert a kind of closure might be seen as corroborating Berlant's main argument. It turns out, we might say, that even Berlant gets lured in by cruel optimism, thinking that the poem is reassuring us about the possibility of staying lost "in a lovely way" when in fact it makes no such promises.

To draw on the terms central to this volume, Berlant's trouble is with regional argumentation. Berlant is a virtuoso noticer, picking up nuances about affects and tones and, through local claiming, tying them to specific aspects of Ashbery's language: the sound of the poem's words, its play with cliché, the rhythm of its lines, and so on. And people have obviously responded to the global theorizing that the close reading, good or bad, makes possible. Berlant's account of how a certain vision of the good life has become a cliché, and their description of how an intimate encounter might help us loosen our attachment to fantasies that are obstacles to our flourishing, are extremely powerful. Where the reading arguably loses its way is somewhere in the region of the regional. Berlant weaves the details that they notice into a pattern that maybe, when seen in relation to the poem as a whole, isn't actually a pattern after all. Their theory of the poem, in other words, turns out to be wrong, even if their theory of cruel optimism is even more correct than they realized.

But Berlant's argument is actually about the problem of middles, which is to say the problem of regional argumentation itself. One thrust of *Cruel Optimism* is that paying attention to things like affect, mood, or vibes is especially useful for thinking about the present. People are all trying to make sense of the middles they find themselves in without knowing how or when they might end. Life happens in the middle, and people experience this as a feeling before they understand it in more rational terms. This is especially true when the old stories that people have relied on to understand their lives—stories about the American dream, the good life, owning a home and having a yard, and so on—have lost their power. Living in moments like ours, Berlant suggests, is a condition of not knowing what the rules are that govern the genre we are living out: Are we in a comedy, a tragedy, a horror movie? Sometimes we think about these questions in expansive terms, using philosophy, or Marxism, or sociology to try to make sense of our lives. We can theorize globally, in other words. But even when we have a strong global theory about of our lives, understanding on some level how our lives are shaped by capitalism or racism or history, say, we still have to do the regional work of figuring out what is going on and how to feel about it. Big ideas, powerful theories, can help us make sense of the world. But even then they do not obviate the patterns that shape the medium-range scale of our day-to-day lives. Ignorance of the law might not be an excuse, but it is for Berlant the precarious position we most often inhabit, constrained by laws and forces that are mostly invisible to us, and without any real assurance of how things will end.

PART V
Global Theorizing

18

Going Global

WILLIAM EMPSON ON
WILLIAM SHAKESPEARE

Noreen Masud

Seven Types of Ambiguity—published in 1930 when its author, William Empson (1906–1984), was just twenty-four—is an inaugural work of close reading and foundational to both British practical criticism and its American counterpart, New Criticism. Empson could persuasively conjure big ideas from scant evidence as an audacious practitioner of global theorizing. How did he do it? Whereas some critics theorize globally through a process of careful, even painstaking, inductive reasoning—see Auyoung in chapter 14—Empson reaches for rhetorical splendor, sleights of hand that leave us exhilarated if unsure how he arrived at his conclusion. These sleights are true to life as to poetry, argues Masud, here, drawing from Empson's 1935 book Some Versions of Pastoral. *Life and poetry are chaotic and confusing and we delight in the tricks that command that chaos, that confusion, into wondrous order. It's difficult; it's easy to fail; but Masud, with humility and wit, licenses us to practice our prose and learn from life and poetry until we, too, can, like Empson, land the spins and twists and backflips of global theorizing.—DS + JW*

MANY FAMOUS close readers would, I suspect, fail a contemporary close reading exam. *Explain yourself clearly*, I say to my students. *Take your time. No leaps in logic. Tether your arguments to textual evidence. Above all: don't pontificate about how the poem inspires you personally. No overblown statements about Life.* What I *don't* say is that, whether we admit it, anyone who loves poetry loves it precisely because we are interested in Big Thoughts about Life. What role do and should these play in close reading?

As a critic with many Big Thoughts about Life, William Empson feels, to me, like the elephant in the close-reading room. Michael Wood calls him "the most brilliant close reader [New Criticism] ever produced."[1] So he should be a model for students and critics alike to follow. He's often treated that way. But, despite three degrees and a university job, I'm not sure I've understood a single one of Empson's close readings. And he pontificates to beat the band. Worst of all: I love him for it.

In this chapter, I try, and mostly fail, to close read Empson's close reading of Shakespeare's Sonnet 94, "They That Have Power: Twist of Heroic-Pastoral Ideas in Shakespeare into an Ironical Acceptance of Aristocracy," which is chapter 3 of his book *Some Versions of Pastoral* (1935). Here, I am doubly hampered. Not only do I not understand Empson's close reading of Sonnet 94; I also don't understand Sonnet 94. And yet, though it's the chapter I can follow least, it's the one that leaves me with most. Empson compels me as a close reader because of the extraordinary power of his "global theorizing": the fifth and final step of close reading, where one explains to the reader *why everything you have just said matters*: what it changes for our reading of the author, of English literature, or even of life itself. I'll read "They That Have Power" for its global theorizing: Empson's dainty, zoomed-out conclusions about why we might read and how we might live. The essay weighs up two questions: What connection, if any, do these theorizations have with the actual work of poetic analysis from which they claim to originate? And what might coerce us, as readers, to accept his necessarily partial long views as the endpoint of close reading?

Any work on *Some Versions of Pastoral* has to acknowledge Empson's complete faith in the reader to know all his literary references. I reread this chapter more than twelve times as I wrote this chapter, but I stopped and started many more times than that. I also had to memorize Sonnet 94, and reread *The Merchant of Venice*, *Measure for Measure*, and both parts of *Henry IV*, to have any chance of keeping up with Empson. So if, like me, you did not originally have Sonnet 94 at your fingertips, here it is:

> They that have power to hurt and will do none,
> That do not do the thing they most do show,
> Who, moving others, are themselves as stone,

---

1. Michael Wood, *On Empson* (Princeton University Press, 2017), 10.

> Unmoved, cold, and to temptation slow:
> They rightly do inherit heaven's graces
> And husband nature's riches from expense;
> They are the lords and owners of their faces,
> Others but stewards of their excellence.
> The summer's flower is to the summer sweet
> Though to itself it only live and die,
> But if that flower with base infection meet,
> The basest weed outbraves his dignity:
> For sweetest things turn sourest by their deeds;
> Lilies that fester smell far worse than weeds.

Sonnet 94 is notoriously difficult. It's part of what's called the "Fair Youth" sequence in the sonnets, where the speaker addresses a beloved but selfish young man. (Empson assumes the speaker is Shakespeare and the addressee is "W. H.," the dedicatee of the first edition of the sonnets.) The octet (or octave, the first eight lines) seems to recommend a mode of behavior where a powerful person has the power to hurt others, but doesn't; is able to move others without becoming moved themselves. These people, Shakespeare notes, are the "lords and owners of their faces." All this seems to describe them positively: they "inherit heaven's riches." Yet the language is ambivalent: such a person is described as "stone" and "cold." Then in the sestet (the last six lines) there's a sharp shift in focus: to the "summer's flower," who is sweet, self-contained, self-absorbed. If that flower meets with infection, though, it becomes worse than the worst weed. Shakespeare concludes: "Lilies that fester smell far worse than weeds." Some kind of metaphorical equivalence is being set up. But how does it work? Is the summer flower the same as the lily, Empson wonders? Is the "owner" the same as the summer's flower? The lily? Both? Neither? And, indeed, is Shakespeare saying that the poem's addressee is equivalent to one, two, or all of these things in its metaphorical implications? Is Shakespeare saying that the addressee is cold? Or should be cold? Should be like the summer flower (and in what way? In its beauty, or in its innocence, or in its self-centeredness, or . . . ?) Or *is* like it (and in which of these ways?)?

In response, perhaps, to this difficulty, Empson's opening to "They That Have Power" makes us a promise: that his work will be easy to follow, moving step by step—almost mathematically—through possibilities:

> . . . you can work through all the notes in the Variorum without finding out whether flower, lily, "owner" and person addressed are alike or opposed.

One would like to say that the poem has all possible such meanings, digested into some order, and then try to show how this is done, but the mere number of possible interpretations is amusingly too great. Taking the simplest view (that any two may be alike in some one property) any one of the four either is or is not and either should or should not be like each of the others; this yields 4096 possible movements of thought, with other possibilities.[2]

The "you" invites us in, informally; the invocation of the Variorum gives one a sense of there being *equipment* to tackle the problem, even if the content of the passage tells us unequivocally that this equipment is of no use. Then Empson breaks the dilemma down mathematically, to give us 4,096 possible interpretations of the poem. 4,096 possible interpretations are worse than none at all. But by performing this designedly stupid mathematics, Empson creates a sense of security. Invoking 4,096 possible interpretations—weirdly—makes understanding seem possible precisely because the number of possible interpretations has been revealed as a finite number.

Empson makes visible a common but embarrassingly necessary problem: that of sussing out a poem's plain meaning. Teaching close reading to first-year undergraduates—who chose to study English at university, but who mostly do not like or trust poetry—has taught me that, ultimately, close reading starts with reading for meaning. My first-years have been taught, at school, quite correctly, that they won't get marks for describing what a poem is about. This has turned into a lack of interest in knowing what a poem might be describing. Unfortunately, if you don't have a supportable case about what is literally happening in a poem—who is speaking and to whom and where they are—no analytic gesture can ever tether itself meaningfully to anything.

But in this case, Empson's mathematical promise of understanding lures us into a false sense of security. We expect the rest of the reading to be this methodically graspable. The difficulty, however, is that Empson paces his close readings so that they're both too slow and too quick: long lists of finicky interpretative possibilities, to make us laugh, and rapid virtuoso triple-turns within a single sentence, to take us three interpretative strides away before we can blink. It's hard to know where the gap in the logic is Empson's, and where it is in fact your failure to follow him: because your attention span is too short, or

---

2. William Empson, *Some Versions of Pastoral*, ed. Seamus Perry (Oxford University Press, 2020), 62. All subsequent citations given in text.

you are too stupid. And often these ambiguities and leaps are encoded within, and inseparable from, lengthy acts of apparent meticulous pedantry. Thinking about the "they" that have "power to hurt," at the beginning of the poem, he unpacks the first four lines:

> They may *show*, while hiding the alternative, for the first couplet, the power to hurt or the determination not to hurt—cruelty or mercy, for the second, the strength due to chastity or to sensual experience, for either, a reckless or cautious will, and the desire for love or for control; all whether they are stealers of hearts or of public power. (64)

Here, again, pedantry is essential; it gives us an unwarranted sense of safety; *and* it gets us nowhere. Empson lays out the possibilities of the poem, methodically, in their various potential couplings. We can see them being laid out, rearranged on the table in front of us. It takes me quite a long time to realize that I don't understand the couplings at all. The tag "for the second" is attached to "the strength due to chastity," but the commas suggest that it could equally be attached to "cruelty or mercy"; the term "for either" probably means "either the first or the second couplet" but it could equally refer to any of the pairs that Empson has presented to us (cruelty/mercy, chastity/sensual experience, and so on). One has to work hard to keep the grammar and punctuation in order: so hard that I, at least, lose track of *where exactly* Empson is getting these various interpretations from (what, for instance, is Empson using as textual evidence for a "reckless will," in these first four lines?). The assured tone sweeps me onward before I really understand that I don't understand.

Empson gets away with it, though, because where he ends up is so seductive. The power of "They That Have Power" turns on his *global theorizing*: the final stage of close reading, in which the whole point of the exercise ought to become clear. What have we got from the literary text, in its busy involuted workings, which couldn't be reached any other way? The final paragraph of Empson's essay begins like this:

> The feeling that life is essentially inadequate to the human spirit, and yet that a good life must avoid saying so, is naturally at home with most versions of pastoral; in pastoral you take a limited life and pretend it is the full and normal one, and a suggestion that one must do this with all life, because the normal is itself limited, is easily put into the trick . . . (79)

This conclusion's been burned on my brain for years, since I first read it; it gave shape to some of the feelings in my first book, and has been an ethic by which

I've scrutinized my own decisions forever after. To put it in other words: if there's any such thing as the human spirit—and let's pretend for a moment that there is: a force that makes human beings uniquely brilliant, exasperating, ingenious, muddle-headed—then not even the best, richest life can accommodate everything that spirit longs for. Empson knew that being human is impossible. It involves wanting to be cuddled close, *and* somehow also wanting to be free and independent. It means wanting to slay the world's dragons, *and* somehow also spend your days studying the tiny patch you were born on. But even the very luckiest life makes us choose. (And most lives aren't the best: most lives are rushed, tragic, deprived.) *Nevertheless*—I think Empson is saying—to live a good life (grown-up, ethical, dignified), one must not complain about this. One must somehow accept life's limits with grace and humor—both its inevitable limits, and those exclusive to your own bad luck—even while a tiny part of you knows, very quietly, that so much in you remains unfulfilled. You must never stop accepting, and you must also never stop knowing. Maintaining this simultaneity has become key to my relationships and my political convictions. The accepting helps me survive the inevitable, agonizing smallness of any progress. The knowing helps me never stop fighting.

I'm placing significant ethical weight, I know, on a close reading of a Shakespeare poem: especially as it's not immediately clear to me how Empson reached that momentous conclusion in the first place. All this might be a rhetorical trick, which takes me in because it sounds authoritative. Somehow he's put two and two together and reached not four but the meaning of life: useful, perhaps, but also logically suspect. Could Empson have got here without involving Sonnet 94? Is the sonnet, and the different tunes he plays upon it, just a pretext for staging this bigger idea?

How you answer depends on what you think close reading is for, and what part you think the reader-of-a-close-reading plays in the process. My own founding assumption is not original: it's that the things we learn from poetry we can *only* learn from poetry, because it's a kind of knowledge which is part-informational, part-musical, part-visceral: form and phrasing and rhythm are as important as content. That's my line whenever I'm goaded to defend poetry. But equally: working with my first-year students has taught me that it's very hard to learn something you don't already sort of know. One class was outraged that Sylvia Plath's speaker in her poem "You're" calls her baby a "little loaf," because it seems dismissive to compare someone to bread when you could call them, say, a rose. Because I am older, though, I know that any person you love is: delicious with or without butter, miraculous as yeast, perfectly shaped, good-smelling, adorably compact regardless of dimensions, comically mundane, and one's staple diet. It takes years to know that love is mostly ridiculous, and anyone's baby is more loaf than rose. So then we might posit that we get out of poems only what we bring to them. Perhaps Empson already knew what he thought about life and the human spirit, before he started on Sonnet 94. And maybe close reading the poem gave him (and us) an occasion to know it all over again, because we cannot know important things just once: we have to learn them again and again, in different forms and textures.

But this is too simple. When my first-years were reading "You're," I reminded them that the internet calls a cat with tucked-up feet a loaf, and obviously nothing is more precious. Of course the students knew about cat loaves. Now the poem made sense. So this was less a case of what the students didn't know, so much as a case of what they *didn't know they were allowed to know when reading a poem*. By far the hardest part of my job is convincing students to bring the wily, sarcastic, irrational, cat-TikTok-watching parts of themselves to the poem in front of them: to let in their knowledge that life is illogical, babies look edible, and two opposing things can be true at the same time. And if Empson's reading of Sonnet 94 does nothing else, it captures some of these inelegant, confused, all-too-human feelings. For instance: the multidirectional sensation of impasse, when—like Shakespeare's speaker—we can't work out whether a person is good or bad, *and* whether we like or despise them for one, the other, or both, *and* whether we *should* like or despise them. In Sonnet 94, Shakespeare's speaker gathers all these contradictory possibilities and puts them side by side: enigmatic and unresolved, just like our feelings about such difficult people. Then he does what we often do when we're faced with unnerving characters: makes an authoritative, insistent statement to hide the fact that one really doesn't know what to think. "Lilies that fester smell far worse than weeds," sniffs the speaker. Empson helps us notice that this is just a rhetorical bluff to hide doubt, and he does this by mimicking Shakespeare's own ambivalent movements in his close reading. Like the speaker, Empson gathers the evidence: owners, lilies, stones, summer flowers. He shuffles it round, trying elements next to each other in different permutations (4,096 possibilities, he tells us). He thinks about what else the problem reminds him of: *Measure for Measure, Henry IV*. Then he sweeps forward, hard, to a haphazardly related conclusion—life is inadequate to the human spirit, et cetera—hoping for the best. In a sense, the doubtful relationship of the global theorizing to his close reading is precisely the part of the close reading that casts the most light on what's happening in Shakespeare's poem: a big statement in the face of irreconcilable doubt.

I'm increasingly inclined to read Empson's close reading as, itself, *about* close reading, and the wishful optimism that underpins it. The pastoral that he describes—"in pastoral you take a limited life and pretend it is the full and normal one"—maps pretty exactly onto what we try to do with close reading. We take the individual case and draw global conclusions from it. It's important, I think, that Empson calls this a "trick." It is a "preten[se]." But still: Empson's global theorizing holds us. They are beautiful. I wonder if Empson himself knows this, because the fundamental conclusion that he draws in his theorization of pastoral is, essentially, "don't ask too many questions": take something that seems limited, in which we can go thus farther but no further, and accept it as all we can reasonably hope for. This seems to me what he does in his close reading: coaxes us to simply accept the jumps of understanding he demands as their own version of pastoral. "The business of interpretation is obviously very complicated," Empson concludes, straight-faced.

19

Little Bit of Ivory

D. A. MILLER ON JANE AUSTEN

Stephanie Insley Hershinow

It's one of the coups of close reading: persuading your reader that something that seemed so trivial that they didn't notice it holds the secret to a global theory. D. A. Miller (1948–) is a master of such triumphs. He attended graduate school in the 1970s at Yale, where literary theory erupted onto the scene to supplant New Criticism. Across his career, Miller has contributed to narrative theory, New Historicism, and queer theory. He has also been one of criticism's most committed close readers. Here, under Hershinow's attentive eye, he queers that classic novelistic convention, the marriage plot, through the work of its most accomplished practitioner, Jane Austen, and through precise attention to something as insignificant as a toothpick. It turns out that the toothpick not only irritates the marriage plot, it offers a clue toward understanding Austen's greatest accomplishment: her Style (capital "S").—DS+JW

CLOSE READING takes something small and tries to turn it into something big. It can help us see a text in a new way, as if with the assistance of a magnifying glass or a microscope. Of course, this shift in scale is also at the heart of a common critique lodged against close reading: that it *over*reads, making mountains out of molehills. In zooming in ever closer to the text, close reading may seem to warp, rather than enhance, our perspective. Its claims for the significance of small things are sometimes convincing, and sometimes not.

In this chapter, I focus on D. A. Miller's ten-page reading of a short scene in Jane Austen's *Sense and Sensibility* (1811) in his book *Jane Austen, or the Secret of Style* (2003). The first close reading in Miller's book, this reading isolates a passage in the novel when the man we'll later identify as Robert Ferrars buys a toothpick case (containing, as was common then, a tiny, reusable, ivory toothpick). He is standing in a jewelry shop, halting the progress of the novel's two heroines, Elinor and Marianne Dashwood. Ferrars is a minor character (the rarely seen brother of a love interest) and the scene in the jewelry shop does little to advance Austen's plot. It is an episode many readers of the novel, even diehard fans, may not remember. But by lingering over this passage, Miller zooms in, focusing on a tiny thing of seemingly no significance: a short episode, a minor character, a toothpick. Yet, Miller uses the scene to draw our attention to the way Austen handles an issue of indisputable centrality to her novel: the institution of marriage and its pull on even those who want nothing to do with it.

Miller's reading is all about the movement between noticing (seeing details and deciding which are significant) and global theorizing (building from those significant details answers to bigger questions). Before I zoom back out to consider Miller's global theorizing, let us first get some sense of the kinds of things Miller notices. He begins by quoting the passage from the novel in full; it takes up just over a page of his book. I'll quote much less, but with an aim—setting the scene for my reading of Miller—of distilling even further what Miller wants us to see. Elinor and Marianne have entered a jewelry shop in London to have some of their mother's jewels placed into new settings. Waiting in line for an attendant, they observe another shopper ahead of them. The narrator, most closely describing Elinor's reaction, suggests that Elinor expects the man will politely allow the ladies to go first. He does not.

> He was giving orders for a toothpick-case for himself, and till its size, shape, and ornaments were determined, all of which, after examining and debating for a quarter of an hour over every toothpick-case in the shop, were finally arranged by his own inventive fancy, he had no leisure to bestow any other attention on the two ladies, than what was comprised in three or four very broad stares; a kind of notice which served to imprint on Elinor the remembrance of a person and face, of strong, natural, sterling insignificance, though adorned in the first style of fashion.[1]

---

1. Qtd. in D. A. Miller, *Jane Austen, or the Secret of Style* (Princeton University Press, 2003), 10. All subsequent citations given in text.

With one long, sinuous sentence, the narrator takes the reader from a more or less straightforward description of Robert's actions ("He was giving orders"), to an ironic assessment of his character ("he had no leisure to bestow"), to insight into what's going on inside Elinor's mind as she watches him ("to imprint on Elinor the remembrance of..."). After this sentence, the scene goes on briefly. We see Elinor's complex negative feelings about the stranger ("contempt and resentment") and Marianne's preoccupation with her own thoughts, until the stranger completes his errand and the women can make their way to the counter.

Miller begins by telling us about the significance of jewelry elsewhere in Austen's work. Rings, pendants, brooches, and so on are all "ubiquitous" in Austen's novels, he tells us, and we can observe a pattern so strong as to constitute a rule: jewelry "must always be *given* to the wearer, and given *only* by a relative or lover, in token of union through marriage or common blood" (11). That is, jewelry *means* "family and marriage" in Austen. If we understand this, we can be all the more struck by Robert's deviation, for he poses the sole exception in Austen's work (according to Miller) to this jewelry-means-family rule. This is Miller's explanation for why this detail is significant. The toothpick case matters not because it follows a pattern but because it *breaks* the pattern. As readers, we benefit here from Miller's long and affectionate familiarity with Austen's novels. He tells us in the introduction to this book that he's read her work since he was a child; here, we see that deep knowledge pay off.

A toothpick is so very personal, something that won't be shared or given away; it won't form an attachment or a relationship with another character the way those other exchanges of jewelry will—the way, for example, Robert's brother will attempt to cement the bond with his lover by giving her a ring containing a lock of his hair (a common love token in the Regency period). In the passage from *Sense and Sensibility*, Miller's close reading goes on to explain, the toothpick case's status outside of the jewelry economy of family and marriage renders it in some sense empty, devoid of the usual significance that jewelry holds. It's meaningless. And, in the next move of Miller's reading, which we can identify as local claiming, he shows us how this quality of emptiness extends to the case's possessor. Elinor bitterly judges Robert to be of "sterling insignificance" as well—not a villain or even a fool, but simply worthless. In Miller's words, a "human toothpick case" (14).

Without explicitly naming it, Miller turns to a question raised by this assessment of Robert: Why does Elinor have such a strong reaction to being made to wait in line? We don't otherwise get the impression that she's entitled or impatient. Miller's reading helps to explain this; Robert bothers Elinor not only because he won't step aside for her but also because, in neglecting to do so, he seems to call into question the whole system of courtship, the social expectations of men's attention to (and intentions for) women. Miller identifies Robert Ferrars as queer; or, as he puts it, as "what might almost be a gay man" (9). Miller's reading isn't just some "gotcha," an attempt to out gay characters in novels written when it was not at all common to name them as such. This kind of recovery work can be valid and certainly common, but it's not what Miller's doing here. Rather, he thinks of Robert's brief intrusion into the novel on an almost allegorical level. That is, Robert's role in this scene is less to represent gay men than to represent an obstacle in the path of courtship in a society where eligible women outnumber eligible men.

Robert gets in the heroines' way. He is immune to their charms. The women, having fallen in social status after their father's death, have been taken to London to find husbands—and Robert makes clear that he has no interest in being the man for the job. This scene is the opposite of the romantic comedy meet-cute in which two characters have a first encounter where sparks fly. The meeting with Robert is instead a serendipitous encounter that goes utterly nowhere. For Miller, the screeching halt Robert brings to the plot's forward movement doesn't just tell us about his character, it also suggests that Austen (who never married despite opportunities to do so) is herself interested in the ways courtship and marriage might be slowed down, thwarted, and avoided. This may come as a surprise to many Austen readers, who are used to associating her with the celebration of heterosexual love and marriage, but that's the power of this minor detail: it forces us to rethink some bigger assumptions we have about how this novel works—and how all of Austen's novels work. This is the moment when Miller pulls it all together, from noticing the toothpick case, through recognizing its local significance as a sign of Robert's emptiness, to offering a global theory of Austen's novels. It's a fun journey, taking us from the toothpick to the dissolution of marriage as an institution.

Miller will take his global theorizing in this reading one step further. His reading of *Sense and Sensibility*—and all of his readings in this book—is grounded in his understanding of what he calls Austen Style: not just a lowercase style that might characterize the way she writes her novels but an uppercase Style that captures her achievement of a transcendent narratorial voice that seems to come from nowhere. Miller sees this point of view as central to Austen's novels and as a powerful loftiness that readers may even aspire to themselves. What does this have to do with Robert? In the final move of Miller's reading of the jewelry store scene, he sees our "human toothpick case" personifying insignificance ... on purpose. That is, Robert Ferrars, the queer interloper in Austen's marriage plot, performs his stylishness (what Elinor calls "the first style of fashion") in such a conspicuous way that he stands not only *against* heterosexuality but also *for* aestheticism, for art itself. His "insignificance" is evidence of his overcoming everyday particularity and becoming a creature of Style. In this, he comes closer than any other character in the novel to its narrator, who likewise surpasses social expectations, defying participation in the social order altogether. For Miller, the voice of Austen's third-person narrator is disembodied, free of all of the messiness that comes with being a person in the world. This gives the narrator an aspirational power the reader is drawn to, mesmerized by. And while this may be true for any reader of Austen, Miller suggests that it is particularly true for queer readers, those who have been made to feel shame for the particularities of their own identities and desires. Reading Austen as a young gay boy, Miller tells us, made him notice her Style in a different way—made him a better reader of Austen. It also helped him notice a minor character like Robert Ferrars.

By drawing our attention to small things and their big implications, Miller also slyly comments on Jane Austen's reputation for triviality. She is sometimes accused of creating fictional worlds that are too slight, too narrow, too inconsequential. She is self-aware about this. In one letter to her nephew, she draws an analogy between her realist fiction and the work of the miniature artist: her novels are akin to a "little bit (two inches wide) of ivory on which I work with so fine a brush, as produces little effect after much labour." (Watercolor artists, especially, in this period would sometimes paint on small bound sheets of ivory that could be erased, something like a reusable sketchbook.) There's self-deprecation in this description, but also an implicit boast. Look how much, she seems to say, I can do with so little.

To make so much with so little. This is the aim of Miller's reading. And what a perfect coincidence that Ferrars is looking at a little bit of ivory when Austen also famously likens her work to a small piece of ivory! This is the kind of connection between text and author that Miller loves—so much so that these thematic and conceptual rhymes across text and time form something of a refrain across his work.[2] We might consider this another way of explaining why *this* particular detail; it's the kind of detail Miller is drawn to as a critic, and he

---

2. For a theorization of how the centering of such connections—often to Miller's own life experiences—affects how close reading works in his writing, see Frances Ferguson, "Now It's Personal: D. A. Miller and Too-Close Reading," *Critical Inquiry* 41, no. 3 (2015): 521–40.

has no interest in making the choice of detail upon which to hang a close reading into an exercise in objectivity.

In the hands of another reader, this connection—ivory to ivory, like the keys pressed to play an octave on the pianoforte—might open out to a consideration of where that ivory comes from, that is, to a reading of Austen's embeddedness in a culture of empire. A strong and compelling vein of criticism on Jane Austen's work seeks to contextualize it in its historical moment; this work shows how her representation of intimate, domestic life is embedded in historical forces much larger than the drawing room: the Napoleonic Wars, the violent oppressions of an expanding British Empire, the brutalities of the transatlantic slave trade. This work is powerful and important, but Miller isn't usually that kind of reader. His work likewise opens Austen up to consider big questions, but his method differs from that of the contextualizing critics. Indeed, he calls his book an "implicit polemic [against] a historicist tradition of understanding Austen" (107–8).

In its place, he sees in Ferrars's "little bit of ivory" a grenade that Austen lobs to blow up her own marriage plot. Does it matter that (spoiler) all three of these characters—Robert, Elinor, Marianne—are married by the novel's final pages? No. Or, not as much as we might expect. It is enough (or, enough for now) to make marriage wait its turn in line. We call this kind of theoretical unraveling of the text "queer theory," and Miller insists that the work of close reading is necessary to achieving these insights because they depend on details smuggled into works that can otherwise seem to uphold more conventional values and to tell more conventional stories. While he chooses close reading as his method, Miller (himself adept both with theory and with close reading) rejects the binary that suggests that one is big and important, the other small and slight. Rather, he suggests, close reading is the gateway to thinking through bigger questions.

I have focused my own attention on Miller's global theorizing in his close reading of this scene, specifically how his close reading makes possible a queer (or, as he puts it, "unheterosexual") reading of Austen's marriage plot. Elsewhere in the book, Miller considers the status of close reading in literary studies. In the final chapter of *Jane Austen, or The Secret of Style*, D. A. Miller envisions a future of literary study in which close reading has fallen out of fashion. In explaining how close reading works, the essays collected in the present volume aim instead to make the practice even more mainstream. With apologies to Miller, close reading isn't, and shouldn't be, the fusty peccadillo of the elbow-patched elite. It's at the center of the work all of us do as critics. And, unlike an ivory toothpick, it's made to be shared.

20

Dirty Projectors

SIANNE NGAI ON ALFRED HITCHCOCK

Kimberly Quiogue Andrews

Aesthetics, in philosophy, is the study of art. Immanuel Kant is the foundational philosopher for modern aesthetics; since his Critique of Judgment *(1790), two categories have dominated the study of art: the beautiful and the sublime. Sianne Ngai (1971–)—one of the greatest aestheticians of the twenty-first century—introduced "our aesthetic categories": the cute, the interesting, and the zany. She has also established the aesthetic importance of envy, irritation, and, as Andrews demonstrates here, anxiety. Andrews is a connoisseur of Ngai's vertiginous leaps. Under Andrews's guidance, we witness how to bring together something we notice in the work of a theorist (here Freud) with patterns we notice locally and regionally in a text (Alfred Hitchcock's* Vertigo*) and globally across other texts, as well (Martin Heidegger's* Being and Time, *Herman Mellville's* Pierre*), to theorize anew about a familiar concept (anxiety). This is close reading at its most audacious, difficult, risky—and thrilling.—DS + JW*

WHEN WE talk about "literature" and "feelings" in the same breath, we're usually talking about an *effect*: that is, the way that stories or poems or plays or films make us feel. One of the major *effects* of literature, in other words, is to *affect* us emotionally. But there's another meaning to that latter word which has become increasingly important in literary studies in the twenty-first century: *affect* as a noun rather than a verb, one that means, roughly, the way that we *demonstrate* emotions. One's affect isn't just how they're feeling, but rather how they show that feeling outwardly, or what behaviors that feeling causes. In the area of literary studies often termed "affect theory," feelings are paramount: but not your feelings as a reader. Instead, this form of criticism analyzes the way texts create emotional states of being on the page or stage or screen. It looks very closely, in other words, at how texts communicate feelings *to* us, and in the process, how they create imagistic or narrative worlds that actively theorize these states of being. One of the foundational critics in this area of study is Sianne Ngai, and in this chapter, we'll take a look at how Ngai close reads some wildly different texts to produce a theory of an emotion—in this case, anxiety—grounded in aesthetic evidence.

Ngai is a notoriously difficult writer to parse. Part of the reason for this is that she is, at heart, a dialectician: a specialist in pointing out the play of opposites, and the way in which our notions of causality are often pointed in precisely the wrong direction. "Doing dialectics" works in many different ways—critics all have their own methods for dealing with seeming paradoxes in literature and art—but for our purposes here, Ngai's method really crashes together the noticing and global theorizing bits of this book's framework. In other words, she uses idiosyncratic constellations of quite small textual details to make very big claims about very abstract concepts. This isn't to say that she skips thinking about texts locally (focusing in on individual parts) or regionally (how those parts belong to a whole). Rather, it's to say that the special quality of Ngai's way of close reading is how she extrapolates big definitions for concepts out of what seems like just a few moments in her chosen texts. So even if the idea of doing something like "revising our entire conception of an emotion" seems well outside what you're able to do right now, pay attention to this chapter to get a sense of just how far noticing, scaled up by this book's steps, can take you.

In "Moody Subjects/Projectile Objects: Anxiety and Intellectual Displacement in Hitchcock, Heidegger, and Melville," an article from 2001 that would later be reprinted as one of the chapters in her 2005 book *Ugly Feelings*, Ngai shows us that what we think of as a *consequence* of anxiety (reductively, a disordered sense of spacetime) is actually a cause (in her words, that it's "a structural effect of spatialization in general").[1] We'll see a little more clearly what this means below, but for now, we can think of it this way: something that's a

---

1. Sianne Ngai, "Moody Subjects/Projectile Objects: Anxiety and Intellectual Displacement in Hitchcock, Heidegger, and Melville," *Qui Parle* 12, no. 2 (Spring/Summer 2001): 18. All subsequent citations given in text.

threat to you is something that you perceive to be outside of yourself. Your recognition of something "over there" that's slowly coming toward you is what causes anxiety. If you think that the future is a looming monster, that's not because you're anxious: you're anxious *because of the very distance between you and the future*. Now, if this sounds like it belongs more in the realm of psychoanalysis than literary studies, that's because it does. Ngai in fact begins her article not with a close reading of any of the figures in the article's title, but with an excursus on Sigmund Freud. Freud's conception of anxiety as having a "projective" quality to it is often read as temporal, as a question of "[w]hen will X happen?" (17). Certainly, this will sound accurate to anyone who has experienced the sharp worry about the future I just described. But Ngai points out that to *project* something is just as much a spatial metaphor as a temporal one, and that this spatial quality of anxiety is much less remarked upon. This moment is the article's inaugural scene of *noticing*.

She attaches this brief analysis of a linguistic duality in a psychoanalytic text to a broad swath of literature by literalizing it: she points out that in Alfred Hitchcock's *Vertigo*, Martin Heidegger's *Being and Time*, and Herman Melville's *Pierre* (three works in three very different genres!), anxiety is front and center as an emotion, and stuff is constantly getting thrown or hurled. This conjunction neatly underscores her claim about the spatial quality of anxious projection, but that argument doesn't really have stakes: that is, it's not yet clear *why it matters* that anxiety can manifest as a spatial phenomenon as well as a temporal one. Ngai's attempt to solve this problem is where her noticing stretches hugely—she leaps into the realm of *global theorizing* by yoking together the aforementioned acts of noticing with the claim that in Western psychoanalytic culture, anxiety has historically been coded as both gendered (male) and as something that attaches in particular to a knowledge-seeking subject. Thus, anxiety is something that is experienced by knowledge-seeking men, and in fact becomes the "male intellectual's signature affect or sensibility" (19). You might feel yourself resisting this claim, as we now tend to think of anxiety as being a feminine-coded emotion (alongside its weaker, less existential subsidiaries: worrying, fretting, fussing). But it's important to remember that Ngai is interested in a relatively specific, Freudian conception of anxiety as that of an originary *fear* (of castration) that "plays a privileged role in the process of gendered ego-formation" (19). What Ngai is pointing out is that in the texts she's analyzing, you get a particularly clear spatial rendering of this "gendered ego-formation"—you get a depiction, in other words, that is potentially richer than that of psychoanalytic writing alone.

For our purposes, Ngai's close reading of Hitchcock's and Melville's anxious male protagonists are the most relevant here, as they demonstrate how to do psychoanalytic criticism on characters without, as it were, psychoanalyzing characters. And this is the tricky bit about reading characters' feelings: they have none beyond the page. It's also not useful, absent a lot of biographical information, to take guesses at the psychological state of authors as a way of interpreting their work. So where does that leave a critic who is interested in something like what Freud famously termed "the unconscious"? What Ngai does brilliantly is something that looks like psychoanalyzing *the text itself*. This is hard to do, so it will be worth taking a long look at how it happens. In *Ugly Feelings*, she characterizes her own method as analyzing "tone," or "a literary or cultural artifact's . . . global or organizing affect, its general disposition or orientation toward its audience and the world" (28). This is a question of form (note the word "organizing"), and as such it is susceptible to close reading. Let's see how she does it.

In both *Vertigo* (a film), and *Pierre* (a novel), the main characters (Scottie and Pierre, respectively) find themselves having dreams or fantasies that involve them falling through space. Scottie's a detective, and he has a nightmare in which he falls into an open grave; Pierre is a writer experiencing writer's block, and he has a semiconscious fantasy of being hurled off the side of a mountain. So far so boring, you might think to yourself: falling is perhaps one of the most common dream motifs we have. And *Vertigo* is literally about the main character's fear of heights! But rather than saying that these falling dreams are simply an allegory for the dreamers' anxiety, Ngai *begins* with that commonplace as a premise and effectively asks: What does the specific rendering of this motif in each text tell us about the nature of anxiety that we might otherwise not see? And here's where another important bit of noticing takes place: she notices that something odd happens in these characters' reveries. In particular, the male characters who are falling are depicted in a way that, paradoxically, "rescue[s]" them from a "potential absorption in sites of a-significance or negativity" (51) often coded as feminine.

Let's unpack that a bit. In her analysis of *Vertigo*, Ngai moves quickly from setting the scene to regional argumentation: "Scottie's dream stages his identification with 'Madeleine''s trajectory as hurled object when it shows him walking in a cemetery and peering into an empty grave . . . an exact reenactment of the phony dream 'Madeleine' describes to him as part of the possession hoax" (29). So we can see how the dream sequence serves to mash together two separate plot moments, demonstrating visually what Scottie is anxious *about* (not death, as it turns out, but rather the two women at the center of the plot). But then Ngai does a dialectical turnaround, abstracting further while still relying on concrete detail: we think the dream is about falling, but in fact, what the film does is to give us "Scottie's initial look at this emptiness" (the grave) and then immediately establish "the aversive turning of his gaze, not showing us the grave's interior . . . but abruptly cutting to a highly defamiliarized, mask-like close-up of the gazer's face, a shot that in turn establishes Scottie as both witness *and* object of his own 'projection'" (30). So what should be a falling-into-nothingness winds up being a shot of the male protagonist's head, nearly filling the screen, negating the nothingness that is the supposed subject of the anxiety in the first place. You can see here, also, the way in which Ngai is using the formal units of film—the edited shot, the cutaway, the special effect—in the same way that we might use a scene in a story, or a line of a poem. In this case, the sudden imposition of an image of Scottie's face *feels* significant, but it's not entirely clear why, which is why Ngai is explaining it to us. (If you look this scene up on YouTube, you'll see what I mean.) Despite the terror of the nightmare, what this weird shot shows us is actually Scottie retaining the ability to "turn away" from nothingness (he's facing us, not the grave)—something the female characters who fall to their deaths in the movie do not get to do.

What's happening here is a fundamental quality of close reading: basically, a whole pile of "noticings," both within and between scenes of the "text," come together to form a reading of the film that is pressed into the service of a global theory of affect. What that theory says, to radically oversimplify, is that anxiety dreams are more complicated than they first appear. First, Ngai has to notice something like a pattern in the film, which she does by noticing all the falling and throwing and "projecting" in space. Then, she zooms in on one scene and shows us how the instance of falling in that scene is linked to other important moments in the film (in this case Madeleine's hoax). Then, she notices the weirdness of the scene *itself*: how its imagery turns what should be nothingness into something. Finally, she has to zoom back out a bit to tell us about the significance of the something (Scottie's face), linking it to her thesis that anxiety in literature is *spatially rather than temporally depicted*, that it's *gendered*, and that it is linked to *knowledge-seeking*. She does this without ever musing about what might be going on in Scottie's head, or in Hitchcock's, or in yours. Instead, she shows us that the imagery of the scene itself "reconstitut[es] the male subject as thrown projection" (30).[2] In doing so, she argues, it refigures our conception of anxiety as one that does not so much project itself onto things as it does *emerge* from the very fact of spatial movement, and further, that by "reconstituting the male subject," it actually grants that subject greater agency in the world of the film. Scottie, in other words, gains control of his space at the exact moment when we expect him to *lose it*, and in doing so, he gains control of his life as a man (he figures out the female duplicity at the heart of the film, and he also gets over his fear of heights. Good job, Scottie!).

These big leaps in thought take a lot of practice. They're almost poetic: how, Ngai seems to be asking, can I possibly yoke together these motifs of throwing or falling, turning away from nothingness, masculinity, and knowledge quests into one big theory about emotion? Ultimately, her readings depend somewhat upon already knowing what to look for—she's interested in the problematics of gender in texts more broadly, and she's also read an enormous amount of psychoanalytic theory—but once she's found details that are suggestive within the frameworks she has in mind, she concretely shows us how the transformations and layerings of those details build to form an affective "tone" that would otherwise be very hard to describe. In close reading *Vertigo*, she stacks images of projectiles (Scottie imagining tossing off a corset, dialogue about throwing women away, women literally being tossed out of windows) and shows that, in the dream sequence we just looked at, there's a culminating reversal in which the male protagonist inhabits "the throw" in order to claim for himself the anxiety-making movement as a redemptive arc (literal and metaphorical) of self-discovery.

This is how you read textual details for psychological significance without attributing an interiority to characters that isn't there. And if your theory is significant enough, you'll see versions of it elsewhere, even in incongruous-seeming places: Ngai reinforces her point in this long article by looking at other texts that are far removed from *Vertigo* in both historical time and in genre, but shows that a similar gender/throwing thing is happening there, too.[3] In Ngai's reading of

---

2. This is, admittedly, a weird construction. Why not just say "thrown object"? In true Freudian fashion, Ngai seems to want us to trip over this double entendre a bit, to realize that "projection" here means not only a literal object projected but also a psychological projection.

3. A quick note about claim significance: you'll notice that Ngai's claim about spatiality, gender, and thrown objects is very *specific*. This is important! You can make all kinds of claims that would apply to a huge range of texts ("older women become invisible") but if they're too general, they won't be significant—they'll just be kind of obvious.

Herman Melville's *Pierre*, she finds a nearly identical reclamation of agency in a projection away from nothingness, and a male character who is similarly worried about his own intellectual exploits as well as his relationships with women. In Melville's novel, things aren't thrown around quite as much as they are in *Vertigo*—so Ngai focuses initially on the vertiginous feelings that Pierre undergoes while trying to navigate both writer's block and a love triangle. Her most extended site of close reading, however, still focuses on a scene in the novel where (potential) projectiles do actually come into play.

Pierre is one of the strangest novels by a man known for writing strange novels, so Ngai has to do a fair bit of scene setting via long block quotations to orient the reader: Pierre, overcome with existentialist angst, throws himself into the space under a rocky overhang, and in a melodramatic soliloquy, beseeches the rock to fall upon him. It doesn't, but even here Ngai manages to find the description telling: in inserting himself into what was a void, Pierre "render[s] *himself* the 'object' of the substance's gravitational force" (46). Much like Scottie's face suddenly looming before us when he's supposed to be looking into an abyss, Ngai sees in this scene Melville rejigging Pierre's experience of anxiety to be an agency-*granting* emotion. This "reconceptualization" (47) of anxious affect intensifies later in the novel when Pierre has a vision of himself as a stone giant hurled off the side of a mountain. He falls, but then he gets back up and flings himself back at the "paternal mass" (49, witness the deliberate Freudian invocation), regaining control of his own trajectory.

In stringing together moments of action that externalize affective intensities, Ngai shows us how films and novels take on a particular "tone" that can encode very surprising and very specific theories of emotion. Ngai's close readings never make conjectures about the nuances of how anyone is feeling at a given moment, neither on the part of the text nor the part of the reader. Instead, the "spatialized renderings" (50) of anxiety in plot and imagery—the patterned and idiosyncratic stuff that literary critics are trained to *notice*—are used to build a type of *global theory* of anxiety that can respond to specific sociocultural circumstances. By establishing at the outset, via a slew of examples ranging from Freud to Kierkegaard to twentieth-century analysts of nineteenth-century culture, that anxiety attaches to masculinity in consequential ways, Ngai lays a foundation for her close readings that does not *valorize* the Freudian idea that only men can be truly anxious because only men bear the original scar of castration fear, but rather demonstrates how that type of psychoanalytic sexism mutates into fascinating and troubling literary form. In some ways, this type of literary analysis is related to standard ideology critique: it shows how texts encode political valence in the warp and weft of their formal fabric. In the case of affect studies, this extends into the very emotions that we often think of as being perhaps the most genuine things about us. As it turns out, even our most ordinary feelings have form, and those forms are politically entangled. But this doesn't mean we should throw our intellectual aspirations out the window (as it were). Far from it! Ngai's layered noticing shows us just how generative it can be to look for feelings in unexpected places, and when we participate in that art of careful attention, we can even dream, like Pierre, of hurling ourselves upright again.

21

The Art of Both-And

JAHAN RAMAZANI ON DALJIT NAGRA

Christopher Spaide

For poetry scholar Jahan Ramazani (1960–), the global *in global theorizing is more than figurative. By* global theorizing, *we mean expanding one's analysis beyond the text at hand to encompass an oeuvre or genre or period or geography. All these are in play for Ramazani, though geography is maybe especially salient: postcolonial theorists foreground how imperialism and colonialism shape culture, and vice versa. Traditionally, global theorizing builds inductively from local claiming and regional argumentation—and Ramazani is gifted at this—but Spaide brings us to a tricky inversion. Ramazani begins with sweeping theories and applies them to a Daljit Nagra's "A Black History of the English-Speaking Peoples." It's a risky endeavor. You don't want to lose the specificity of the poem by checking boxes: yes, the poem fits the theory in this way; no, not in this way. You must allow the poem to stand in its specificity and for the theories to illuminate the uniqueness of the poem. Under Ramazani's thoughtful gaze, we begin to see the histories of the world and of poetry to which Nagra responds. We see whom Nagra is borrowing from, arguing with, revising, rejecting, and why those interventions matter, how they form a singular maximalist poetic missive to modernism, and to us.—DS + JW*

YOU'RE DOING a close reading of a poem: How close are we talking? Do you want something *close* close, an extreme magnification putting your poem's ittybittiest details into sharp relief? A reading sensitive to unassuming words and unspoken thoughts, precisely timed pauses and punctuation marks, inflections and innuendoes just this side of subliminal? Or would you prefer the opposite: a reading with sweep, distance, perspective, comprehensiveness—virtues, paradoxically, not of closeness but of standing far back? Is what's "close" about your reading its attention to histories and geographies, systems and interconnections, a contextual universe too vast to ever grasp in full? If you had to choose: Do you want the little things, or the big picture? Sure, I'm doing that familiar trick, reducing a vast field of possibilities to two mutually exclusive choices. (Red pill or blue pill? Go big or go home? Would you rather fight a horse-sized duck or one hundred duck-sized horses?) But at least I'm giving you a choice. Robert Frost, the American poet laureate of pessimism, once wrote a short poem about humans' inability to look any farther or any closer than an unenlightening middle distance. He titled it "Neither Out Far Nor In Deep": not an either-or but a neither-nor.

Want a close reader practiced in the art of both-and, whose bifocal readings can switch, in a moment's reorientation, between looking out far and looking in deep? Try Jahan Ramazani. Throughout a career of looking out farther and farther, from his early studies of single authors and genres to his later mappings of poetry's traversals across media and geographies, Ramazani's chief method has remained the same: the closest of close readings of individual poems, seen in all their irreducible multidimensionality. A critic of great, long, taxonomizing lists, Ramazani relishes listing the countless qualities that make poetry *poetry*: its "physical, musical, visual, sensual, semantic, sonic, individual, intersubjective, and other dimensions," or its "compression, metaphoric density, self-reflexivity, sonic self-awareness, visual form, and other shifting features."[1] Doing justice to even a handful of those qualities, turning over multifaceted lines and noticing how variously their verbal surfaces catch the light, a Ramazani reading makes any poem under consideration appear unprecedentedly and unrepeatably distinct. But his reading's value never ends there, with close reading for close reading's sake. As Ramazani has pushed poetry to the fore of postcolonial, transnational, and global studies, he has repeatedly proven that a single poem, sensitively read, can test and contest the most totalizing theoretical models. He looks out far to look in deep, in deep to look out far, each look lending perspective or contrast to the next.

For the respective virtues, as well as the compatibility, of looking out far and looking in deep, let's consider Ramazani's book chapter "Modernist

---

1. Jahan Ramazani, *Poetry and Its Others: News, Prayer, Song, and the Dialogue of Genres* (University of Chicago Press, 2013), 7, 15.

Inflections, Postcolonial Directions."[2] Its buoyantly rhyming title belies a hugely ambitious undertaking, which Ramazani summarizes in three questions: "How does postcolonial poetry in particular converge with and diverge from modernism? How do postcolonial poems understand their relation to modernism? And what literary-historical models are most productive in mapping their relationship?" (102). If you're new to questions like these, Ramazani makes it easy to play catch-up: his first endnote provides working definitions of his two "endlessly debated" keywords, *postcolonial* ("typically ascribed to imaginative works written in the shadow and aftermath of Western colonialism") and *modernist* ("usually understood as innovative writing developed in early-twentieth-century Europe and America") (276). If you're the least bit familiar with these questions, you know that Ramazani has crowded enormous helpings of theory and literature—several disciplines, over a century of writing, an atlas-wide expanse of poetry—onto a tiny scholarly plate. You could study postcolonial poetry or modernism for a lifetime and never exhaust either. How could anyone dream of "mapping their relationship" in a single book chapter?

Ramazani does it with three close readings. His chapter's halves model two opposing but compatible approaches, which he characterizes in photographic terms: first a "close-up poetry zoom" on "self-theorizing poems," then a "wide-angle conceptual lens" taking in "global analytic models" (108, 102). In his chapter's first half, Ramazani conducts a close-up zoom on two postcolonial poems that speculate on their relation to modernism: "This is not a riot policeman" by the South African Jewish poet Karen Press, which riffs on the representational switcheroos of the Belgian surrealist artist René Magritte (such as a painting of an apple titled "This is not an apple"), and "Quest" by the Jamaican poet Lorna Goodison, a preadolescent reminiscence of first listening to T. S. Eliot's "The Journey of the Magi" in a Caribbean classroom. Both readings get as close as close can be: Ramazani dwells for a paragraph on the complications of Press's one-word opening line "Look:," and listens in to the music and the diction of Goodison's "steplike, variable trimeter tercets," "seamlessly incorporating Eliotic diction, Jamaican Creole, and other ingredients" (106–7).

---

2. "Modernist Inflections, Postcolonial Directions" first appeared in *A History of Modernist Poetry*, eds. Alex Davis and Lee M. Jenkins (Cambridge University Press, 2015), 459–78; Ramazani incorporated the chapter, lightly revised, in his *Poetry in a Global Age* (University of Chicago Press, 2020), 101–16, 276–79. I quote from the revised version; all subsequent citations given in text.

And both readings end by standing back, taking that late, daring step in a close reading that this book calls *global theorizing*. From the sturdy, charted ground of the local—a text, its contexts and intertexts, a crisscrossing of angles taking everything in—these readings extrapolate findings on modernism, postcolonialism, and their tracery of interrelations. Out of a single poem, they create something portable: a general claim whose variables can be filled, algebra-like, with a world of other examples and counterexamples.

So looking in deep can lead to looking out far: What about the inverse? How might "a wide-angle conceptual lens"—a panoramic survey of theories of modernity, modernism, and postcolonialism, offering nothing short of full-scale accounts of history, empire, the workings of the modern world—capture something as intricate and idiosyncratic as a poem? Ramazani models that comprehensive looking in his chapter's second half, which introduces four theoretical models for the relation between modernism and postcolonialism, then concentrates all that scholarship on a single extravagant frame-breaking poem: "A Black History of the English-Speaking Peoples" (2011), by the Punjabi British (or Black British) poet Daljit Nagra.[3] You could call what Ramazani is doing global theorizing in reverse, a drastic zooming-in from stratospheric generalities to grounded textual particulars. You could think of it as testing out a theory with a text, an exercise that can tell you plenty about both: the range and flexibility of the former, the conventionality and deviations of the latter. But you could also worry that it's a risky maneuver, even the antithesis of what we're told close reading is for. Indiscriminately apply a one-size-fits-all theory, the worry goes, and all texts end up looking the same. (Carelessly applying theory is like carelessly applying sunscreen: what should be a delicate and thorough act of care turns into something clumsy, imbalanced, ickily slick.) Close reading poetry is often a case of "reading for difference," in Helen Vendler's phrase: not reading poems, plural, for what they share (themes, genres, rhetorical approaches, theoretical consistency) but reading for the aesthetic distinction, singular, of each poem, each stanza, each matchless line.[4] So if we're looking for differences, what's the use in starting out by keeping your distance, thinking in the blurry terms of generalizations

---

3. In Great Britain, the racial and political label "Black" has historically included nonwhite Britons of African, Caribbean, and South Asian descent; Nagra claims it here and in several other poems.

4. See Helen Vendler, "Shakespeare's Sonnets: Reading for Difference," *Bulletin of the American Academy of Arts and Sciences* 47, no. 6 (March 1994): 33–50.

and aggregates? What could be further from attentively reading a text, in all its letter-precise granularity?

In his reading of Nagra, Ramazani exemplifies three tactics for incorporating theory into a close reading, avoiding apparent risks and reaping the distinctive rewards. His first tactic is never to test only one theoretical model, presented without counter-arguments or alternatives. Instead he surveys the range of scholarship on his big theoretical question—what's modernism's relation to postcolonialism?—and draws out several conflicting models, which he brings into dialogue within the controlled environment of Nagra's poem. In a cool two thousand words, Ramazani cites several syllabuses' worth of theorists (Gayatri Chakravorty Spivak, Kwame Anthony Appiah, Fredric Jameson, Arjun Appadurai) and artists and authors (from Pablo Picasso and Langston Hughes to Press and Goodison). While he takes care to note variations, disputes, and internal contradictions, he also realizes the necessity of reduction; midway through a close reading is no time to strike up a lecture series. Miniaturizing the field to flashcard proportions, Ramazani narrows down four models for the relation between modernism and postcolonialism:

1. diffusionism—modernist innovations begin in European metropolises and spread to postcolonial peripheries;
2. resistance—in Salman Rushdie's words, "the Empire writes back to the Centre," struggling against colonial impositions like Western modernism (109);
3. a singular modernity—modernism and postcolonialism alike respond to capitalist modernity, whose structures manifest differently in the global North and South; and
4. alternative modernities and modernisms—different cultures make modernism their own, whether through "cultural appropriation, indigenization, vernacularization, creolization, or hybridization" (111).

The diffusionist model moves from the center outward; the resistance model, from the peripheries inward. A singular modernity homogenizes; alternative modernisms diversify. Are they overly simplistic, these one-sentence reductions, with their mathematical clarity and neat symmetries? For a discussion section or research paper for your postcolonial theory seminar, no question. But for a many-angled close reading of one multidimensional poem, they're just right. Miniaturized and flattened, sure, but also easy to deploy and manipulate, like the tools in a Swiss Army knife.

Ramazani's second tactic is to grant as much authority to his chosen text as to any theory. If a single captivating line of a poem resists the most enduring theoretical model, that's an occasion not only to reread the poem but to rethink the theories. When Ramazani, "swapping out the wide-angle for a close-up lens," turns to Nagra's five-section, eighty-line poem, his first ponderings put theory and text on an even footing: "What do we learn about the conceptual models by looking at them anew from the perspective of this poem? And what do we learn about this and other modernist-inflected postcolonial poems by applying these various critical templates?" (112). He wastes no time answering those questions; he never pauses to paraphrase the poem, and even refrains from name-checking the exuberantly titled collection in which it appears.[5] Eyes on the conceptual prize, Ramazani gets right to his four models, which he tests in the order he introduced them. His first model, diffusionism, finds footing in Nagra's very first line, which situates the poem in London, within earshot of a performance of William Shakespeare: "A king's invocations at the Globe Theatre." "If ever there was a literary exemplar of diffusion across countless works of postcolonial and diasporic literature," Ramazani confirms, "it is Shakespeare, his plays disseminated from the Globe to every region of the globe" (113). The shout-out to Shakespeare is only the first of Nagra's diffusionist allusions. Beyond quoting canonical British authors (Thomas Babington Macaulay, Matthew Arnold) and fellow Anglophone postcolonial poets (Derek Walcott, Seamus Heaney), Nagra's poem rewrites one modernist predecessor in particular, W. H. Auden's "Spain" (1937). That contentious political poem, written during the tumult of the Spanish Civil War (1936–39), gives Nagra an anvil-shaped stanza-shape (two five-beat lines, an indented three-beat line, another five-beat line), a triptych-like structure (past, present, and future), and a modernist sense of a divided self, unable to forget he is "morally complicit in wrongdoing (war for Auden, empire for Nagra)" (113).

So far, so good: Ramazani's first model sheds some selective light. "But doesn't the empire write back to the center?" he wonders (114). Answering that question leads him to unexamined stretches of Nagra's poem, including its title—a defiant Blackening of Winston Churchill's four-volume work *A History of the English-Speaking Peoples*, remembered today for its openly racist Anglocentrism. But Ramazani also revisits aspects of the poem he's just

---

5. All quotations of "A Black History of the English-Speaking Peoples" are from Daljit Nagra, *Tippoo Sultan's Incredible White-Man-Eating Tiger Toy-Machine!!!* (Faber, 2011), 50–53. Imagine: Ramazani resisted name-checking *that*.

discussed, finding them unexhausted by his first, diffusionist model. Nagra's reworking of "Spain," Ramazani reflects, is not simply a case of metropolitan modernism spreading unencumbered through postcolonial culture, meeting no resistance. Far from accepting Auden's influence unquestioningly, Nagra turns Auden's words against him. Specifically, Nagra seizes on the most notorious phrase in "Spain," publicly decried by George Orwell and eventually cut by Auden himself: "necessary murder," a callous characterization of deaths in the Spanish Civil War. Sandwiching Auden's phrase between the contexts of European colonialism and of mass migration in the time of decolonization—"Between *Mayflower* and *Windrush*/(with each *necessary murder*)"—Nagra stretches out Auden's moral complicity to global, century-spanning proportions.[6] In Ramazani's judicious summary, even as Nagra "embraces Auden's complex view of ethical responsibility in history," he "ties his English predecessor's work to the logic of imperialism" (113–14). It's a conflicted relation to the modernist past, blending allegiance and dissent, and Ramazani clarifies it with a surprising fusion of two theoretical models, diffusionism and resistance.

Ramazani's third tactic for incorporating theory into his close reading is to take every new theoretical frame as an opportunity to read for difference. More can be more, Ramazani's juggling of conceptual models seems to say: whenever he pulls out one model and swaps in another, his attention is drawn to a different excerpt, a different aspect, a different virtue of Nagra's poem. Neither diffusionism nor resistance suits the poem's fifth and final section, as Nagra's speaker strolls along the Thames River, haunted by the material goods and historical evils of imperial extraction: "the waters of Britannia bobble / with flotillas of tea and white gold / cotton and sugar and the sweetness-and-light // blood lettings." But his third model, a singular modernity, easily accommodates this nightmarish vision of worldwide capitalism, as "the waters of Britannia" overflow with commodities plundered from the global south—as well as "blood lettings" excused in the name of "sweetness and light," a phrase for a virtuous English culture, popularized by the Victorian poet and critic Matthew Arnold. More than any other of Ramazani's models, a singular modernity clarifies Nagra's closing image of "multinationals lying along the sanitised Thames":

---

6. In 1620, the English settlers known as the Pilgrims crossed the Atlantic Ocean on the *Mayflower* and established the Plymouth Colony, the third permanent English colony in the Americas. In 1948, the *Empire Windrush* traveled from Jamaica to England, carrying the largest group of West Indian migrants to date; the post–World War II generation of migrants from Commonwealth countries to the United Kingdom soon became known as the Windrush generation.

"The history of British imperialism has culminated in multinational corporations, which perpetuate the empire's earlier patterns of exploitative accumulation, yet sanitize that history," Ramazani writes (114). "Lying," Ramazani picks out, is a mischievous pun. By "lying" (as in taking up photogenic real estate) along Britain's storied river of culture and commerce, multinationals can continue "lying" (as in deceiving, as in cleaning up their imperialist act).

And it's the last of Ramazani's four models—alternative modernities and modernisms—that best clarifies the poem's self-critical midpoint. It's here that Nagra's speaker-poet turns away from the lowercase-g globe (or the capital-G Globe Theatre) and begins questioning himself and his polyvocal poetics. Maybe, he fears, he's a descendant not only of his Punjabi ancestors but of the British historian and colonial statesman Thomas Babington Macaulay, who notoriously spoke of Indian inferiority and boasted of "*the imperishable empire of our arts*": "So does the red of Macaulay's map run through / my blood?" Maybe he's compromised, a sellout hoping the "academy might canonise / his poems for their faith in canonical allusions" ("presumably," Ramazani smirkingly notes, "in works such as the book you are reading") (115). But Nagra's speaker resolves to be no one thing, and Ramazani's pluralist reading of this hybridized self-portrait—which "combines insider and rebel, perpetuator and opponent, mimic and insurgent" (115)—grants him that:

> Is my voice phoney over these oft-heard beats?
> Well if my voice feels vexatious, what can I but pray
>   that it reign Bolshie
> through puppetry and hypocrisy full of gung-ho fury!

A reader more distractible than Ramazani could spend all day with lines like these, picking apart their mash-up of registers and regions. In this quatrain, literary archaism ("oft-heard," "vexatious," the compacted Yeatsian construction "what can I but") abuts hip-hop's terminology ("beats" or backing tracks, the pun on micro- and megaphones in "phoney") and polysyllabic slant-rhyming (*phoney-Bolshie-fury, puppetry-hypocrisy*).[7] Nagra's global English ping-pongs between Latinate and Anglo-Saxon words, between the British slang *Bolshie* ("left-wing" or by extension "uncooperative," from the Russian political party *Bolshevik*) and the American confection *gung-ho* ("enthusiastic," a military

---

7. For the best-known appearance of this construction in Anglophone poetry, see W. B. Yeats's "The Circus Animals' Desertion": "What can I but enumerate old themes?" *The Variorum Edition of the Poems of W. B. Yeats*, eds. Peter Allt and Russell Alspach (Macmillan, 1987), 629.

motto derived from the Mandarin *kung ho*, "work together"). But rather than enumerating every ear-catching effect, Ramazani synthesizes a portrait of Nagra's hybrid "voice," which holds together the quatrain and the poem: "In a vexed, angry, pumped-up, humorously theatrical voice, Nagra performs the English literary tradition he is part of, yet restively parts from," pronouncing modernist poetics "not sotto voce but through a postcolonial megaphone." With that memorable image for Nagra's boisterous, souped-up, culture-crossing style, Ramazani concludes, but not before adding one last symphonic list: "He Blackens, indigenizes, hybridizes, and postcolonizes modernism" (115). The dozens of scholars he gratefully cites provide usefully abstract accounts of the processes of Blackening, indigenization, hybridization, and postcolonialism writ large. Thanks to Ramazani's close reading, we can see those processes happening on the page, in real recitable time, on the memorably precise levels of the rhymed syllable, the borrowed stanza, the inimitable voice.

The paradigmatic close reading, as we encounter it in poetry classrooms and see it modeled in anthologized snippets of criticism, is often about the poem, the whole poem, and nothing but the poem. If that's your standard, then one of Ramazani's bifocal readings, pairing wide-angle with close-up lenses, can alternately seem too distanced and too narrow: they look out *too* far, look in *too* deep. If you want a comprehensive reading of all eighty lines of Nagra's "Black History," front to back—let alone a reading textbook-thick with context, stretching from the imperial past preceding the poem to the late-capitalist waste land it portends—you'll have to write it yourself. But one reason I admire Ramazani is that he continually broadens my sense of the scales, plural, of close reading. Far from a process that digests individual poems and extrudes poem-sized insights, Ramazani's close readings consider seemingly everything, from fascinating phrases to entire scholarly fields, and land on discoveries that feel impossible to measure precisely: how a single word—"Look:"—can tug on an allusive web that spans periods, regions, and media; or how irregularly shaped theories, when applied to the same poem, can join one another in seamless, mosaic-like unity. These discoveries, dizzying in their shifting scales, remind me, of all things, of Ramazani himself. We've never met, and I should know him primarily on a last-name basis, the standard for book spines, academic citations, and any number of other professional courtesies. But whenever I think of this globe-spanning, word-magnifying, scale-defying close reader, I find it hard not to call him by his first name, Jahan: from the Persian, meaning "world."

Practical Materials

Reading Close Readings

In the introduction to this book, when we described what close reading is, we offered a brief close reading of William Carlos Williams's "The Red Wheelbarrow" and broke it down into our five steps. We wanted that reading to show each step of close reading clearly, and to serve as a straightforward way to teach those steps. But once you have learned the steps, then they can help you read and understand literary criticism, which is usually more surprising and complicated than our example and also more fun and interesting.

When you're reading an article or book and want to trace its argument to understand it better—maybe you feel thrilled by it, maybe you feel confused by it, maybe you want to agree or disagree with it—that's when it's worth identifying its moves. Now that you've learned the steps of close reading, you can practice reading close readings. This section, and the following activities, will help you. First, we'll show you a close reading and how identifying its steps helps you understand what it's saying, and then we've selected six brief close readings from recent scholarship for practice. We have a worksheet (with some suggested solutions) to guide you.

Before we jump in, here are the steps again for your quick reference:

> **Step 1: Scene Setting.** The close reader begins by setting the scene, describing what's happening at that moment in the text and what's relevant for the close reading that's about to arrive.
>
> **Step 2: Noticing.** The close reader focuses more tightly by *noticing* a detail. Noticing is often expressed as bafflement or surprise—something's missing, something's in excess, something's odd. Why this word rather than

another? Why this punctuation mark? Why repeat that word? What has caught your attention, what has snagged you, where are you stuck?

Step 3: Local Claiming. After noticing a detail, the close reader makes a claim about how to understand what they've noticed. The close reader does this by saying how that detail works in its immediate context.

Step 4: Regional Argumentation. The close reader now reaches beyond the immediate context to say how that detail sheds light throughout the text by connecting it to other details.

Step 5: Global Theorizing. The close reader reaches beyond the text to connect the reading to the author's oeuvre, the text's genre, form, period, or historical context.

"The Red Wheelbarrow" Again, a Wild Close Reading

First, let's look at another close reading of "The Red Wheelbarrow," one that wasn't written as a demonstration, which we are catching from the wild. This one is by the scholar Hugh Kenner from his book *A Homemade World*, published in 1974. Kenner's is a fun and useful reading of Williams's poem—although you wouldn't want to write an essay for a class exactly like his reading. It's messy compared to our example; that's partly because it's not written to teach students, and also because Kenner is fairly idiosyncratic for his own era, and now is out-of-date as well. Messy can be interesting! By examining his reading we can see that although it's old-fashioned, and strange, and also brilliant, it still follows the same steps as our example. It still works the way other close readings work, and our steps still help you figure out what Kenner is saying and how. We'll show you how to break it down.

We see Kenner move through the first few steps: scene setting, noticing, and into local claiming:

> Not what the poet says, insisted Williams; what he makes; and if ever we seem to catch him saying ("So much depends upon . . ."), well, he has cunningly not said what depends. He has levered that red wheelbarrow into a special zone of attention by sheer torque of insistence. Attention first encounters the word "upon," sitting all alone as though to remind us that "depends upon," come to think of it, is a rather queer phrase. Instead of tracing, as usage normally does, the contour of a forgotten Latin root, "depends upon" ignores the etymology of "depend" (de + pendere = to hang from). In the substantial world "upon" goes nicely with "wheelbarrow": so

much, as it were, piled upon. In the idiomatic world, inexplicably, "upon" goes with "depends." In the poem, since we're paying unaccustomed attention, these two worlds are sutured, and "depends" lends its physical force, an incumbency as though felt by the muscles, to what must be a psychic depending.[1]

1. *Scene setting:* The very first sentence initiates Kenner's argument—*Not what the poets says, insisted Williams; what he makes*—by setting up a distinction between *saying* and *making*. This is a kind of scene setting, because no one would disagree that saying something and making something are different, but we don't know why that matters yet: it's just a general assertion. The real scene setting comes next, when Kenner points out that Williams insists, without explanation, that the red wheelbarrow is important: *he has cunningly not said what depends. He has levered that red wheelbarrow into a special zone of attention by sheer torque of insistence.*

Kenner's scene setting does its work through its use of adjectives and adverbs. He describes Williams as "cunning," suggesting that he thinks Williams's withholding of information is deliberate and strategic, even manipulative, delimiting our sense of it as possibly accidental. He describes the attention that Williams gives the wheelbarrow as "special" and his focus on the wheelbarrow as a kind of force, "sheer torque." Williams insists on attention to the wheelbarrow and, as a result, compels his readers to pay that attention. Although Williams is *saying* that "so much depends" on the wheelbarrow, he's forcing us to pay attention through how he's *making* the poem.

2. *Noticing:* Kenner notices two words. This is similar to what we did in our close reading: we focused on one word in our reading, "glazed," but Kenner puts his finger upon the words "depends" and "upon."

> *Attention first encounters the word "upon," sitting all alone as though to remind us that "depends upon," come to think of it, is a rather queer phrase. Instead of tracing, as usage normally does, the contour of a forgotten Latin root, "depends upon" ignores the etymology of "depend" (de + pendere = to hang from).*

Kenner notices this "rather queer phrase"—he just means that it's weird—and then explains why it's odd, why he noticed it in the first place. He noticed these two words together because there's a tension if not contradiction between something hanging (*depends*) and resting (*upon*). It's fine if you didn't notice this, and it's definitely fine if you don't know Latin. Different people, with

---

1. Hugh Kenner, *A Homemade World: The American Modernist Writers* (Johns Hopkins University Press, 1989), 59–60.

different expertise or different interests, notice different things—that's part of why it's useful and even fun to read other people's close readings. Really, all that's happening here is that Kenner has noticed that an ostensibly normal idiomatic phrase is weird once you stop to pay attention to it, and, really, a nearly infinite number of things are weird once you slow down enough to notice.

3. *Local claiming:* In this step, the close reader makes a claim by saying how to understand the detail that they've noticed.

> *In the poem, since we're paying unaccustomed attention, these two worlds are sutured, and "depends" lends its physical force, an incumbency as though felt by the muscles, to what must be a psychic depending.*

To paraphrase what Kenner is saying: the poem mashes two words together that don't really go together—"depends" and "upon"—and then commands that the reader feel how strange this is. The effect, he argues, is that the poem instructs us to unite several distinct forces at once: etymology and idiom; the physical and the psychic; hanging and resting.

Maybe you don't agree with him—that's okay! Maybe you don't think "depends" and "upon" are all that strange together, you might disagree that our attention is directed to this, and you might even more firmly dispute that the poem transforms a relationship between objects into one of ideas and feelings. It's fine to disagree because if someone can disagree, that's how we know it's an argument in the first place.

Kenner's argument, even in this step of local claiming, has already started opening up toward an account of the whole poem, pointing toward regional argumentation and beyond to global theorizing. He has shown us how attention to a tiny piece of the poem causes one to see the poem in a new way. And on top of that, his claim about the whole poem is that this is what art does: it says something in a special way so that you pay attention to it differently, encounter it anew. (This idea of art connects a lot of modernism; literary theory describes it as *defamiliarization*.) So now we can begin to understand what Kenner meant when he wrote, at the beginning of this reading, *Not what the poet says, insisted Williams; what he makes.* What matters is how art changes our reality: that it makes a difference in how we encounter the world.

Kenner goes on to regional argumentation and global theorizing, but those don't immediately follow this quotation; this is part of what we mean by it being a little messy. In Kenner's case, he repeats steps 1–3 a few times and then uses regional argumentation to tie his different local claims together (go read *A Homemade World* for more!).

Your Turn

Here are six close readings that we've excerpted from recently published scholarship. You don't need to be an expert in any of these topics; you don't need to have read any of the original texts (much less these full essays or books) to follow these close readings. You can still identify the steps. The first three are close readings of poems, and numbers four, five, and six are close readings of fiction.

As you read, label each of the five steps. (Hint: we've chosen close readings that we think demonstrate each of the five.) There are some suggested ways to map them at the end of this section.

From Kristin Grogan's article "Thorns Served on Honey: Lyric Difference in Lola Ridge's 'The Ghetto'"

> Consider a scene in which an "old stooped mother" lights the Shabbat candles:
>
> On Friday nights
> Her candles signal
> Infinite fine rays
> To other windows,
> Coupling other lights,
> Linking the tenements
> Like an endless prayer.
>
> Everyone in the tenements—from the elderly observant to the secular young people to whom the poem pays so much attention—are implicated in this metaphor of attachment. The image of the shabbat candles is an apt figure for both the poetic sequence and the poem's social vision of individuals who are coupled, linked, and drawn into a greater whole. [Lola] Ridge's conceit also maps onto an anarchist vision of social relation in which individuals exist with full autonomy but in relations of solidarity with one another, a vision that she was exposed to through the Ferrer Center and her work with Goldman. In the capacious sequence of "The Ghetto," Ridge braids Whitmanian universalism, anarchist individualism, and tropes from ethnographic journalism about the Lower East Side.[2]

2. Kristin Grogan, "Thorns Served on Honey: Lyric Difference in Lola Ridge's 'The Ghetto,'" *American Literary History* 35, no. 4 (Winter 2023): 1617–37, 1623.

From Erica McAlpine's book The Poet's Mistake

In "She dwelt among th' untrodden ways," [William Wordsworth] uses only simple tenses to describe Lucy's actions in the past:

> She dwelt among th' untrodden ways
> Beside the springs of Dove,
> A Maid whom there were none to praise
> And very few to love.
>
> A Violet by a mossy Stone
> Half-hidden from the Eye!
> —Fair, as a star when only one
> Is shining in the sky!
>
> She *liv'd* unknown, and few could know
> When Lucy ceas'd to be;
> But she is in her Grave, and oh!
> The difference to me.

The actual moment of Lucy's death occupies an unknown place in time—"few could know / When Lucy ceas'd to be." And yet her life and death are unequivocally separate when it comes to the poem's grammar. Before Wordsworth announces her death in the second line of the third stanza, she performs simple, past-tense actions: "She dwelt," "she *liv'd*," she "ceas'd." Once she is pronounced dead, Wordsworth switches to the present tense: "she is in her Grave." Part of the slowly enunciated "difference" to which the poet refers in that final line is represented by this linguistic change: from "dwelt" to "*liv'd*" to "ceas'd" to "is," Lucy effects a transformation from a child who occupied life actively to one whose sole action is merely being—but only in the grave. The sequence is similar in "There was a boy," where Wordsworth depicts the boy at the beginning of the poem in various states of past-tense play—he "blew," "he hung"—only to give him presence at the end through "the grave in which he lies." But none of these changes create confusion; rather, Wordsworth clearly delineates between life and death by ensuring that all of life's former actions remain in the past tense, while all of death's current actions (to be, to lie, to slumber) receive everlasting presence. The verbs associated with the living Lucy never lead continuously forward the way "has carried" does; only her death is continuous. Wordsworth's grammatical difference forces the reader to feel the sudden shift between life and death, between "she dwelt" and "she is," all the more acutely.³

From Walt Hunter's book Forms of a World: Contemporary Poetry and the Making of Globalization:

> The poems in the first section of [Claudia Rankine's] *Citizen* are not recognizably "poetic": their language is the ordinary, spoken kind; there is no elaborate figuration; there is hardly a sense of stanza, or line break, or rhyme, or meter. There is no dreamlike sensation of being in a different world, a meaning that "lyrical" prose sometimes carries. One of the poems recounts a visit to a trauma therapist, who reacts to the presence of a black figure approaching her house with "Get away from my house. What are you doing in my yard?" The poem continues:
>
> > It's as if a wounded Doberman pinscher or a German shepherd has gained the power of speech. And though you back up a few steps, you manage to tell her you have an appointment. You have an appointment? she spits back. Then she pauses. Everything pauses. Oh, she says, followed by, oh, yes, that's right. I am sorry.
> > I am so sorry, so, so sorry.
>
> Rankine describes these anecdotal scenes "as a way of talking about invisible racism—moments that you experience and that happen really fast. They go by at lightning speed, and you begin to distrust that they even happened, and yet you know that you feel bad somehow." These are microaggressions, moments that may seem insignificant, in comparison to greater moments of violence, but that come as shocking and unexpected. This poem is in the genre of the prose anecdote: someone is listening to someone else, and she is talking about a strange, violent, and disturbing thing that happened to her. Readers are situated firmly in the everyday world, a world constructed from individual misrecognitions that channel historical prejudice. Very little here is obscured through figuration or rhetoric, hardly anything that recalls lyric poetry's proclivities for lies or playful obfuscations. Still, the anecdote is more than a report or documentation of an incident, transcribed faithfully. At the moment in which the therapist realizes her error, the poet's voice interpolates a remark, "everything pauses," widening the meaning of the verb "pauses" and complicating the poetic mediation of the account. This repetition, which turns the reporting of

---

3. Erica McAlpine, *The Poet's Mistake* (Princeton University Press, 2020), 37–38.

the incident into a poetic trope, is an index not only to the realism of the language—it is common enough to have the feeling, while remembering a violent scene, that "everything suddenly froze"—but also to its constructedness, a shaping gesture of the poet. By calling this prose poetry "lyric," *Citizen* makes an argument for the malleability of lyric as a genre. In its juxtaposition of heterogeneous forms, the book is a companion volume to Rankine's 2004 collection of poems *Don't Let Me Be Lonely: An American Lyric*. There, Rankine explores life after 9/11 by collaging citations from other texts, images captured on television screens, anatomical drawings, clip art, and logos. This "image stream" brushes against meditations on racialized violence, cancer, and Zoloft, focalized through the first-person "I." Commentary on *Don't Let Me Be Lonely* reveals some of the concerns that subtend both books.[4]

From Dora Zhang's book Strange Likeness: Description and the Modernist Novel:

Here is the opulent drawing room at Lancaster Gate in Henry James's *The Wings of the Dove* (1902) in which Merton Densher awaits an interview with the wealthy aunt of the penniless young woman he wishes to marry. Certain readerly expectations of visual specificity are thwarted in this passage, but we will also see that it seeks out a particular, if somewhat hazy, feature of the space, one that points toward the new likenesses sought by modernist description.

He couldn't describe or dismiss them collectively, call them either Mid-Victorian or Early—not being certain they were rangeable under one rubric. It was only manifest they were splendid and were furthermore conclusively British. They constituted an order and abounded in rare material—precious woods, metals, stuffs, stones. He had never dreamed of anything so fringed and scalloped, so buttoned and corded, drawn everywhere so tight and curled everywhere so thick. He had never dreamed of so much gilt and glass, so much satin and plush, so much rosewood and marble and malachite. But it was above all the solid forms, the wasted finish, the misguided cost, the general attestation of morality and money, a good conscience and a big balance.

Densher cannot treat the objects in the room collectively, but James himself certainly proceeds to do so. Since they cannot be arranged under a

---

4. Walt Hunter, *Forms of a World: Contemporary Poetry and the Making of Globalization* (Fordham University Press, 2019), 50–51.

single label, "Mid-Victorian or Early," we might expect more finely distinguished specifications. But James proceeds in the opposite direction. Although there are allusions to objects, he makes no attempt to comprehensively decorate the narrative space with particular items. The preference for pluralized materials and qualities over individualized and particular objects is one of the most insistent features of this passage. So Michael Levenson attributes "the great provocation" of James's late work to "its refusal of what one may call the novelistic norm of descriptive specificity . . . which takes as its foundation . . . in J. L. Austin's phrase, 'moderate-sized specimens of dry goods.'" This refusal of descriptive specificity together with his eschewal of visual concreteness is key to James's reputation for vagueness. And yet if at the end of the description we know very little about the specific chairs, curtains, or carpets that lie within the Lancaster Gate drawing room, we are also left in little doubt about its overall effect, the impression it creates, so to speak, in the air. James's vagueness is not simply a refusal of specification altogether. Commenting on the "underdescription" of characters' bodies in *The Other House* and *The Awkward Age*, David Kurnick observes that "the attribution of some definite physical effect is often a means to evade positing any actual corporeal *trait*." So Harold Brookenham possesses an "acuteness, difficult to trace to a source, of his smooth fair face," and his father has "a pale, cold face, marked . . . by a hardness of line in which, oddly, there was no significance, no accent." Meanwhile, Nanda, whom we first encounter via the "faded image" of a photograph, is described by Vanderbank as having "no features" because "'she's at the age when the whole thing—speaking of her appearance, her possible share of good look—is still, in a manner, in a fog.'" We could also compare Nanda's fogginess with a later description of the much older Adam Verver in *The Golden Bowl*. "Mr. Verver then, for a fresh full period . . . had been inscrutably monotonous behind an iridescent cloud. The cloud was his native envelope—the soft looseness, so to say, of his temper and tone, not directly expressive enough, no doubt, to figure an amplitude of folds, but of a quality unmistakable for sensitive feelers." In each case, the absence of defined traits—or particularized objects, to hearken back to the description of Lancaster Gate—is combined with the evocation of a strongly felt though nonlocalized effect. How should we understand James's "underdescriptions"? To begin with, we can reframe the question by asking why we read such passages as thin or vague in the first place. That we do so reveals the extent to which we associate description with a relatively narrow idea of visualization. When we say that Lancaster Gate is underdescribed, we mean it cannot be easily imagined as a picture, or to use Elaine Scarry's terms (discussed in the introduction), the description doesn't give us instructions for imagining a visual perception. We could say of James something similar to Walter Scott's observation of Ann Radcliffe, that if six artists tried to render the first description of the castle of Udolpho, "they would probably produce six drawings entirely dissimilar to each other, yet all of them equally authorized by the printed description." This idea of visualization, often imagined through a transmedial thought experiment like the one proposed by Scott, is often taken to be synonymous with description tout court. Accordingly, critics have proposed that Jamesian description interferes with the process of world imagining. "Reading entails an immense labor of imaginative construction," Scarry writes, but as Kurnick points out, "this process of world-imagining must feel all but effortless to function successfully." James's readers, however, are made to feel the labor involved in reconstructing the sensory scene on the basis of the descriptive information on the page: his descriptions seem designed not to enable but rather to block perceptual mimesis. More precisely, they block visualization. But are there other forms of perceptual mimesis that Jamesian descriptions are enabling? If we understand James's likenesses to be about something other than how things look, they turn out to be in fact quite precise, hardly underdescribed at all. In the case of Lancaster Gate, he does not give us an inventory or spatial plan of sideboards, tables, or footstools, but we know that whatever is there is made of gilt, glass, satin, plush, rosewood, marble, and malachite and that it is scalloped, fringed, buttoned, corded, gilded, drawn, and curled. James's descriptive mode remains indefinite with respect to individual objects, but it is quite specific with respect to qualities and effects. The general impression of luxurious materials and ornate aesthetics are clear even if the Balzacian inventory has disappeared. The descriptive referent has become an impression on a perceiver that is irreducible to any one of its component parts. Insofar as they issue instructions for imagining acts of perception, I propose that James's descriptions instruct us above all to imagine what it is like to feel an atmosphere.[5]

5. Dora Zhang, *Strange Likeness: Description and the Modernist Novel* (University of Chicago Press, 2020), 61–63.

From Claire Jarvis's book Exquisite Masochism: Marriage, Sex, and the Novel Form:

> When the maddened Catherine says she thinks she will "feel the same distress underground" that she does alive, she imagines a world that solders the physical body to the soul—or metaphysical self—that inhabits it. She imagines death as a premature burial, which connects physical feeling to emotional feeling. If her "shattered prison" irritates her, it also binds her to the world she inhabits with Heathcliff; it is no surprise that the consummation Heathcliff eventually imagines with Catherine depends on the blending of their bodies' physical traces. Both imagine a physical afterlife that unites their bodies with their metaphysical selves, whereas the novel's other characters imagine a separate world beyond the physical one where their metaphysical selves find rest or recuperation. For both Catherine and Heathcliff, then, death is not something that separates one's body from one's soul, but the event that seals the two together unmistakably. One peculiar aspect of Brontë's cosmology is that the blended world of Catherine the Elder and Heathcliff offers more sustaining pleasure and satisfaction than does the conventional Christian world imagined by the other characters. In this way, the physical landscapes in *Wuthering Heights* separate into the Christian physical world, organized by pain and suffering caused by violence escapable only upon death, and the blended metaphysical world, organized by states of attenuation, anticipation, and the suffering that attends these states.[6]

From Jesse McCarthy's article "Form and the Anticolonial Novel":

> Anne-Lise François uses the "open secret" as a way to refer to a literary text's "nonemphatic revelation—revelation without insistence and without rhetorical underscoring," "a mode of recessive action that takes itself away as it occurs." François applies the term to very different ends, but if I may be allowed to hijack the concept, I think it is remarkably apt for understanding the function of torture in the anticolonial novel. Consider another scene from Yacine's *Nedjma*:
> "So the gentleman is a student?"
> "Student," Lakhdar gasped.

---

6. Claire Jarvis, *Exquisite Masochism: Marriage, Sex, and the Novel Form* (Johns Hopkins University Press, 2016), 37–38.

The inspector hung his crop back on his belt. He picked up a wet rope that was lying on the edge of the sink. The other two inspectors stopped kicking him. Lakhdar kept his head buried in his arms, on the floor.

While he was waiting to be tortured, he had prepared himself. . . . He wouldn't deny his presence at the demonstration. He wouldn't mention the old revolver he had buried near the river. If the torture became unendurable, he had decided to give the names of his pro-French schoolmates; besides the investigation would prove they were innocent.

Part of the effect of this scene relies on its sparse and laconic description; the more significant implication emerges quietly from the free indirect discourse, which makes clear to us that Lakhdar has been able to premeditate the foreseeable outcome of his political activity. The presumption that the state will not only detain you but also almost certainly torture you if you are caught engaging in subversive activity is a naturalized and internalized fact of Lakhdar's world. A subsequent description of waterboarding in the novel is similarly uninflected, as though the routine and predictability of its occurrence were seamlessly continuous with the rest of the narration. This kind of recessive scene, which reveals without seeking to draw attention to itself, is key to the anticolonial novel's mission of drawing out the "open secret" of a daily operation, a fact of life (like starvation in Walrond's story) that stands in metonymically for the hegemonic open secret of the colonial situation as such.[7]

Worksheet

Complete this worksheet for each close reading above.

1. Identify *scene setting*: How does the close reader identify what's relevant for the reading that's about to arrive?
2. Identify *noticing*: Which detail has caught the close reader's attention?
3. Identify *local claiming*: How should we understand what has been noticed, and how that detail is working in its immediate context?
4. Identify *regional argumentation*: How does the close reader connect this detail to other details in the text, providing an interpretation of the text as a whole? Does an abstract term or concept appear at this step?

7. Jesse McCarthy, "Form and the Anticolonial Novel: William Gardner Smith's *The Stone Face*," *Novel* 55, no. 1 (May 2022): 70.

5. Identify *global theorizing*: How does this reading connect with ideas beyond this particular text? Does an abstract term or concept appear at this step?
6. Putting it together: Can you summarize the overall argument in your own words in a sentence or two?
7. *Reflection*: With what steps did you have trouble? What steps did you find most difficult to identify and why? How could the close readers have signposted their steps more clearly? Are steps split across sentences? Are sentences split across steps?
8. *Evidence*: How long is the quotation from the literary text? How is that quotation handled? When does it appear, and why there? When is it analyzed? How does the close reading explain the warrants by which evidence counts as evidence?
9. *Expertise*: Does the close reading cite or refer to other scholarship? Between what steps? How does it help the close reader move to the next step? What knowledge do they assume that their implied reader already knows?
10. *Extras*: Are there sentences in these close readings that do not fall under the steps? What are they doing?

Identifying Steps: Suggested Maps

Identifying the steps in scholarship is a matter of interpretation. This is not the same as saying anything goes. It's also not saying there's a single right answer. You might disagree with someone else about whether such-and-such a phrase is a matter of scene setting or noticing: Is the phrase neutral observation or does it point out something non-obvious?

The goal is to see the argumentative skeleton of what you read and so to understand how that argument works. If you find it tricky to identify a step, or if you disagree with how we've identified a step, recognize that difficulty as legitimate and informative. You are learning about yourself, your strengths and inclinations. You are also learning about what you are reading. If you are having trouble identifying local claiming, for example, maybe that's because the writer downplayed or condensed it. Maybe, if you were their editor, you would recommend an extra sentence highlighting that step. Maybe they'd respond that they made that choice for specific reasons.

In other words, identifying the steps is like every other kind of interpretation. The richest moments are often those of ambiguity or friction.

We, Dan and Johanna, diagrammed each of these close readings independently and compared notes—we agreed on the following after some debate. You might disagree with us; if so, see if you can articulate why. These brilliant close readings weren't written to exemplify our steps, so some sentences, for example, might bridge two steps, or sometimes orders are inverted; we've made judgment calls and you can, too.

The excerpt from Kristin Grogan's "Thorns Served on Honey: Lyric Difference in Lola Ridge's 'The Ghetto'"

1. *Scene setting*: "Consider a scene in which an 'old stooped mother' lights the Shabbat candles"
2. *Noticing*
      and
3. *Local claiming*: "Everyone in the tenements—from the elderly observant to the secular young people to whom the poem pays so much attention—are implicated in this metaphor of attachment"— *These two steps are combined in a single sentence by Grogan, who is noticing the metaphor and immediately preceding it with the local claiming about it.*
4. *Regional argumentation*: "The image of the shabbat candles is an apt figure for both the poetic sequence and the poem's social vision of individuals who are coupled, linked, and drawn into a greater whole."
5. *Global theorizing*: "[Lola] Ridge's conceit also maps onto an anarchist vision of social relation in which individuals exist with full autonomy but in relations of solidarity with one another, a vision that she was exposed to through the Ferrer Center and her work with Goldman. In the capacious sequence of 'The Ghetto,' Ridge braids Whitmanian universalism, anarchist individualism, and tropes from ethnographic journalism about the Lower East Side."

The excerpt from Erica McAlpine's *The Poet's Mistake*

1. *Scene setting*: "In 'She dwelt among th' untrodden ways,' [William Wordsworth] uses only simple tenses to describe Lucy's actions in the past:"
2. *Noticing*: "The actual moment of Lucy's death occupies an unknown place in time—'few could know / When Lucy ceas'd to be.' And yet her life and death are unequivocally separate when it comes to the poem's

grammar. Before Wordsworth announces her death in the second line of the third stanza, she performs simple, past-tense actions: 'She dwelt,' 'she *liv' d*,' she 'ceas'd.' Once she is pronounced dead, Wordsworth switches to the present tense: 'she is in her Grave.'"

3. *Local claiming*: "Part of the slowly enunciated 'difference' to which the poet refers in that final line is represented by this linguistic change: from 'dwelt' to '*liv'd*' to 'ceas'd' to 'is,' Lucy effects a transformation from a child who occupied life actively to one whose sole action is merely being—but only in the grave."

4. *Regional argumentation*: "But none of these changes create confusion; rather, Wordsworth clearly delineates between life and death by ensuring that all of life's former actions remain in the past tense, while all of death's current actions (to be, to lie, to slumber) receive everlasting presence. The verbs associated with the living Lucy never lead continuously forward the way 'has carried' does; only her death is continuous."

5. *Global theorizing*: "The sequence is similar in 'There was a boy,' where Wordsworth depicts the boy at the beginning of the poem in various states of past-tense play—he 'blew,' 'he hung'—only to give him presence at the end through 'the grave in which he lies.' . . . Wordsworth's grammatical difference forces the reader to feel the sudden shift between life and death, between 'she dwelt' and 'she is,' all the more acutely."—*McAlpine has a sentence of global theorizing before regional argumentation, and another one after it.*

The excerpt from Walt Hunter's *Forms of a World*

1. *Scene setting*: "The poems in the first section of [Claudia Rankine's] *Citizen* are not recognizably 'poetic': . . . Very little here is obscured through figuration or rhetoric, hardly anything that recalls lyric poetry's proclivities for lies or playful obfuscations."—*There's a lot of scene setting!*

2. *Noticing*: "Still, the anecdote is more than a report or documentation of an incident, transcribed faithfully. At the moment in which the therapist realizes her error, the poet's voice interpolates a remark, 'everything pauses,' widening the meaning of the verb 'pauses' and complicating the poetic mediation of the account."

3. *Local claiming*: "This repetition, which turns the reporting of the incident into a poetic trope is an index not only to the realism of the

language—it is common enough to have the feeling, while remembering a violent scene, that 'everything suddenly froze'—but also to its constructedness, a shaping gesture of the poet."
4. *Regional argumentation*: "By calling this prose poetry 'lyric,' *Citizen* makes an argument for the malleability of lyric as a genre."
5. *Global theorizing*: "In its juxtaposition of heterogeneous forms, the book is a companion volume to Rankine's 2004 collection of poems *Don't Let Me Be Lonely: An American Lyric*. There, Rankine explores life after 9/11 by collaging citations from other texts, images captured on television screens, anatomical drawings, clip art, and logos. This 'image stream' brushes against meditations on racialized violence, cancer, and Zoloft, focalized through the first-person 'I.' Commentary on *Don't Let Me Be Lonely* reveals some of the concerns that subtend both books."

The excerpt from Dora Zhang's *Strange Likeness*

—*We, Dan and Johanna, had fun analyzing how Zhang builds her close reading of Henry James's* The Wings of the Dove. *It's a complicated and skillful performance. She keeps a tight focus on the quotation and moves through the steps in several phases. In the first phase before the block quote, to introduce the argument, she runs through scene setting, noticing, local claiming, and global theorizing, skipping regional argumentation. Then, after the block quote, in the second phase, she skips scene setting but spends time on noticing, local claiming, and briefly goes back to noticing; this phase builds up a lot of detail about the passage that's just preceded it. Zhang then states her question—"How should we understand James's 'underdescriptions'?"—and to answer it, she works backward from global theorizing to regional argumentation, and then she goes forward again from scene setting to noticing, to local claiming, to regional argumentation, to return finally to global theorizing. In this third phase, she needs the global theorizing to itself serve as the scene setting for the last phase.*

First phase: A

1. *Scene setting A*: "Here is the opulent drawing room at Lancaster Gate in Henry James's *The Wings of the Dove* (1902) in which Merton Densher awaits an interview with the wealthy aunt of the penniless young woman he wishes to marry."

2. *Noticing A*: "Certain readerly expectations of visual specificity are thwarted in this passage"
3. *Local claiming A*: "but we will also see that it seeks out a particular, if somewhat hazy, feature of the space"
5. *Global theorizing A*: "one that points toward the new likenesses sought by modernist description."

Second phase: B

2. *Noticing B:* "Densher cannot treat the objects in the room collectively, but James himself certainly proceeds to do so. Since they cannot be arranged under a single label, 'Mid-Victorian or Early,' we might expect more finely distinguished specifications. But James proceeds in the opposite direction. Although there are allusions to objects, he makes no attempt to comprehensively decorate the narrative space with particular items. The preference for pluralized materials and qualities over individualized and particular objects is one of the most insistent features of this passage."
4. *Regional argumentation B*: "This refusal of descriptive specificity together with his eschewal of visual concreteness is key to James's reputation for vagueness. And yet if at the end of the description we know very little about the specific chairs, curtains, or carpets that lie within the Lancaster Gate drawing room, we are also left in little doubt about its overall effect, the impression it creates, so to speak, in the air. James's vagueness is not simply a refusal of specification altogether."

Third phase: C

2. *Noticing C:* "In each case, the absence of defined traits—or particularized objects, to hearken back to the description of Lancaster Gate—is combined with the evocation of a strongly felt though nonlocalized effect. How should we understand James's 'underdescriptions'?"
5. *Global theorizing C:* "To begin with, we can reframe the question by asking why we read such passages as thin or vague in the first place. That we do so reveals the extent to which we associate description with a relatively narrow idea of visualization. When we say that Lancaster Gate is underdescribed, we mean it cannot be easily imagined as a picture, or to use Elaine Scarry's terms (discussed in the introduction), the description doesn't give us instructions for

imagining a visual perception. We could say of James something similar to Walter Scott's observation of Ann Radcliffe, that if six artists tried to render the first description of the castle of Udolpho, 'they would probably produce six drawings entirely dissimilar to each other, yet all of them equally authorized by the printed description.' This idea of visualization, often imagined through a transmedial thought experiment like the one proposed by Scott, is often taken to be synonymous with description tout court. Accordingly, critics have proposed that Jamesian description interferes with the process of world imagining."

5. *Regional argumentation* C: James's readers, however, are made to feel the labor involved in reconstructing the sensory scene on the basis of the descriptive information on the page: his descriptions seem designed not to enable but rather to block perceptual mimesis. More precisely, they block visualization. But are there other forms of perceptual mimesis that Jamesian descriptions are enabling? If we understand James's likenesses to be about something other than how things look, they turn out to be in fact quite precise, hardly underdescribed at all.

1. *Scene setting* C: "In the case of Lancaster Gate, he does not give us an inventory or spatial plan of sideboards, tables, or footstools,
2. *Noticing* C: "marble, and malachite and that it is scalloped, fringed, buttoned, corded, gilded, drawn, and curled"
3. *Local claiming* C: "James's descriptive mode remains indefinite with respect to individual objects, but it is quite specific with respect to qualities and effects. The general impression of luxurious materials and ornate aesthetics are clear even if the Balzacian inventory has disappeared."
3. *Regional argumentation* C: "The descriptive referent has become an impression on a perceiver that is irreducible to any one of its component parts."
4. *Global theorizing* C: "Insofar as they issue instructions for imagining acts of perception, I propose that James's descriptions instruct us above all to imagine what it is like to feel an atmosphere."

The excerpt from Claire Jarvis's *Exquisite Masochism*

1. *Scene setting*
    and

2. *Noticing*:
   and
3. *Local claiming*: "When the maddened Catherine says she thinks she will 'feel the same distress underground' that she does alive, she imagines a world that solders the physical body to the soul—or metaphysical self—that inhabits it. She imagines death as a premature burial, which connects physical feeling to emotional feeling."—*Jarvis moves very quickly through the first few steps: all three appear in the first sentence, and the second sentence elaborates the local claiming further.*
4. *Regional argumentation*: "If her 'shattered prison' irritates her, it also binds her to the world she inhabits with Heathcliff; it is no surprise that the consummation Heathcliff eventually imagines with Catherine depends on the blending of their bodies' physical traces. Both imagine a physical afterlife that unites their bodies with their metaphysical selves, whereas the novel's other characters imagine a separate world beyond the physical one where their metaphysical selves find rest or recuperation. For both Catherine and Heathcliff, then, death is not something that separates one's body from one's soul, but the event that seals the two together unmistakably."
5. *Global theorizing*: "One peculiar aspect of Brontë's cosmology is that the blended world of Catherine the Elder and Heathcliff offers more sustaining pleasure and satisfaction than does the conventional Christian world imagined by the other characters. In this way, the physical landscapes in *Wuthering Heights* separate into the Christian physical world, organized by pain and suffering caused by violence escapable only upon death, and the blended metaphysical world, organized by states of attenuation, anticipation, and the suffering that attends these states."

The excerpt from Jesse McCarthy's "Form and the Anticolonial Novel"

1. *Scene setting*: "Anne-Lise François uses the 'open secret' as a way to refer to a literary text's 'nonemphatic revelation—revelation without insistence and without rhetorical underscoring,' 'a mode of recessive action that takes itself away as it occurs.' François applies the term to very different ends, but if I may be allowed to hijack the concept, I think it is remarkably apt for understanding the function of torture in the anticolonial novel."
2. *Noticing*: "Part of the effect of this scene relies on its sparse and laconic description; the more significant implication emerges quietly from the

free indirect discourse, which makes clear to us that Lakhdar has been able to premeditate the foreseeable outcome of his political activity."
3. *Local claiming*: "The presumption that the state will not only detain you but also almost certainly torture you if you are caught engaging in subversive activity is a naturalized and internalized fact of Lakhdar's world."
4. *Regional argumentation*: "A subsequent description of waterboarding in the novel is similarly uninflected, as though the routine and predictability of its occurrence were seamlessly continuous with the rest of the narration."
5. *Global theorizing*: "This kind of recessive scene, which reveals without seeking to draw attention to itself, is key to the anticolonial novel's mission of drawing out the 'open secret' of a daily operation, a fact of life (like starvation in Walrond's story) that stands in metonymically for the hegemonic open secret of the colonial situation as such."

For Instructors

- We've provided these six sample close readings, but feel free to use others that are relevant for your classes; we recommend excerpts of between one paragraph and two pages.
- Identifying the steps in an excerpt of criticism or scholarship can be adapted to work as a lecture, a homework assignment, a group activity, a quiz, or more.
- Don't shy away from difficulty or disagreements. As with close reading a literary text, moments of puzzlement or friction are signs of something interesting. Try to get as clear as possible about that puzzlement. Is a student not able to locate a step? Do students disagree about which step is where? Those are moments in which the text is doing something worth paying attention to—something that clarifies what its argument is about and how it's making it—though such moments aren't always the most apposite for students to emulate in their own writing.

Writing Close Readings

In the previous section, we offered exercises to help you practice reading the close readings you encounter in literary criticism. This section has exercises to help you refine the skills you need to write your own close readings.

We have exercises for each of the five steps. As you'll see, we've arranged them out of order. In the written version of your close reading you'll begin with step 1, setting the scene. But for most people, the process of writing begins with step 2, noticing. You read; you notice a detail; you formulate a local claim about it, and then, at that point, you might go back and think about how to set the scene for someone else to understand that claim. So we're starting with activities for step 2. Then we'll have step 3, local claiming, then we'll return to step 1, scene setting, before offering some activities for step 4, regional argumentation, and step 5, global theorizing. Then, in the next section of activities, "Using Close Reading," we'll show you how to assemble your close readings into genres of writing.

Step 2: Noticing

To notice well, it helps to see the text you're close reading as a series of choices. To do that, you need to slow down and heighten your attention. You need to remember that a text is not a natural artifact—it's not a rock that's been rolled around in a river—but a made one—like a spaceship that's crash landed in your backyard. Why is it the way it is? Don't just pay attention to what it says, or what it's about, but how it says it, how it creates effects. These activities are designed to help you improve at the step of noticing, to pay attention to details that—if you look not just at them but through them, as if they were keyholes or telescopes—show you everything.

- Put your finger on it, say why
  - Put your finger on something small enough to fit underneath it—a word, a grammatical mark, a space—that you found weird or surprising, and explain why it's weird or surprising to someone else. Take everything seriously: remember how Robert Stagg shows us that nothing is too basic for noticing. For more inspiration, go to Adrienne Brown's chapter on noticing how Toni Morrison teaches us how to notice race and racism in literature and also to notice when they are evaded. Or visit Summer Kim Lee's chapter on how Barbara Johnson notices that there's an odd contradiction between who's

silenced versus who claims they are. Or, if you aren't actually surprised by the text's language, that might also be surprising! Look at how Katie Kadue writes about how Christopher Ricks notices cliché.
- Put your finger on it, change it, say what
  - Put your finger on one word, and come up with an alternative that's a near synonym. Rewrite the line or sentence with that alternative word; what difference does that substitution make? Look at how Jeff Dolven and Joshua Kotin describe Helen Vendler's practice of empathetic reading, imagining being the writer and playing out the alternative paths a text could have taken.
- If you're having trouble getting started or going with your gut, sharpen yourself up with this list of details to notice:
  - Opposite qualities of words: long or short, Latinate or Germanic in etymological origin, abstract or concrete
  - Parts of speech: pronouns, adjectives, verbs, adverbs, conjunctions
  - Things that aren't words: grammatical symbols, spaces, use of the page
  - How would you describe the sentences? The grammar? Choose 1–3 adjectives.
  - Puzzles: What's missing? What's ambiguous? At what point are you confused?
  - Situation (Speaker): Who is speaking? What do you know about them? What do you not know? What is their class, background, taste, age? If they lived today, what would they wear, what car would they drive, what music would they listen to? What does that tell you?
  - Situation (Setting): What is the setting? What do you know about it? When is it, in terms of year, time of day, season? What is the weather? What don't you know?
  - How would you describe the tone? How would you describe the style? How would you describe the text's speed or pace? If it's a poem, how would you describe the form? Choose 1–3 adjectives.
  - How would you describe the text's organization or construction?
  - Is there a gap between the text as a whole and the speaker or narrator? How are they aligned or not?
  - How does the text begin? How would you describe that beginning with 1–3 adjectives? What happened before it began? What impels it to begin?
  - How does the text end? Does the end satisfy you, and if so, in what way? If not, why? Why does the end count as an ending?
  - Repetitions: What gets repeated in terms of words or images, or stylistic or formal techniques?

- What does the text know about the world? About history? About art and culture? About other books? What does the speaker or narrator know about the world, history, art and culture, or other books? Where do you see evidence of this?
- What are the text's assumptions? What does it assume about you, its reader? Who does it think you are? What does it think you know? What does it think you like, and what does it think you agree with already? What does the text assume about the world? About other people? Where do you see evidence of this?
- How does the speaker or narrator want you to feel about them? What do they want you to think about them? Where do you see evidence of this?
- What does the text want from you, or for you? How does it want you to feel about it? Does it want to delight and please, does it want to infuriate or frustrate? Does it want to lull or string you along, or does it want to challenge and puzzle you? Does it want to teach you, and if so, what? Is it easy or hard to resist it? Where do you see evidence of this?
- What does the text think about its own art form? If it's a novel, what does it think novels do or are? If it's a play, what does it think plays do or are? If it's a poem, what does it think poems do or are? Where do you see evidence of this?

—Now do the "put your finger on it" activities again. You must move from noticing lots of aspects of the text to letting one detail emerge to you as particularly rich and significant.

More activities:

- Notice new details by spending more time with the text
  - Read it out loud, read it out loud again, read it out loud for someone else, record yourself reading it out loud; what new detail did you notice?
  - Write it out longhand, write it out on a computer; what new detail did you notice?
  - Memorize it; what new detail did you notice?
  - Draw it, sing it, dance it, write it as an equation, write it as a graph, write it as a chart, write it as a map, write it as an experiment, write it as a scene if it's a poem, write as a poem if it's a scene; what new detail did you notice?

- Say what's lost in translation
  - Paraphrase the text in your own words, then think about what is lost
  - If you speak or read another language, translate the text (even a sentence, even clumsily!); what is lost?
- Say how the text works by rearranging or erasing it
  - Print out the text and rearrange it; how does this clarify its original structure or form?
  - Print out the text and black out a tiny detail (a word, a grammatical symbol); how does this alter what's left?
- Index the text
  - Compile a list of what you've noticed as a personal index to the text
  - In a group, compare your indices; make a giant overall index to the text on the board, online, or elsewhere

For Instructors

- We often spend the first weeks of a course teaching students how to notice—it really does take a long time for many of them to stop summarizing or identifying a theme—and we will say "more specific" and "what can fit under your finger" frequently during that time. We like to ask students to come to every class with one detail that they've noticed in the text to be discussed that day; we often ask them to write it down and turn it in (an easy way of taking attendance and figuring out what they are paying attention to) or else to write it on the board as they walk into the room.
- In seminar-style courses, the things that they've noticed can work very well to start discussion—you can ask someone what they noticed, knowing they'll be ready—or you can start discussion by asking the whole class one thing from the list of things to notice that we provide here.
- In smaller or in larger courses, many of these exercises can be adapted into quiz or exam questions or essay prompts. For example: "Choose one adjective that describes this novel's style, and write a paragraph in which you analyze a quotation to support your description of it" or "What do we know about the speaker of this poem? What information is missing but would be useful to know? Write a paragraph about what you would like to know and how it would help clarify a question you have about the poem."

Step 3: Local Claiming

How do you move from a detail that you notice to a claim about it? If you have a particular enough detail—or one that's described tightly and specifically enough—you are well on your way to a claim. There's probably already a claim lurking in your noticing, so now what you have to do is pull it to the surface, open it up, and make it clear. It might be obvious for you that what you noticed is worthy of attention—but it might not be for your reader—and it is even less obvious that what you noticed should be understood in the specific way you think it should be. This comes down to stating how someone else should understand what you've noticed. Other versions of this include: how what you noticed works and thereby helps the text work, how it functions to create a particular effect in the text, how the text uses or changes based on the detail you noticed. You are *not* summarizing or describing—you are saying something someone could disagree with, and even if that disagreement feels minor, it matters.

Julie Orlemanski shows how, in a chapter of Erich Auerbach's *Mimesis*, a local claim is shaped both by imagining how a detail in the text might have been interpreted in its historical context, and also by your sense of it, so that a local claim is both inevitable and contingent—it could have gone otherwise for other people, but not for you. Omari Weekes, reading Hortense Spillers, unpacks how she formulates a local claim about how Maud Martha's contradictory desires could be read as incoherence or naiveté but should be read instead as genius. Lindsay Reckson's chapter on Kevin Quashie's attention to sound in Lucille Clifton's poetry traces how he moves from registering individual syllables to making a local claim about sound's power. In Natalia Cecire's chapter on Judith Butler, she shows us how Butler makes a local claim that the narrator of Nella Larsen's *Passing* steps in to voice what a character can't. Farah Bakaari, in writing about Eleni Coundouriotis's careful dissection of perspective in Yambo Ouologuem's novel *Le Devoir de violence*, shows how she makes a local claim about how the reader doesn't have access to a character's point of view.

Once you have one specific thing that you've noticed, you can answer the following series of questions. This activity is designed to help you strengthen this skill of local claiming, the leap between what you see and what you say about it.

- What did you notice? Identify it as particularly as possible, using fewer than ten words, and even better if fewer than five.
- What is surprising, confusing, interesting, weird, or cool about what you noticed? Why did you notice it? (This is less of a question about

you and what you're interested in, and more of a question about the text and what made this detail stick out.)
- Do you have a question about what you noticed that you are trying to answer?
- How would the text be different if what you noticed were different?
- What is this detail's importance in the text?
- How do you want someone to understand what you noticed?
- Can you write what you noticed and how you want someone else to understand your claim about it in one sentence?
- Tinker with your claim—what words did you choose? What are possible synonyms or alternatives for your words? Are you using an adjective? Is it exact?
- What are alternative claims? How are they meaningfully different from what you're saying? (They are your counter-arguments.)
- Once you have your local claim—what rests on it? What must your reader believe if they believe you? What can they see if they see what you've shown them?

The point here is that the detail you noticed could give rise to any number of potential claims. Draw a chart like this for what you noticed, your local claiming, and other possible claims.

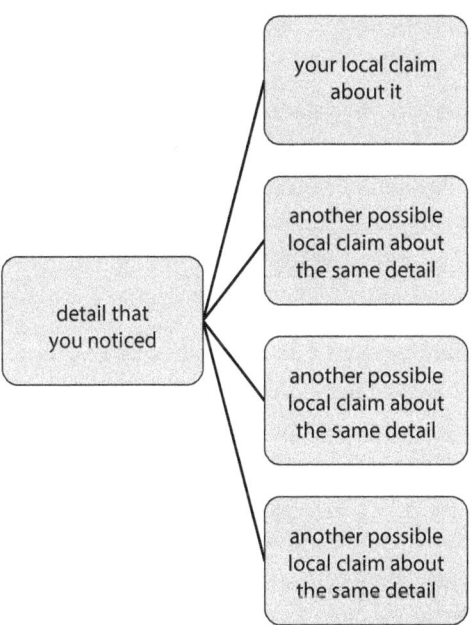

For Instructors

- We explain to students that the five-paragraph essay and the compare-and-contrast essay will prevent them from making strong claims. We know that making a claim is anxiety-producing for many students—they worry they might be wrong—but we reassure students that if they work through an idea carefully and thoughtfully, their claim will be strong. We tell them how these exercises will help. It is useful to remind anxious students that the local claim should be focused only on one circumscribed moment in the text; they don't have to explain very much, just one thing in one place.
- We like to draw the previous chart on the board, working with the class to complete it as a shared example by using a detail from the text that someone has noticed (though not one they might be writing about) and collaboratively coming up with many possible alternative claims that serve as counter-arguments.
- The series of questions above can serve as a worksheet; have students complete it as homework after they become proficient at noticing.
- Once students have some comfort with the steps of noticing and local claiming, you can ask them to write short paragraphs of those two steps as homework or as quiz or exam questions.

Step 1: Scene Setting

Scene setting includes a special kind of summary; it's a description that prepares your reader to notice the same detail that you noticed and to understand why you noticed it. Literary texts, even tiny moments in literary texts, might be described in many ways. You need to limit the information, offering only what's salient for your readers to set up and highlight the noticing that's to come. Here are activities to help you sharpen your scene setting:

- If you've already noticed a detail in a literary text, write a scene-setting description of its context—don't include the noticing! Think about how to help your reader enter the world of the text in the ways that are relevant for what you'll help them see once they get there. We call this step scene setting to suggest a stage or film set: What is the backdrop for your argument?
  - What informational context does your reader need? Where are we? What do we know and where do we stand? Jane Hu, in her chapter on

Eve Kosofsky Sedgwick, shows us how she situates the beginning of a close reading in real places.
- What senses does your reader need to recognize your noticing as noticing? Think about how powerfully Beci Carver conjures Angela Leighton's evocation of a poem's sound, from footfall to rain.
- Write a scene setting that's three or four sentences long. What gets included? What gets left out? What gets expanded or even added? Remember how Oren Izenberg's chapter on Erich Auerbach's close reading of Virginia Woolf's *To the Lighthouse* showed how Auerbach sets the scene by subtly transforming the detail that he's noticed.
- Now write a one-sentence scene setting. What gets included and what gets left out?

- To practice scene setting, read this excerpt, the first paragraph of Kazuo Ishiguro's novel *Never Let Me Go*, and complete the activities below:

> My name is Kathy H. I'm thirty-one years old, and I've been a carer now for over eleven years. That sounds long enough, I know, but actually they want me to go on for another eight months, until the end of this year. That'll make it almost exactly twelve years. Now I know my being a carer so long isn't necessarily because they think I'm fantastic at what I do. There are some really good carers who've been told to stop after just two or three years. And I can think of one carer at least who went on for all of fourteen years despite being a complete waste of space. So I'm not trying to boast. But then I do know for a fact they've been pleased with my work, and by and large, I have too. My donors have always tended to do much better than expected. Their recovery times have been impressive, and hardly any of them have been classified as "agitated," even before fourth donation. Okay, maybe I *am* boasting now. But it means a lot to me, being able to do my work well, especially that bit about my donors staying "calm." I've developed a kind of instinct around donors. I know when to hang around and comfort them, when to leave to themselves; when to listen to everything they have to say, and when just to shrug and tell them to snap out of it.[8]

- First, noticing
  - What detail do you notice? (Remember that it has to be on the page and small enough to fit under your finger.)

8. Kazuo Ishiguro, *Never Let Me Go* (Knopf, 2005), 3.

- Or, if you'd like to skip to scene setting, here are a list of details we noticed in this excerpted paragraph (and there are of course so many more possible details to notice than just these!)
    - Kathy doesn't give us a whole last name, just an initial.
    - Kathy tells us her name in the first sentence.
    - Kathy tells us her age in the second sentence.
    - We don't know who "they" are ("they've been pleased . . .").
    - Kathy changes her mind to admit that she is "boasting."
    - Kathy uses casual idioms, for example "waste of space" (also "by and large," "kind of," and "snap out of it"). We're thinking again of Katie Kadue's chapter on Ricks writing about cliché as something to notice here.
    - "Agitated" is in quotation marks (as is "calm") as if it's someone else's word. We're thinking again about Summer Kim Lee's chapter on how Barbara Johnson notices who is speaking.
- Now, practice scene setting with one of those details
    - Write a three-to-four sentence description that highlights the backdrop to what you've noticed so that it will help your reader notice it too. Then write it again in one sentence. Do not, however, say what you've noticed yet!
        - For example, using the last detail noticed above, that Kathy puts the word "agitated" in quotation marks.
            - Three sentences that set the scene for that detail to pop out: "Kathy H., the narrator of *Never Let Me Go*, is plainspoken as she introduces herself. She tells her name, her age, and explains a little bit about her success in her work as a carer. Although what being a carer entails is a little mysterious, Kathy—mostly—speaks casually and without any particular professional jargon or elevated vocabulary. We have the sense that she is speaking straightforwardly and that we are hearing her own voice."
            - One sentence that sets the scene for that detail to pop out: "Kathy H., the narrator of *Never Let Me Go*, mostly speaks casually and without any particular professional jargon or elevated vocabulary as she introduces herself."

Here's the next iteration of our chart, now with scene setting included. The point here is that scene setting should lead firmly and directly to noticing with no acknowledgment of another possible path.

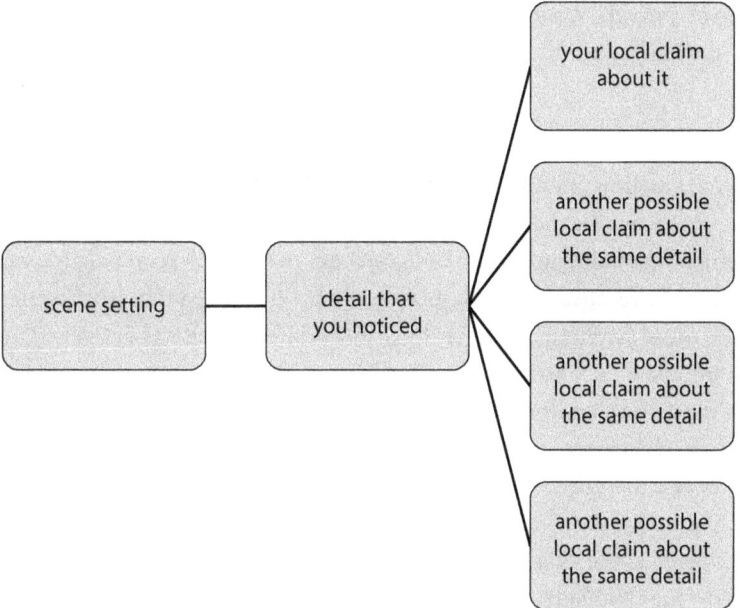

For Instructors

- You can substitute in any other brief excerpt from a literary text to teach this step and adapt the activities as necessary.
- You can scaffold student writing toward a longer essay by asking them to complete these steps as homework or as in-class activity. For example, once they have completed the noticing and local claiming step, you could ask them to come to class having written a one-sentence scene setting for their own essay.
- Once students have some comfort with the steps of scene setting, noticing, and local claiming, you can ask them to write short paragraphs of those three steps as homework or as quiz or exam questions.
- We like to draw the previous chart on the board, and diagram out a sample close reading, coming up with the examples to fill in each bubble in class as discussion or as a small-group activity.
- For another in-class activity, ask students to work off of a scene setting sentence to predict what the noticed detail will be. (The scene setting sentence should not have the noticing in it already.) This could be a sentence you write, or one that a student writes. You could have students swap sentences of their own or work in small groups on the one

you provide. A successful scene setting will suggest what detail will be noticed, and students should be able to predict it correctly, if roughly.

Step 4: Regional Argumentation

Regional argumentation expands outward from local claiming in three ways. First, it reaches further in the text, drawing together details and making an argument about the text as a whole. Second, in doing so, regional argumentation usually reaches further conceptually by invoking a term that brings together those far-flung details in the texts or different aspects of the text under an umbrella of an abstract idea. Third, in stating how a larger concept can be seen in the linking done by regional argumentation, this step also involves clarifying other potential counter-arguments that would use a different concept or use the same one in a slightly different way. The activities below ask you to practice all three of these aspects of regional argumentation.

Looking at the chapters on regional argumentation in this volume, we can see how they highlight these three aspects. Emily Ogden, writing about Robert Penn Warren's literary criticism, shows how he interprets the parts of a text to fit together as a whole. Elaine Auyoung also deals with the sometimes uneasy jostling of pieces within a framework, though for her—reading Alex Woloch on Jane Austen—the pieces are characters. The second aspect is emphasized in Pardis Dabashi's chapter; she directly considers the status of abstract terms in her discussion of how Qolamhossein Yousefi urges specificity but also must rely on generalization to think about a poem as a whole. Brian Glavey considers counter-arguments at the regional level when he discusses how Lauren Berlant interprets—and arguably misinterprets—a poem by John Ashbery.

- In order to develop a regional argument, you first need a local claim. Once you have a local claim, answer the following questions:
  - If your local claim is about the content of your text, how does it also apply to the way the text is written? How does your local claim connect to your text's tone, form, or style? To the way it begins or ends? To its mood or vibe? To what it wants from its reader?
  - What other details or aspects of the text are similar? How and why are they similar? Are they exactly the same or do they share a rough family resemblance with your noticing? Does your local claim also apply to them? Do you need to adjust it to have it apply to them? Your regional argument must do more than identify a theme: you need to say how to understand that theme and/or how it works in the text. *Do not let your regional argument lapse back into noticing or scene setting.*

- Write out your regional argument in one sentence. Pay attention to each word—is each word the right word? Tinker with it. What are possible synonyms or alternatives for your words?
- In your regional argument, are you using a more abstract conceptual term? What is it? Is it the exact right term? What are some near synonyms? What are some close-relative alternatives?
- To keep your regional argumentation as an argument, identify three possible near-miss counter-arguments. They can use synonyms of your conceptual term.
- What rests on your regional argumentation? What must your reader believe if they believe you? What can they see if they see what you've shown them?
- Using your scene setting, noticing, local claiming, and regional argumentation, write a one-paragraph close reading of roughly 350 words.

Here's our chart, updated to include regional argumentation. As with local claiming, it's important to imagine possible counter-arguments to clarify and strengthen your own.

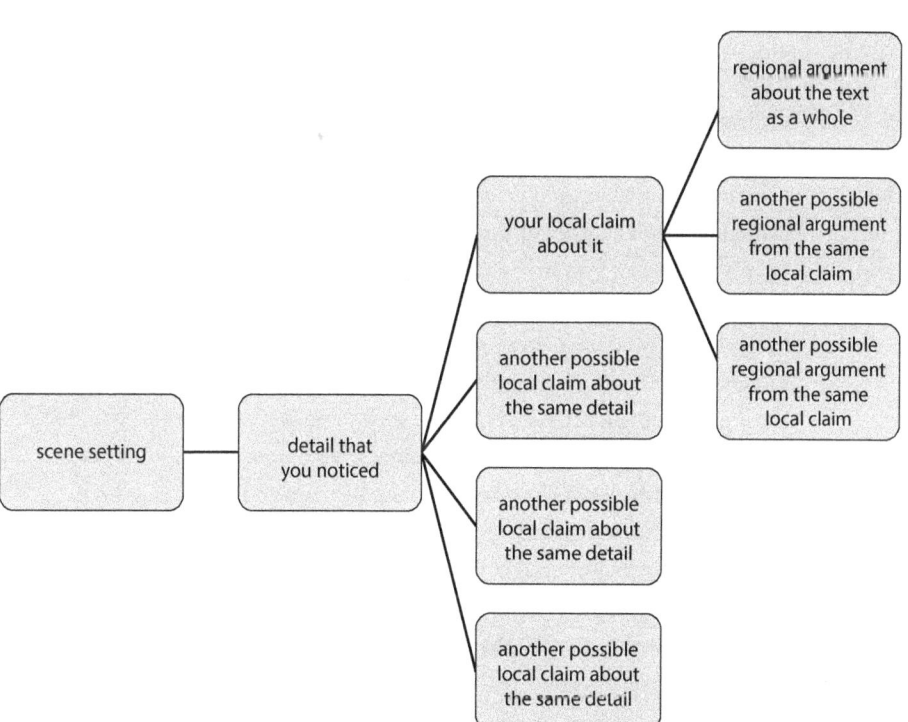

For Instructors

- Johanna explains the way the steps work via an analogy to what someone might say when they're having a conflict with a friend who, say, has been inconsiderate. You might first set the scene: "I know you've been having a hard time, and I've tried to be there for you." Then notice a specific example: "You didn't return my messages this past weekend." Then make a local claim about that specific example: "And that made me feel really upset, like you weren't supporting me in return." Then regionally argue: "I worry that our friendship is uneven." (Or even get to global theorizing: "Friendships that are uneven aren't real friendships.")
- To teach students to connect many details across single texts, we like to reach back to the "Index" activities from the section on noticing.
- To teach students to connect a text's content to its tone, form, or style, we like to reach back to the list of things to pay attention to in the section on noticing. You can ask students to answer those questions—and other noticing questions—again after they've written their local claim.
- Ask them to come up with synonyms for their abstract term or concept that are close but not quite right. (Or was one of them better than the one they first had?)
- As with all the other steps, we like to draw the chart on the board, and diagram a sample close reading, coming up with examples to fill in each bubble in class as discussion or as a small-group activity. It's particularly helpful, at this step, to fill in the counter-arguments, each of which probably uses a slightly different conceptual term (which students may have already listed, as in the previous activity).
- As with all the other steps, you can scaffold student writing toward a longer essay by asking them to complete these steps as homework or as in-class activity. For example, once they have completed the scene setting, noticing, and local claiming steps, you can ask them to come to class with their regional argumentation. (We'll note that if you ask students to develop a close reading step by step, you can break down the writing process clearly and with accountability.)
- Once students have some comfort with the steps of scene setting, noticing, local claiming, and regional argumentation, you can ask them to write 350-word paragraphs of those three steps as homework or as quiz or exam questions.

Step 5: Global Theorizing

In global theorizing, your close reading springboards off the individual text; you begin to participate in scholarly or theoretical conversations. Maybe these are conversations about literary form or genre, maybe they are about an author's oeuvre, or maybe they are about historical or cultural context, or some combination. In global theorizing, you connect your close reading to a larger set of ideas to show the broadest relevance of your thinking. You are now addressing readers who may not know or care about the particular text you've been close reading. The stakes of your argument grow.

To succeed at this step, you need to figure out what—more broadly—you are talking about. You can think about what kinds of arguments the different theoretical movements and schools of thought in literary criticism tend to make; look back at the third section of our introduction. You can also focus your research via the conceptual term that you probably used in the previous step. (And if you didn't then, you need to elucidate it now.) So, for example, if you are thinking about *Never Let Me Go* and euphemism—our example for scene setting—you will research what scholars have written on Ishiguro, for sure, and also you'll read about what scholars have written about euphemism in literature, or how power or authority shape dialogue in novels.

In her chapter, Stephanie Insley Hershinow shows how D. A. Miller moves from a barely mentioned toothpick held by a barely mentioned character in Jane Austen's *Sense and Sensibility* to a startling and sharp idea about how genre and style work, terms that he uses to locate commonalities between new historicism and queer theory. Kimberly Quiogue Andrews shows how Sianne Ngai makes connections between texts to develop an account of affect theory, or how emotions are communicated by texts. Noreen Masud writes about how practical critic William Empson jumps to some of the biggest claims for literature, those about life and the human spirit, and how those feel both unjustifiable and also just right. Christopher Spaide works through how the postcolonial theories that Jahan Ramazani brings to close reading poetry allow him to leap into global theorizing.

Unlike the essays written by professional scholars and critics—by those who have been trained to be professors—undergraduate essays usually reach global theorizing only at the very end of an essay, often as a gesture. An essay by a strong English major may invoke a conceptual term as early as their local claim, but it does not, generally speaking, have the room or time to research how their close reading connects to a larger scholarly conversation. The task in most senior theses is to take this next step and write a graduate-level essay. Graduate close readings should reach global theorizing, even if the research is minimal. In the next section of pedagogical activities, we'll offer some structures for how to incorporate close reading into essays of different scholarly genres and lengths.

Refining your global theorizing skills means becoming self-aware about the kind of argument you're making, and performing research so you can make it better.

- Go back to the third section of the introduction, "What Close Reading Has Been." Which of the following schools of thought are making arguments that share some similarities with yours? Are they concerned about the same topics? Do they discuss the same texts? Do they use the same conceptual terms?
  - New Criticism
  - Deconstruction
  - Feminist theory
  - Queer theory
  - New Historicism
  - Marxism
  - Postcolonial theory
  - Psychoanalysis
  - Affect theory
  - Narratology
  - Afropessimism and critical fabulation
- Identify the conceptual term that you use in regional argumentation. Find one reputable scholarly article or book published after the year 2000 that is relevant for your conceptual term.
  - Find it by talking to your professor, the librarian specializing in your discipline at your college or university's research library, by searching on your library's database or MLA Bibliography
  - Make sure it was published by a university press—that's a rough way of making sure it's reputable
  - From its bibliography, find three more reputable scholarly articles or books
- Don't read all scholarship the same way you read literature, attentive to every little detail. Instead, at least on your first reading, pay attention to

what the argument is. What is its local claim, its regional argumentation, its global theorizing? If you haven't done the activities from the previous section on "Reading Close Reading," go back and do those. If you want to see how close reading can be built into a longer essay, check out the next section, "Using Close Reading."

Here's the final iteration of the same chart, now through global theorizing. As with scene setting, global theorizing shouldn't be framed rhetorically as one possible step among many, but the full, inevitable follow-through of regional argumentation.

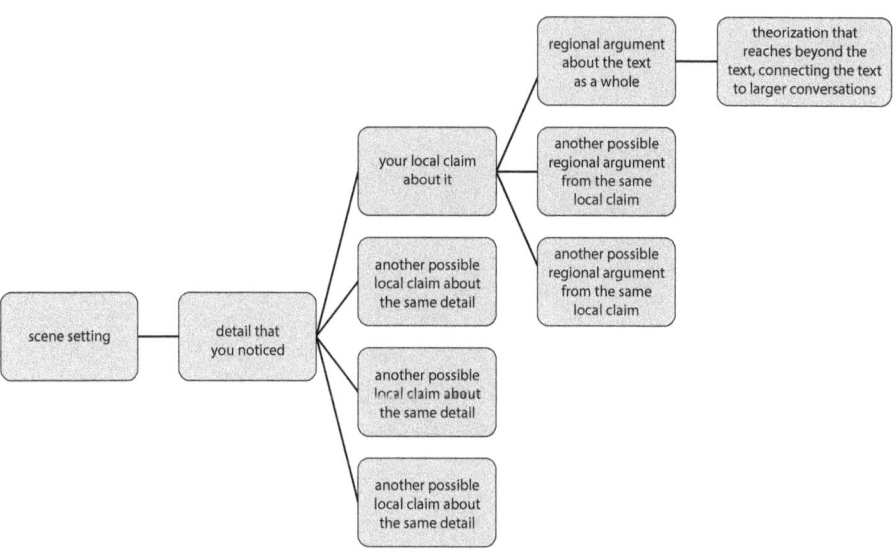

For Instructors

- When teaching research, it can be helpful to have a librarian do a presentation, or to have various faculty members or advanced graduate students present to more junior students on their own research techniques. But the main part of teaching global theorizing is teaching students to recognize the concepts at stake in their work.
- We like to assign annotated bibliographies in which students write the local claiming, regional argumentation, and global theorizing of each scholarly article or book they read under the bibliographic information.

- For graduate students, we sometimes ask them to group the scholarly conversations into clusters or even family trees.
- A big part of teaching global theorizing is teaching *chutzpah*, particularly for students who might feel out of place in their classrooms, who suffer from impostor syndrome, or who aren't sure if they are prepared as well as their peers. We affirm that they also have something to contribute, even if it's something small, to a larger ongoing scholarly conversation—that they are scholars.

Using Close Readings

Close readings can stand alone in shorter writing and they also can be components of longer essays. This section teaches you how to use them as foundational building blocks. A close reading can be as short as a paragraph, around 300 words. But a close reading that runs through all five steps can be as long as five double-spaced pages, around 1,500 words. With this kind of variation, how can you use them as a stable element of something larger?

Here are the most common genres of academic writing at both the undergraduate and graduate levels that involve close reading a literary text, and the approximate length of each genre:

- discussion board post or similar: 50–300 words
- short answer essay on an exam: 300 words
- informal response essay: 1–2 double-spaced pages/300–600 words
- in-class exam essay: a few pages/600–800 words
- shorter essay: 5–7 double-spaced pages/1,500–2,100 words
- conference paper: 8 double-spaced pages/2,400 words
- longer essay: 10–12 double-spaced pages/3,000–3,600 words
- senior thesis/academic journal article: 25 double-spaced pages/7,500 words
- dissertation chapter: 25–45 double-spaced pages/7,500–13,500 words

Discussion board posts come in different forms. They may include a prompt—like "identify a moment that perplexed you," "how should we understand the author's use of this particular word?" "why does the text begin this way?" or "choose a keyword"—and for those, you can often answer with only one of the steps, or perhaps one step and the subsequent one. Noticing answers a prompt like "identify a moment that perplexed you"; local claiming responds to questions like "how should we understand the author's use of this particular word?"; and regional argumentation responds to "why does the text begin this way?" For "choose a keyword," you could answer with noticing, local claiming, regional argumentation, or even global theorizing. You could also respond with two adjoining steps (noticing and local claiming, or local claiming and regional argumentation, or regional argumentation and global theorizing) so that you can make a case for the meaningfulness of your keyword by showing how it ramifies in significance. Discussion board posts also may be open-ended, asking you to write a paragraph or so; in that case, they are more like short-answer questions on an exam.

Short answers on an exam are almost always full paragraphs that respond to a question or a prompt. These usually consist of scene setting, quoting the text probably only once, noticing, and at least local claiming, and perhaps regional argumentation; they rarely reach as far as global theorizing.[9]

Informal response essays are usually assigned as homework. In our experience, students find this genre confusing, because it might appear that they're being asked to write about an emotional response to a text. Instead, think of a response essay as a simple close reading; your response to the text consists of showing your professor how you interpret it. Like a short answer, a response essay should contain at least the first three steps of scene setting, noticing, local claiming, and probably will reach regional argumentation. But it's not a single paragraph—you might write as much as two double-spaced pages. You should begin with a brief introduction, but rather than organizing each body paragraph to center on a single step, or having each paragraph contain all of the steps, focus each body paragraph on a quotation from the text. In the first body paragraph, you might start with scene setting, quote from the text and then write about noticing, or you might start with noticing and then quote. This first body paragraph might then include local claiming, making an argument about what has been noticed. The next paragraph might use only regional argumentation to reframe the quotation from the previous paragraph, or it might quote from another moment of the text to regionally argue across the text, or it might include both local claiming to interpret that new quotation and then build to regional argumentation by the end of the second page. You may even reach global theorizing.

The in-class exam essay is akin to a reading response, though it might be more formal in tone or style, but, even writing by hand in a blue book, you should be able to move through the steps. We expect that an essay like this would include scene setting, noticing, local claiming, and regional argumentation, and perhaps touching on global theorizing in the last few sentences. Remember to anchor body paragraphs with quotations, and to engage with potential counterarguments, using the implications to build your way to the next step.

So far, we have discussed close readings that are one double-spaced page/300 words, two double-spaced pages/600 words, and what could be the equivalent of up to three double-spaced pages. Let's imagine these as blocks.

---

9. For more advice, see Eric Hayot, "The Uneven U," *The Elements of Academic Style* (Columbia University Press, 2014), 59–73.

To write the next kind of essay, *the shorter essay* of 5–7 double-spaced typed pages or 1,500–2,100 words, you will start to combine blocks. After a brief introduction, you will have two or three close readings, moving from scene setting through regional argumentation for each, and hopefully building to global theorizing by the end of the essay (it often works as a conclusion for essays of this length). Your close readings will be connected, but the way they should be connected is that each should build on the regional argumentation of the one before. That regional argumentation informs the next close reading's scene setting. You can organize the close readings in different ways, with shorter ones first or last. You could include two or three close readings. You should not be able to rearrange the close readings. They work cumulatively; each depends on the previous one. Start with your clearest close reading and move to the one that you could only recognize once you have learned how to understand the first one. Your blocks could look like any of these or more (representing different close readings in grayscale):

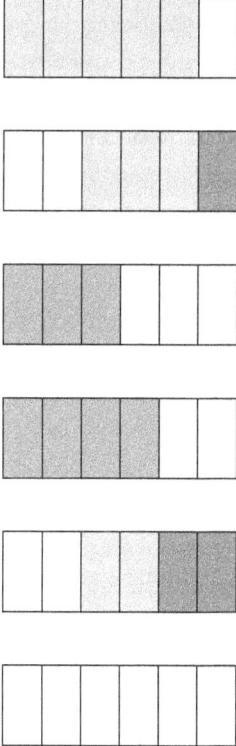

After you've moved beyond 7 pages/2,100 words, you are probably discussing more than one text, and so your essay won't be purely close reading. You might be discussing multiple literary texts, but more likely you are using theory, criticism, and/or other scholarship to frame your discussion of literature. Your close readings are still the core of your essay. Close reading is how you make your evidence into evidence. But close readings might comprise less than half of the essay's total length.

What do we mean when we say that you're using scholarship to frame your discussion of literature? Usually this happens in at least two ways and you should do both. The first uses scholarship to situate the literary text in relation to its contexts, and the second draws on an abstract idea. For example, Kate Marshall's *Novels by Aliens* has the subtitle: *Weird Tales and the Twenty-First Century*; contemporary fiction draws on one scholarly conversation, weirdness on another, and Marshall sets up her book at this intersection. Or, as another example, Jennifer Fleissner, in her book *Maladies of the Will*, writes about nineteenth-century American novels and larger conceptual accounts of how the will works.

Once you have written a single close reading through regional argumentation, you should have a rough version of at least the two most important conceptual frames. First, simply by choosing a text, you know whether you're writing about, say, sixteenth-century drama in Ireland or twenty-first-century poetry in Canada. Second, you should already have some sense of a conceptual term (like Marshall's "weird" or Fleissner's "will") that might be particularly important in a particular time and place but also has a longer or larger theorization. In the previous section's activities, we wrote about how regional argumentation usually reaches further conceptually than local claiming by invoking a larger and more abstract term that unites the literary text under an umbrella of an abstract idea. And global theorizing requires connecting your close reading to a larger conversation, and as we wrote in the previous section, you focus your research via the conceptual term that has probably already emerged for you.

When you write an essay that's not just close reading, you place your concepts first; you use them to frame the close reading that follows. Just the way that noticing often comes first when you're reading, but scene setting comes first for your own reader, you can think about the whole close reading coming first for you—from scene setting through global theorizing—but once you write a longer essay, you frame all of that conceptually with research before even scene setting orients your reader in the close reading that will serve as evidence for it all.

As you write a longer essay, rather than think about it as one 12- or 25-page chunk, divide it into sections, each with a specific purpose. When you read articles or chapters, pay attention to how they break down into sections: how many sections there are, what each one's job is, the order they come in. In the essays that graduate students and professional scholars write, a brief close reading will often start off the essay, but more sustained close readings usually appear later.

If you're writing *a conference paper*—we're thinking here of conferences like the Annual Convention of the Modern Languages Association at which graduate students and professors present, but this is adaptable for some undergraduate presentations too—you might have about 8 double-spaced pages, or 2,400 words. Conference papers tend to break down like this:

- 1-page or less introduction that begins with an efficient example—a scene, anecdote, stanza, disagreement, puzzle—that lays out the problem or question that your argument will address, followed by a statement of that argument, whether it is a local claim, a regional argument, or a global theory. (For example, Johanna recently gave a conference paper on how the analogies in Emily Dickinson's poems should count as logical reasoning, and how that changes our idea of how poetry can be philosophical.) While this efficient example isn't always a 1-page/300-word close reading that gets to global theorizing, it often is.
- 3–4 pages that come out of the research you've done that set up the conceptual frames for your argument, whether they are theoretical, literary critical, cultural, historical, philosophical, or something else. Usually there are two groups, of around two pages each: one is on the relevant scholarship on the author and the text that you're discussing, and the other is the relevant scholarship on the abstract term that emerges from your close reading. (In Johanna's paper, she drew on the scholarly conversation about the particular author or texts, in this case, how scholars have written about Dickinson, particularly her imagery, and the scholarly conversation about an abstract idea, here analogy as logical reasoning).

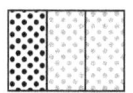

- 2–3 pages of close reading (Johanna close-read two poems by Dickinson, the second very quickly)

- 1 page of global theorizing. (Johanna clarified how recognizing logical reasoning in poetry means that poems can be philosophical in their forms and not just in their content.)

All together:

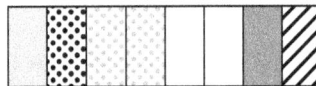

We would like to add that this organization is descriptive of what a lot of people do and not prescriptive of what you must do. It's fun to experiment! What's important is to have a clear organization that supports your argument; and if you're writing about a literary text, close reading is an important component.

In a *longer essay* of 10–12 double-spaced typed pages or 3,000–3,600 words—the kind of essay that an undergrad might write at the end of a course—we would expect it to have the following organization, though again this is descriptive rather than prescriptive:

- 1-page introduction that states the argument, whether it ends with a local claim, a regional argument, or a global theory
- 4–5 pages that come out of the research you've done that set up the conceptual frames for your argument, whether they are theoretical, literary critical, cultural, historical, philosophical, or something else
- 4–5 pages of close reading
- 1–2 pages of implications

All of these pieces together:

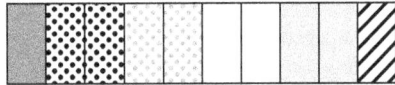

A senior thesis usually shares the same structure as *a final essay for a graduate school seminar*—25 double-spaced pages or 7,500 words—because both of them are asking students to mimic the professional requirements of *an academic journal article*. This means that you can go read articles in such journals as *PMLA, American Literary History, English Literary History, Modernism/modernity, J19*, and many more, and see models there. (Go look up your professors' articles!) What you'll find is, often, the following:

- 2–3-page introduction that begins with an efficient example—a scene, anecdote, stanza, disagreement, puzzle—laying out the problem or question that the argument will address and then stating that argument, ending with global theorizing
- 8–9 pages of conceptual frames, some combination of theoretical, literary critical, cultural, historical, philosophical, or something else, usually in at least two parts
- 8–9 pages of close reading, usually in two or more parts
- 2–5 pages of further global theorizing

All of these pieces together:

If you look at models of academic articles, you'll see that many are divided into sections, either with numbers or spacing or asterisks between them. Those sections usually include the four that are listed above, though often the conceptual frames section will be subdivided into its different conversations and the close reading section will also be subdivided into individual close readings.

Finally, *a dissertation chapter* is 25–45 double-spaced pages or 7,500–13,500 words. On its shorter end, it is identical to an academic article, and indeed, many graduate students publish chapters of their dissertations as journal articles. But it's more elastic, so any of the sections above might be longer or there might be an additional conceptual frame brought in, or an extra close reading or two, or more room for the implications. For models of dissertation chapters that are longer than academic articles, go look at the first books of many professors, which are often based on their dissertations. (And then go look up the actual dissertations and see how effective the revision process can be, especially with some time and institutional support.)

For an activity: map out the sections of your essay. Here's a 25-page block. Try it different ways.

For Instructors

- We've brought in Legos, Duplos, or other kinds of blocks of different colors to class to show students how to put together the sections of different genres of academic writing. What is germane, here, is how each section builds off the one before.
- If students are writing longer essays—especially the first time they are writing a longer essay, such as a senior thesis—consider assigning one section at a time. It can be easier to tell them to write a close reading section, or a conceptual frame section, and perhaps revise those before assembling them, rather than writing a full draft, even if it is a rough draft.

ACKNOWLEDGMENTS

We'd like to thank our teachers from whom we learned to read closely. Johanna takes this opportunity to thank Peter Reinke, her high school English teacher at Germantown Friends. Dan thanks the late Rich DuRocher, who introduced him to close reading at St. Olaf.

We also thank our students, from whom we also learn more about close reading every time we teach it. It is an honor to write something that we hope will be broadly useful; if it is, it's due to what we gained by sharing our classrooms with our students. We tested out this material in our fall 2024 semester courses. We thank the students in West Virginia University's Foundations of Literary Study: Vincenza Altieri, Eleni Ambatis, Konnor Brown, Elena Brunty, Abigail Davis, Rebecca Deimler, Lauren Erwin, Greta Giuliano, Carina Haines, Talia Jordan, Alexis Lindsey, Christopher Meyer, Cala Palmer, Sarabeth Parsons, Morgan Ranck, Sarah Seif, Gabrielle Stillion, and Alexandria VanMeter. We thank, too, the students in Emory University's Methods of Literary Study and Research: Syd Clark, Peter Daddazio, and Madison Kraft.

We're grateful for Anne Savarese at Princeton University Press; she understood this project immediately and guided it through the publication process with deftness and insight. We also appreciate the help of James Collier, Jill Harris, Leah Caldwell, and Emma Wagh.

Thank you to our contributors. The twenty-two people whose essays are included here were indispensable interlocutors who helped us conceptualize this book. Their contributions exceed the pages that bear their names. Thank you in particular to Kimberly Quiogue Andrews, Brian Glavey, Oren Izenberg, Joshua Kotin, and Julie Orlemanski; all gave us illuminating and helpful feedback.

We thank our friends who talked with us about this book; they felt our excitement about it and offered more back to us: Brian Glavey, Joshua Kotin, Anne O'Donnell, Daisy Pitkin, Jillian Wein Riley, Rose Casey—Dan's and Johanna's mutual friend who introduced us in 2019; Paul Buchholz, Kevin McNellis, Nick Sturm, and Nathan Taylor. We thank Scott Newstok, a champion and avid tracker of close reading who kept us apprised of scholarship and trends as he discovered them.

We thank our families. Johanna thanks her parents—Howard Winant and Deborah Rogow—for their unflagging support for this book and also nearly everything she does. She told her father about this book project early on; she walked her mother through the last pieces to fall in place while they walked through gardens together. She thanks her siblings, Carmen and Gabe, who also bring together thinking and teaching, the life of the mind and the world in need of repair. She's grateful for her husband, Geoff Hilsabeck, whose love makes everything from the most local to the most global possible. Dan thanks his parents, Stu and Carol, his brothers, Andy and Alex, who all cheered on this book throughout the process. He thanks his wife, Masha, a companion in close reading the texts, aesthetic and otherwise, of everyday life: lately, the textual obsessions of their offspring, deeply strange works of fiction such as *The Color Kittens* and *Little Fur Family*.

Dan and Johanna thank each other. *Close Reading for the Twenty-First Century* was a total delight because of our collaboration. This has been a once-in-a-career experience. It has affirmed for us the value of what we do as scholars every day, and also why we should do it together.

This book looks forward into the future. We dedicate it to our children: to Esther and Ezekiel Hilsabeck, both learning to read in these years; and to Eulia Vlasova Sinykin, uttering her first words. You belong to this century, and it to you. We joyfully entrust the future to you; you have our confidence and our hearts.

CONTRIBUTORS

Kimberly Quiogue Andrews is associate professor of English at the University of Ottawa. She is the author of *The Academic Avant-Garde: Poetry and the American University* and the poetry collection *A Brief History of Fruit*.

Elaine Auyoung is associate professor of English at the University of Minnesota and affiliate faculty of its Center for Cognitive Sciences. She is the author of *When Fiction Feels Real: Representation and the Reading Mind*.

Farah Bakaari is assistant professor of English at the University of California, Berkeley.

Adrienne Brown is associate professor in the departments of English and Race, Diaspora, and Indigeneity at the University of Chicago.

Beci Carver is based at the University of Exeter. Her book *Granular Modernism* was published by Oxford University Press in 2014, and her new book *Modernism's Whims* is forthcoming in 2025. She has published widely on modernism and its penumbrae.

Natalia Cecire is associate professor of English and American literature at the University of Sussex.

Pardis Dabashi is assistant professor of English and film studies at Bryn Mawr. She is affiliated faculty in the Middle Eastern Studies Program and the Comparative Literature Program. She is the author of *Losing the Plot: Film and Feeling in the Modern Novel*.

Jeff Dolven teaches poetry and poetics, especially of the English Renaissance, at Princeton University. He is the author of *Senses of Style* and **A New English Grammar*, and is an editor-at-large at *Cabinet* magazine.

Brian Glavey is associate professor of English at the University of South Carolina and the author of *The Wallflower Avant-Garde*. He is completing a book on postwar American poetry and the aesthetics of relatability.

Stephanie Insley Hershinow is associate professor at Baruch College and the Graduate Center, CUNY. She is the author of *Born Yesterday: Inexperience and the Early Realist Novel* and editor of the Norton Library editions of *Emma* and *Sense and Sensibility*.

Jane Hu is assistant professor of English at the University of Southern California.

Oren Izenberg studies the long history of poetry and poetics. He is the author of *Being Numerous: Poetry and the Ground of Social Life*, and teaches at the University of California, Irvine.

Katie Kadue is assistant professor of English at Binghamton University. She is the author of *Domestic Georgic: Labors of Preservation from Rabelais to Milton*.

Joshua Kotin teaches at Princeton University. He is the author of *Utopias of One* and coauthor (with Jeff Dolven) of *Parkland Mysteries*. He directs the Shakespeare and Company Project.

Summer Kim Lee is assistant professor in the Department of English at University of California, Los Angeles.

Noreen Masud is lecturer in English Literature at the University of Bristol, UK, and an AHRC/BBC New Generation Thinker. She wrote *Stevie Smith and the Aphorism: Hard Language* and *A Flat Place*.

Emily Ogden is professor of English at the University of Virginia and the author of *On Not Knowing: How to Love and Other Essays*.

Julie Orlemanski is associate professor of English at the University of Chicago and co-editor of the *Norton Anthology of English Literature, Eleventh Edition*. She is currently writing about fictionality and literary personhood.

Lindsay Reckson is associate professor of English at Haverford College. She is the author of *Realist Ecstasy: Religion, Race, and Performance in American Literature* and the editor of *American Literature in Transition: 1876–1910*. She is the Faculty and Curriculum Innovation Director for the Graterford Archive, a community-based archive that lifts up the creative, life-affirming, and liberatory work of people incarcerated at Graterford State Correctional Institution (1929–2018).

LIST OF CONTRIBUTORS

Dan Sinykin is associate professor of English at Emory University and the author of *Big Fiction: How Conglomeration Changed the Publishing Industry and American Literature*.

Christopher Spaide is assistant professor of English at the University of Southern Mississippi, focusing on twentieth- and twenty-first-century poetry.

Robert Stagg is assistant professor of English and director of the New Variorum Shakespeare at Texas A&M University. He is the author of *Shakespeare's Blank Verse: An Alternative History*.

Omari Weekes is assistant professor of English at Queens College, CUNY. He is currently working on his first book, tentatively titled *Lurid Affinities: Sex and the Spirit in Post–Civil Rights Black Literature*.

Johanna Winant is associate professor at Reed College. She is the author of the book *Lyric Logic*.

INDEX

Abrams, M. H., 55
academic journal articles, 255, 261
Achebe, Chinua, 133
Aebischer, Paul, 112
aesthetics, 201–8
aesthetics of spectacle, 136
affect theory: close reading and, 34; global theorizing and, 201–8, 251; regional argumentation and, 176–83, 248
"The Affective Fallacy" (Wimsatt and Beardsley), 176–77
Africanist presence, 82–83, 84–87
Afropessimism, 35–36, 116–23
Alexander, Elizabeth, 143
alliteration, 118–19, 180
anaphora, 117–19
"Andrew Marvell" (Ricks), 93–95
Andrews, Kimberly Quiogue, 34, 201–8, 251
Ansatzpunkte (points of departure), 108, 111–12
anthropology, 132–39
antiblack violence, 116–17, 122
anxiety: affect theory and, 34, 201–8, 251; close reading and, 98, 103, 104, 244; *Le Jeu d'Adam* (*The Play of Adam*) and, 113–14; noticing and, 84–87
Appadurai, Arjun, 213
Appiah, Kwame Anthony, 213
Arendt, Hannah, 89
Aristotle, 169n4
Armstrong, Louis, 84–87
Arnold, Matthew, 214
The Art of the Novel (James), 46–54, 244–45

Ashbery, John, 34, 176–83, 248
assonance, 118–19, 180
Auden, W. H., 214–15
Auerbach, Erich: close reading and, 27–31; global theorizing and, 40–41; *Le Jeu d'Adam* (*The Play of Adam*) and, 107–15, 242; local claiming and, 107–15, 242; scene setting and, 27–28, 39–45, 109, 245; Woolf and, 27–28, 39–45, 245
Austen, Jane: global theorizing and, 195–200; narratology and, 35, 151–59, 248; postcolonialism and, 32; regional argumentation and, 151–59
Austen, Jane—works: *Mansfield Park*, 32; *Pride and Prejudice*, 151–59; *Sense and Sensibility*, 195–200, 251
Austin, J. L., 125
authorial choice, 73–79, 80–81
autotheory, 35
Auyoung, Elaine, 18, 35, 151–59, 248

Bakaari, Farah, 35, 132–39, 242
banality of evil, 89n1
Baraka, Amiri, 117
Baudelaire, Charles, 171n8
Beardsley, Monroe, 176–77
beholding, 119–20
Being and Time (Heidegger), 201, 203
"Bells for John Whiteside's Daughter" (Ransom), 162–66
Beowulf, 171n8
Berlant, Lauren, 33–34, 176–83, 248
biopower, 127n6

Black Aliveness, or a Poetics of Being (Quashie), 116–23
Black femininity, 140–47
Black feminism, 27–28, 121–22, 125. *See also* Spillers, Hortense
"A Black History of the English-Speaking Peoples" (Nagra), 209–17
Black interiors, 143–44
Black Lives Matter movement, 122
Black studies: deconstruction and, 26–27, 140–47; local claiming and, 116–23, 124–31, 140–47; noticing and, 80–87; in the twenty-first century, 35–36
blackness, 82–83, 84–87
Blake, William, 76–77
The Bluest Eye (Morrison), 81
Bodies that Matter (Butler), 124–31
Book of Kings (Ferdowsi), 171n8, 173
Borgquist, Alvin, 117–18
Bourdieu, Pierre, 34
Bright Fountain (*Cheshme-ye roshan*) (Yousefi), 168–75
Brontë, Emily, 228, 235–36
Brooks, Cleanth, 24, 160–61, 163, 165–66, 169n4
Brooks, Gwendolyn, 140–47
Brown, Adrienne, 27, 80–87
Butler, Judith, 27–28, 124–31, 242

Campion, Jane, 101–4
Cardinal, Marie, 84–87
Carver, Beci, 22, 55–62, 245
Cather, Willa, 83, 84
Cecire, Natalia, 27, 124–31, 242
"Characteristics of Negro Expression" (Hurston), 143–44
characterization, 154–57
Chauvin, Derek, 116–17
Christian, Barbara, 27–28, 125, 130–31
Churchill, Winston, 214
Citizen (Rankine), 224–25, 232–33
Claiming History (Coundouriotis), 132–39, 242
clichés: Berlant on, 179, 182–83; Ricks on, 88–96, 238, 246; Warren on, 163–65
"Clichés" (Ricks), 88–93, 95–96

Clifton, Lucille, 116–23, 242
close reading: academic writing and, 255–62; concept and example of, 1–10, 36, 219–21 (*see also specific steps*); conversation and, 19–20; deconstruction and, 21, 25–28, 29; drama and, 66; Marxism and, 21, 29, 30–31, 32, 34; New Criticism and, 21–25, 28–29, 158, 160–62; New Historicism and, 21, 29–32; postcolonialism and, 21, 26, 29, 31–32, 35, 251; psychoanalysis and, 21, 34; as skill, 17–18; in the twenty-first century, 34–35; understanding and, 11–17
Cole, Henri, 78
colorism, 145–46
conference papers, 255, 259
conversation, 19–20
Coundouriotis, Eleni, 35, 132–39, 242
Critical Approaches to Literature (Daiches), 168
critical fabulation, 35, 36
Critique of Judgment (Kant), 201
Cruel Optimism (Berlant), 33, 176–83, 248
Culture and Imperialism (Said), 31–32

Dabashi, Pardis, 34, 167–75, 248
Dahomey (present-day Benin), 133
Daiches, David, 168
Dante, 20
deconstruction: close reading and, 21, 25–28, 29; local claiming and, 124–31, 140–47; noticing and, 80–87, 97–104
Derrida, Jacques, 25, 27, 28
Le Devoir de violence (Ouologuem), 35, 133–39
differentiation, 153
discussion board posts, 255
dissertations, 255, 261
Dolven, Jeff, 18, 20, 22, 72–79, 239
Dominguez, Véronique, 112
Donne, John, 24
Du Bois, W.E.B., 117–18
"Dust" (Shamlu), 169–75
Dylan, Bob, 92–93

Eichmann, Adolf, 89n1
Eliot, T. S., 93–95, 211–12

empathetic reading, 72–79, 239
Empson, William, 22, 88, 93, 187–94, 251
Epic of Gilgamesh, 171n8
essays, 255, 256–59, 260
ethnography, 132–39
exams, 255, 256–59

Farrokhzad, Forugh, 168
Faulkner, William, 81, 84
feminism: affect theory and, 34, 176; deconstruction and, 26, 27; noticing and, 97–104. *See also* Black feminism
The Feminist Difference (Johnson), 102–3
Ferdowsi, Abolqasem, 168, 171n8, 173
Fleissner, Jennifer, 258
Floyd, George, 116–17, 122
footfall, 55–62, 245
Foucault, Michel, 26, 29, 127n6
"The Fourth Dimension of a Poem" (Abrams), 55
free indirect discourse, 126n4, 128–29
Fresh Air (Shamlu), 169–74
Freud, Sigmund, 34, 99, 203–4
Frost, Robert: deconstruction and, 25; New Criticism and, 23–24; New Historicism and, 30; pessimism and, 210; psychoanalysis and, 33–34; understanding and, 14–16
Frost, Robert—works: "Neither Out Far Nor In Deep," 210; "The Road Not Taken," 23–24, 25, 30, 33; "Stopping by Woods on a Snowy Evening," 14–16

Gates, Henry Louis, Jr., 26, 35
gender: anxiety and, 203–8; deconstruction and, 27–28; local claiming and, 124–31, 140–47; noticing and, 97–104. *See also* queer theory
Gender Trouble (Butler), 124–25
"The Ghetto" (Ridge), 222, 231
Gilmore, Ruth Wilson, 126n3
Glavey, Brian, 34, 176–83, 248
global theorizing: Auerbach and, 40–41, 109, 112; Berlant on, 182–83; Butler and, 129; concept of, 3–4, 8–10, 40–41, 219; conversation and, 19; Empson and, 187–94; exercises, 251–54; identification of, 222–37; Kenner and, 221; Miller and, 195–200; Ngai and, 201–8; Ramazani and, 209–17, 251
Goodison, Lorna, 211–12, 213
"A Greyhound in the Evening After a Long Day of Rain" (Oswald), 56–59
Griffiths, Eric, 22, 65–71
Grogan, Kristin, 222, 231

Hafez, 168, 171n8
Hamlet (Shakespeare), 65–71
Hartman, Saidiya, 35
Hazoumé, Paul, 133
Heaney, Seamus, 214
Hearing Things (Leighton), 55–62, 245
Hegel, G.W.F., 30
Heidegger, Martin, 201, 203
Hemingway, Ernest, 84
Henry IV (Shakespeare), 188, 193
hermeneutic circle, 107, 112–13, 115
Hershinow, Stephanie Insley, 35, 195–200, 251
Hill, Geoffrey, 92
A History of the English-Speaking Peoples (Churchill), 214
Hitchcock, Alfred, 34, 201–8
A Homemade World (Kenner), 219–21
Homer, 171n8
"How Should One Read a Book?" (Woolf), 72–73
Hu, Jane, 34, 46–54, 244–45
Hughes, Langston, 213
Hunter, Walt, 224–25, 232–33
Hurston, Zora Neale, 143–44

"I Shall Be Free" (song), 92–93
"Ignorance of the Law Is No Excuse" (Ashbery), 178–83, 248
Iliad (Homer), 171n8
incandescence, 142
internal focalization, 126n4

irony, 24, 26, 29, 160–66
Ishiguro, Kazuo, 245–46
Izenberg, Oren, 28–29, 39–45, 245

James, Henry: on novel, 39; psychoanalysis and, 34, 46–54, 244–45; scene setting and, 34, 46–54, 244–45
James, Henry—works: *The Art of the Novel*, 46–54; *The Wings of the Dove*, 225–27, 233–35
Jameson, Fredric, 30–31, 213
Jane Austen (Miller), 195–200, 251
Jarvis, Claire, 228, 235–36
Le Jeu d'Adam (*The Play of Adam*), 107–15, 242
Jim Crow laws, 125–26
Johnson, Barbara, 26, 97–104, 238, 246
Johnson, Samuel, 88
Johnston, Freya, 66
Jordan, June, 117
"The Journey of the Magi" (Eliot), 211–12

Kadue, Katie, 22, 88–96, 238, 246
Kant, Immanuel, 201
Keats, John: deconstruction and, 26, 97–101; on negative capability, 115n4; New Criticism and, 24, 72–79, 92; noticing and, 72–79, 97–101; Persian literary traditions and, 171n8
Keats, John—works: "To Autumn," 74–79; "Ode on a Grecian Urn," 24, 26, 97–101; "Ode to a Nightingale," 77
Kenner, Hugh, 78, 219–21
Kotin, Joshua, 18, 20, 22, 72–79, 239
Kuhn, Thomas, 16
Kurnick, David, 47

Larsen, Nella, 27, 124–31, 242
Leavis, F. R., 88
Lee, Summer Kim, 26, 97–104, 238, 246
Leighton, Angela, 22, 55–62, 245
Lipton, Peter, 14
local claiming: Auerbach and, 107–15, 242; Berlant on, 182–83; Butler and, 124–31; concept of, 3–4, 6–7, 9, 219; conversation and, 19; Coundouriotis and, 132–39, 242; exercises, 242–44; identification of, 222–37; Kenner and, 219–20, 221; Miller and, 197–98; Quashie and, 116–23, 242; Spillers and, 140–47; understanding and, 11–17; Vendler and, 76; Yousefi and, 170–71
Lorde, Audre, 117

Macaulay, Thomas Babington, 214, 216
MacLeish, Archibald, 98
Magritte, René, 211–12
Maladies of the Will (Fleissner), 258
Mallarmé, Stéphane, 98
"Mama's Baby, Papa's Maybe" (Spillers), 140
Mansfield Park (Austen), 32, 157
Marshall, Kate, 258
Marvell, Andrew, 92, 93–95
Marx, Karl, 30–31
Marxism: affect theory and, 34, 176; close reading and, 21, 29, 30–31, 32, 33
Masud, Noreen, 22, 187–94, 251
Maud Martha (Brooks), 140–47
McAlpine, Erica, 223–24, 231–32
McCarthy, Jesse, 228–29, 236–37
Measure for Measure (Shakespeare), 188, 193
Melville, Herman, 34, 84, 201–8, 251
The Merchant of Venice (Shakespeare), 188
metaphysical poets, 24
Miller, D. A., 35, 195–200, 251
Milton, John, 73, 92
Mimesis (Auerbach), 27, 39–45, 107–15, 242
Mitchell, Koritha, 122n7
modernism, 209–17, 221, 225–28
"Moody Subjects/Projectile Objects" (Ngai), 201–8, 251
Morrison, Toni, 26–27, 80–87
"Muteness Envy" (Johnson), 97–104

Nagra, Daljit, 209–17
narratology: close reading and, 35; global theorizing and, 195–200; local claiming and, 132–39; regional argumentation and, 151–59, 248
Nazi regime, 89n1

Nedjma (Yacine), 228–29, 236–37
negative capability, 115
Neill, Sam, 103
"Neither Out Far Nor In Deep" (Frost), 210
Never Let Me Go (Ishiguro), 245–46
New Criticism: affect theory and, 176–77; Auerbach and, 108–9; close reading and, 21–25, 28–29, 158, 160–62; deconstruction and, 25–26, 28; global theorizing and, 187–94; noticing and, 65–71, 72–79, 88–96; regional argumentation and, 160–66; scene setting and, 56–62; Yousefi and, 169
New Historicism, 21, 29–32
New Science (Vico), 27
Ngai, Sianne, 34, 201–8
Nietzsche, Friedrich, 167, 170
noticing: Auerbach and, 109; Butler and, 127–29, 131; concept of, 3–4, 5–6, 218–19; conversation and, 19; Coundouriotis and, 134–35; exercises, 238–41; Griffiths and, 65–71; identification of, 222–37; Johnson and, 97–104, 238, 246; Kenner and, 219–21; Miller and, 196–97; Morrison and, 80–87; Ngai and, 201–8; Quashie and, 118–20; Ricks and, 88–96; skill and, 18; understanding and, 11–17; Vendler and, 72–79; Yousefi and, 170–71
Novels by Aliens (Marshall), 258

"Ode on a Grecian Urn" (Keats), 24, 26, 97–101
"Ode to a Nightingale" (Keats), 77
The Odes of John Keats (Vendler), 72–79
Ogden, Emily, 24, 160–66, 248
The One vs. the Many (Woloch), 151–59
"'An Order of Constancy'" (Spillers), 141–42
Orientalism (Said), 31
Orlemanski, Julie, 28–29, 40, 107–15, 242
Orwell, George, 71, 89–92, 95–96, 215
Oswald, Alice, 56–61
Other, 132–39
Ouologuem, Yambo, 35, 133–39

"Pad, Pad" (Smith), 60–61
paradigms, 16
"Paranoid Reading and Reparative Reading" (Sedgwick), 47
parentheses, 42–43
Passing (Larsen), 28, 124–31, 242
performative audacity, 107, 113–14
performative language, 125
Phillips, Natalie, 71
The Piano (1993 film), 101–4
Picasso, Pablo, 213
Pierre (Melville), 34, 201–8, 251
Plath, Sylvia, 192–93
Playing in the Dark (Morrison), 80–87
Poe, Edgar Allan, 84
Poetics (Aristotle), 169n4
point of view, 132–39
"Politics and the English Language" (Orwell), 89–92, 95–96
Ponge, Francis, 98
postcolonialism: close reading and, 21, 26, 29, 31–32, 35, 251; global theorizing and, 209–17; local claiming and, 132–39
Pound, Ezra, 78
The Pound Era (Kenner), 78
practical criticism, 22–24, 65. *See also* Empson, William; Ricks, Christopher
Press, Karen, 211–12, 213
Pride and Prejudice (Austen), 151–59
psychoanalysis: close reading and, 21, 33–34; scene setting and, 46–54, 244–45. *See also* affect theory
psychoanalytic feminism, 127
"Pure and Impure Poetry" (Warren), 162–66

Quashie, Kevin, 35, 116–23, 242
queer theory: Berlant and, 179; deconstruction and, 26, 27; local claiming and, 124–31; Miller and, 195, 198–200; psychoanalysis and, 46–54, 244–45; scene setting and, 46–54, 244–45
"Quest" (Goodison), 211–12

race and racism, 24, 26–27, 116–17, 122
"The Race for Theory" (Christian), 130–31
racial passing, 125–28
racial uplift, 126
Ramazani, Jahan, 32, 209–17, 251
Rankine, Claudia, 224–25, 232–33
Ransom, John Crowe, 24, 162–66
rape, 99–104, 132–36
Reckson, Lindsay, 35, 116–23, 242
"The Red Wheelbarrow" (Williams), 3–10, 219–21
regional argumentation: Auerbach and, 109; Berlant and, 176–83, 248; concept of, 3–4, 7–8, 9, 219; conversation and, 19; Coundouriotis and, 136; exercises, 248–50; identification of, 222–37; Kenner and, 221; Ngai on, 204–5; skill and, 18; understanding and, 12; Warren and, 160–66; Woloch and, 151–59; Yousefi and, 167–75
"A Rehearsal of Hamlet" (Griffiths), 65–71
"reply" (Clifton), 117–21
Richards, I. A., 21–23
Ricks, Christopher: on clichés, 88–96, 238, 246; New Criticism and, 22, 65, 167
Ridge, Lola, 222, 231
"The Road Not Taken" (Frost), 23–24, 25, 30, 33
Romanticism, 24
Romeo and Juliet (Shakespeare), 12–14, 16
"A Room of One's Own" (Woolf), 142
Rumi, 168

Sa'adi, 168
Sacks, Peter, 100–101
Said, Edward, 31–32
scene setting: Auerbach and, 27–28, 39–45, 109, 245; Berlant on, 182–83; Butler and, 127–28; concept of, 3–5, 41, 218; conversation and, 19; Coundouriotis and, 134–35; exercises, 244–48; identification of, 222–37; Kenner and, 219–20; Leighton and, 56–62, 245; Morrison and, 84; Ngai on, 204–5, 207; Sedgwick and, 46–54,

244–45; skill and, 17; understanding and, 12–13; Vendler and, 73
Sedgwick, Eve Kosofsky, 26, 33, 46–54, 244–45
senior theses, 255, 261
Sense and Sensibility (Austen), 195–200, 251
Seven Types of Ambiguity (Empson), 187
sexual violence, 99–104, 132–36
Shakespeare, William: global theorizing and, 187–94; New Criticism and, 65–71, 73, 187–94; noticing and, 65–71; postcolonialism and, 214; understanding and, 12–14, 16
Shakespeare, William—works: *Hamlet*, 65–71; *Henry IV*, 188, 193; *Measure for Measure*, 188, 193; *The Merchant of Venice*, 188; *Romeo and Juliet*, 12–14, 16; Sonnet 94, 187–94
shame, 34, 46–54, 244–45
"Shame, Theatricality, and Queer Performativity: Henry James's *The Art of the Novel*" (Sedgwick), 46–54, 244–45
Shamlu, Ahmad, 168, 169–75
Sharpe, Christina, 35, 119n3, 121–22
"She dwelt among th' untrodden ways" (Wordsworth), 223–24, 231–32
skill, 17–18
slavery: Black studies and, 35, 121–22; deconstruction and, 26; Morrison on, 80; narratology and, 200; postcolonialism and, 32; Spillers on, 140, 141–42, 145
Smith, Stevie, 60–61
Some Versions of Pastoral (Empson), 187–94
Sonnet 94 (Shakespeare), 187–94
The Sovereignty of Quiet (Reckson), 116–23
Spaide, Christopher, 32, 209–17, 251
"Spain" (Auden), 214–15
Spenser, Edmund, 73
Spillers, Hortense, 26, 140–47, 242
Spitzer, Leo, 109
Spivak, Gayatri Chakravorty, 213
Stagg, Robert, 22, 65–71, 238
Stevens, Wallace, 98

"Stopping by Woods on a Snowy Evening"
(Frost), 14–16
stream of consciousness, 39–45, 146
Swift, Taylor, 142

Tate, Allen, 162
Tennyson, Alfred Lord, 57
tetrameter, 56–59
"The Three Wise Men of Gotham Who Set
Out to Catch the Moon in a Net"
(Oswald), 59–61
"They That Have Power" (Empson),
187–94
"This is not a riot policeman" (Press),
211–12
"To Autumn" (Keats), 74–79
To the Lighthouse (Woolf), 39–45, 245
Toulmin, Stephen, 15
transatlantic slave trade, 133, 200
travel narratives, 132–33

Ugly Feelings (Ngai), 201–8, 251
understanding, 11–17
Understanding Poetry (Warren and Brooks),
160–61, 163, 165–66
"Upon Appleton House" (Marvell),
93–95

Vendler, Helen: Keats and, 72–79; New
Criticism and, 22, 23, 167; noticing and,
72–79, 239; on reading for difference, 212
Vertigo (Hitchcock), 34, 201–8
Vico, Giambattista, 28, 30–31

Walcott, Derek, 214
Warren, Robert Penn, 24, 160–66, 248
Weekes, Omari, 26, 140–47, 242
Wellek, René, 109
Where Shall I Wander? (Ashbery), 178–83,
248
Wilderson, Frank, 35
Williams, William Carlos, 3–10, 219–21
Wimsatt, William K., 162, 169n4, 176–77
The Wings of the Dove (James), 225–27,
233–35
Wittgenstein, Ludwig, 34
Woloch, Alex, 35, 151–59, 248
Wood, Michael, 188
Woolf, Virginia: Auerbach and, 27–28,
39–45, 245; on incandescence, 142;
Morrison and, 81; scene setting and,
28–29, 39–45, 245; Vendler and, 72–73
Woolf, Virginia—works: *To the Lighthouse*,
39–45, 245; "A Room of One's Own," 142
The Words to Say It (Cardinal), 84–87
Wordsworth, William, 24, 171n8, 223–24,
231–32
Wuthering Heights (Brontë), 228, 235–36
Wyatt, Thomas, 61–62

Yacine, Kateb, 228–29, 236–37
Yeats, W. B., 76–77
"You're" (Plath), 192–93
Yousefi, Qolamhossein, 34, 167–75, 248
Yushij, Nima, 168

Zhang, Dora, 225–27, 233–35

GPSR Authorized Representative: Easy Access System Europe - Mustamäe tee 50, 10621 Tallinn, Estonia, gpsr.requests@easproject.com

www.ingramcontent.com/pod-product-compliance
Lightning Source LLC
Chambersburg PA
CBHW031431160426
43195CB00010BB/694